# CATALYSTS FOR CHANGE

Philanthropic organizations, or foundations, are a major source of the funding needed in community revitalization efforts, particularly in the USA. *Catalysts for Change* provides new models and new thinking for how philanthropic groups can work to better their communities.

With the current economic climate forcing shrewd spending, foundations need all the guidance they can find on how to appropriately channel their funds in the best way. But how can these sorts of community projects be analyzed for effectiveness? Is there a quantitative rather than qualitative element that can be studied to give real feedback to those investing in projects? Arguing against a one-size-fits-all model, the authors illustrate the importance of context and relationships in the success of these projects.

Filling a gap in the literature on the many ways in which philanthropic organizations and community development intertwine, the authors use their own first-hand experiences and research to forge a new path for academic research in an area where it has been lacking. Drawing first on the history of philanthropic funding, the authors then look at developments in the last 20 years in detail, focusing on four key case studies from across the United States.

**Maria Martinez-Cosio** is an Associate Professor at the School of Urban and Public Affairs at the University of Texas, Arlington. She received her Ph.D. in Sociology from UC San Diego. Her research interests include private foundations' role in community development, civic participation by immigrants in urban redevelopment, Latino parent involvement in urban education, and qualitative research methods.

**Mirle Rabinowitz Bussell** is a Continuing Lecturer and Academic Coordinator in the Urban Studies and Planning Program at UC San Diego. She received her Ph.D. in Urban Planning from UCLA. Her research interests include the relationship between philanthropy and community development, the role of CDCs in neighborhood revitalization, quality of life planning at the grassroots level, and the relationship between gender and planning.

# The Community Development Research and Practice Series

## Volume 2

This series serves community developers, planners, public administrators, and others involved in practice and policymaking in the realm of community development. The series provides timely and applied information for researchers, students, and practitioners. Building on a 40-year history of publishing the Community Development Society's journal, *Community Development* (www.comm-dev.org), the book series contributes to a growing and rapidly changing knowledge base as a resource for practitioners and researchers alike.

For additional information please see the series page at www.routledge.com.

Community development as reflected in both theory and practice is continually evolving. This comes as no surprise as our communities and regions constantly change. As a practice focused discipline, change is the only constant in the community development realm. The need to integrate theory, practice, research, teaching, and training is even more pressing now than ever, given uncertain and rapidly transforming economic, social, environmental, and cultural climates. Current and applicable information and insights about effective community development research and practice are needed.

In partnership with Routledge, the Community Development Society is delighted to present this new book series serving community developers, planners, public administrators, citizen activists, and others involved in community development practice, research, and policymaking. The series is designed to integrate innovative thinking on tools, strategies, and experiences as a resource especially well-suited for bridging the gaps between theory, research, and practice. It is our intent that the series will provide timely and useful information for responding to the rapidly changing environment in which community development researchers and practitioners operate. The Community Development Society was formed in 1970 as a professional association to serve the needs of both researchers and practitioners. That same year, the Society began publishing *Community Development*, its journal promoting exchange of ideas, experiences, and approaches between practice and research. *Community Development Research and Practice* builds on this rich legacy of scholarship by offering contributions to the growing knowledge base.

The Community Development Society actively promotes the continued advancement of the practice and theory of community development. Fundamental to this mission is adherence to the following core Principles of Good Practice. This new book series is a reflection of many of these core principles.

- Promote active and representative participation towards enabling all community members to meaningfully influence the decisions that affect their lives.
- Engage community members in learning about and understanding community issues, and the economic, social, environmental, political, psychological, and other impacts associated with alternative courses of action.
- Incorporate the diverse interest and cultures of the community in the community development process; and disengage from support of any effort that is likely to adversely affect the disadvantaged members of a community.
- Work actively to enhance the leadership capacity of community members, leaders, and groups within the community.
- Be open to using the full range of action strategies to work towards the long-term sustainability and well-being of the community.

## Series editor introduction

*Catalysts for Change: Twenty-first century philanthropy and community development* as a volume in this inaugural year of the new series is an excellent example of the tenets of good practice principles in action. Authors Maria Martinez-Cosio and Mirle Rabinowitz Bussell foster a richer understanding of the scope and context of foundations' community development activities with this original and impactful work. Drawing on case studies as well as analysis of foundations' qualitative and quantitative effects, they find critical indicators of positive work, including the need for meaningful community engagement and collaborative efforts across sectors.

This is an exciting addition to the literature, reflecting changes taking place in strategic approaches to charitable investments. One of the newer trends evidenced in some foundations' community development efforts is that of concentrated interventions—comprehensive community initiatives—seeking to convey greater impact than providing smaller support for numerous philanthropic projects across many areas. One of the recommendations from the authors is that the "goal for private philanthropies is not the transfer of community development models from one underserved community to another; rather, it is a deeper understanding of different approaches to realizing significant community revitalization and the type of innovation that is possible at the local level." This focus on calibrating the activities and approaches to local situations and collaborating with community partners is of paramount importance as past efforts for "one-size-fits-all" grants programs have not succeeded. It also reflects a systems theory framework, certainly a paradigm shift in the making. In other words, communities are systems and in order to elicit positive collective impact, developing tailored approaches based on local conditions and relationships is needed for driving complex comprehensive change in communities. Calibrating strategic investments and activities can lead to a host of beneficial outcomes, not least of which is helping foster more engagement, capacity, and community well-being.

The role of foundations in community development is an area that has not been explored in much depth—until now. This book responds with a comprehensive and constructive analysis with significant implications for community development. I invite you to fully delve into this volume, as I think you will find it both beneficial and inspiring. Further, continue to explore the series as new volumes are added, and we do hope you will find it a valuable resource for supporting community development research and practice.

Rhonda G. Phillips

Editor, *Community Development Research and Practice Series*

# CATALYSTS FOR CHANGE

Twenty-first century philanthropy and community development

*Maria Martinez-Cosio and Mirle Rabinowitz Bussell*

Routledge
Taylor & Francis Group

LONDON AND NEW YORK

First published 2013
by Routledge
2 Park Square, Milton Park, Abingdon, Oxon OX14 4RN

Simultaneously published in the USA and Canada
by Routledge
711 Third Avenue, New York, NY 10017

*Routledge is an imprint of the Taylor and Francis Group, an informa business*

*British Library Cataloguing in Publication Data*
A catalogue record for this book is available from the British Library

*Library of Congress Cataloging-in-Publication Data*
Martinez-Cosio, Maria.
Catalysts for change : 21st century philanthropy and community
development / Maria Martinez-Cosio and Mirle Rabinowitz Bussell. --
1 Edition.
pages cm. -- (The community development research and practice series)
Includes bibliographical references and index.
1. Charity organization. 2. Community development. I. Bussell, Mirle
Rabinowitz. II. Title.
HV40.M4197 2013
307.1'4--dc23
2012048802

ISBN: 978–0-415–68322–7 (hbk)
ISBN: 978–0-415–68323–4 (pbk)
ISBN: 978–0-203–40551–2 (ebk)

Typeset in Bembo by
GreenGate Publishing Services, Tonbridge, Kent

Printed and bound in Great Britain by
TJ International Ltd, Padstow, Cornwall

To Dalia, Noah, Daniel, and Sofia

# CONTENTS

# ILLUSTRATIONS

## Figures

## Tables

# ABBREVIATIONS

| | |
|---|---|
| AHP | Affordable Housing Program |
| CalEndow | California Endowment |
| Caltrans | California State Transportation Department |
| CAN | Community Action Network |
| CBP | Community Building in Partnership |
| CCBI | Cleveland Community Building Initiative |
| CCC | Center for Community Change |
| CCE | Center for Community Engagement |
| CCI | comprehensive community initiatives |
| CCRP | Comprehensive Community Revitalization Program |
| CDBG | Community Development Block Grants |
| CDC | community development corporation |
| CNC | Coalition of Neighborhood Councils |
| COS | charity organization society |
| DART | Dallas Area Rapid Transit |
| DSNI | Dudley Street Neighborhood Initiative |
| EEI | Environmental Enterprise Initiative |
| EIS | Elementary Institute of Science |
| FCE | Foundation for Community Empowerment |
| GAO | General Accounting Office |
| GCCB | Germantown Community Collaborative Board |
| GIFT | Giving Indiana Funds for Tomorrow |
| HCZ | Harlem Children's Zone |
| HUD | U.S. Department of Housing and Urban Development |
| IPO | initial public offering |
| IRS | Internal Revenue Service |
| JCNI | Jacobs Center for Neighborhood Innovation |
| KKK | Ku Klux Klan |
| LAUF | Los Angeles Urban Funders |
| LISC | Local Initiatives Support Corporation |

| | |
|---|---|
| LLC | limited liability corporations |
| NCDI | National Community Development Initiative |
| NCP | New Communities Program |
| NCRP | National Committee for Responsive Philanthropy |
| NFI | Neighborhood and Family Initiative |
| NII | Neighborhood Improvement Initiative |
| NPI | Neighborhood Partners Initiative |
| NSP | Neighborhood Strategies Project |
| NTC | Neighborhood Transformation Center |
| OCS | Office of Community Services |
| OMDC | Orange Mound Development Corporation |
| OMG | Organization and Management Group |
| RCI | Rebuilding Communities Initiative |
| SCAP | Southern California Association for Philanthropy |
| SDSU | San Diego State University |
| SDUSD | San Diego Unified School District |
| SEDC | Southeastern Economic Development Corporation |
| TAP | The Atlanta Project |
| VOCAL | Voices of Community at All Levels |

# PREFACE

The funding landscape for community development in low-income neighborhoods is at crisis levels. The continued ripple effects of the 2008 global recession have exacerbated a pre-existing pattern of federal, state, and local retrenchment, particularly in distressed urban neighborhoods that lack the political clout and networks needed to direct attention, and resources, to the numerous challenges they face. Across the country people are struggling on a daily basis to improve the physical, economic, and social infrastructure of their communities. Piecemeal efforts to cobble together funding sources are often ineffective and time consuming, but what are the alternatives? This book investigates a growing effort spearheaded by philanthropic entities seeking to catalyze comprehensive community development. Often working on the ground with the communities they fund, these foundations are exploring new approaches to maximizing their investment and effecting change. The results have been mixed, and measuring success is difficult. By presenting an overview of these innovative approaches, this book provides an analysis of foundation-driven comprehensive community initiatives (CCIs) across the country. Larger trends are explored and then elucidated by a series of detailed case studies that investigate the inner-workings, challenges, and positive outcomes that have been realized to date. We know from the historical record that there is no magic bullet for community development in underserved urban neighborhoods, but nonetheless it is imperative for the internal stakeholders—residents, nonprofits, and community organizations in these communities—as well as the external stakeholders—local and state governments, education agencies, and the business community—to add to their toolkits of interventions and approaches. The research presented in this book focuses on one such tool.

As researchers with more than 20 years of experience in observing and analyzing community change, we still struggle to present a balanced view of the newest efforts to disrupt the dynamics that led to the decline of urban neighborhoods. There are no easy answers to improving the quality of life in poor communities, and good intentions abound. But in the end, those most impacted by the newest revitalization iteration are the residents that call that community home.

CCIs that seek to integrate public and private partners with residents to address the multiple challenges of a declining community and improve the quality of life, present a promising approach to a balanced, and more just, process of neighborhood revitalization. By balanced, we mean programs that recognize the role of residents as equal participants in decision-making; balanced by incorporating social justice as a key element in understanding the decline of these neighborhoods; balanced through the spreading of financial risk among a variety of collaborative funders; and balanced in recognizing the complex nature of low-income communities within the context of the broader economic, cultural, social, and political systems that impact them.

The role of foundations in activating these endeavors cannot be underestimated. Private and public foundations offer the type of funding, technical skills sets, long-term commitment, and risk-taking that leads to innovation in responding to the disinvestment and neglect that contributed to the decline of low-income neighborhoods across the country. Many foundations, both large and small, are convening strategic partnerships involving public partners, the corporate community, scholars, nonprofits, and other foundations to more effectively address the complex problems that keep residents in low-income neighborhoods, particularly children, from achieving success.

The challenge for these CCIs remains effectively engaging low-income residents as equal partners. While those of us involved in this type of work are paid to attend meetings, read up on the latest scholarship on CCIs, and attend conferences to learn about the newest community interventions, residents often do not face these advantages. Poverty-level wages, lack of health care, inadequate childcare, threats to safety including gangs, language differences, and a distrust of government and institutional forces are formidable obstacles for attaining true partnerships for achieving comprehensive change. Throughout this volume we offer many innovative approaches to bridging this divide and catalyzing systems-wide changes at the neighborhood level.

Many people generously provided their assistance and support during the research and writing of this book. The biggest thanks of all goes to the people who live, work, and genuinely care about City Heights and southeastern San Diego. Their graciousness and honesty was crucial to the completion of this book. Of particular note, for Maria Martinez-Cosio, the parents in the Rosa Parks Parent Room generously welcomed her and answered her many questions. Residents invited her into their homes and took her to their celebrations. For Mirle Rabinowitz Bussell, the members of the housing team at Jacobs Center for Neighborhood Innovation (JCNI) accepted her into the fold. The residents' eloquent articulation of their community knowledge was a powerful reminder of the necessity of collaborative planning.

We offer a heartfelt thanks to the residents, nonprofit staff members, city of San Diego staff members, and volunteers who continue to advocate for the betterment of these two unique communities. The residents of City Heights and the Diamond Neighborhoods in southeastern San Diego are clearly co-authors of this effort, and we are cognizant of the role we play in accurately representing residents' views. This is a profound responsibility. As one City Heights parent shared with us, "we are tired of being guinea pigs" as new interventions continue to target this community. We hope we do justice to their trust in us.

We received invaluable guidance and insights from numerous other individuals. Rhonda Phillips was a constant champion of the book and provided early and continuous encouragement. Bud Mehan, Professor Emeritus at UC San Diego, deserves special recognition for his unwavering support. Amy Bridges provided sage advice at an early stage in the process that helped guide the direction of our work. Stuart Henry, Director of the School of Urban Affairs at San Diego State University (SDSU), provided a visiting scholar position to Maria Martinez-Cosio during a semester research leave granted by Barbara Becker, Dean at the School of Urban and Public Affairs at UT Arlington. A grant from the Lincoln Institute of Land Policy afforded us access to resources and a community of scholars that provided instrumental insights and served as the starting point for this volume. Ann Foss, Steven Rogers, and Kathy Tran served as very capable research assistants.

We are also thankful for the candid comments and access to information we received from current and former staff and board members at Price Charities and JCNI. We value all of these relationships on many different levels, but ultimately we take complete responsibility for the work presented in this volume.

This effort could not have been completed without the endless patience and support of our loved ones. While Lynn Rabinowitz sadly passed away before the project was completed, we know that she believed in our work and would be immensely proud of the final volume. We thank our families—Steve, Sofia, and Daniel, and Stuart, Dalia, and Noah. We now have a reply to the oft-repeated question in both of our households—yes, the book is finally done.

Maria Martinez-Cosio
Mirle Rabinowitz Bussell
September 2012

**PART I**

# The scope and scale of philanthropic investment in community development

# 1

# THE CHANGING LANDSCAPE OF FOUNDATION-LED COMMUNITY DEVELOPMENT

On a warm evening in 2006, hundreds of people filled a large portable tent set up in the parking lot of an old strip mall in southeastern San Diego. Men, women, and children of different racial and ethnic backgrounds eagerly awaited the start of the meeting. The excitement was palpable. Everyone was in attendance to learn about a proposal to provide this low-income community with opportunities for affordable homeownership. This was big news in a community that had not seen new housing built in many years. The meeting was not convened by a public agency, redevelopment authority, or community development corporation (CDC), the typical developers of affordable housing. Rather, a private family foundation, the Jacobs Family Foundation, was spearheading the effort as part of a larger comprehensive plan: it was preparing to catalyze comprehensive community redevelopment in this neighborhood five miles east of downtown San Diego. The foundation was driven by a clearly defined mission that emphasized resident engagement in community development and, ultimately, resident ownership of community assets. In a community known for a historical legacy of neglect, nominal public investment, and a weak infrastructure of nonprofit social service organizations, the Jacobs Family Foundation offered some a glimmer of hope that perhaps the time had finally come to elevate the quality of life for the 85,000 residents who lived in this section of southeastern San Diego. Others expressed skepticism and questioned whether or not a foundation lacking historical ties to the community could or should successfully undertake such an ambitious and potentially transformative plan.

Four miles to the north, a similar scenario was playing out. The City Heights neighborhood, often referred to as San Diego's "Ellis Island" due to the large number of immigrants and refugees who reside there, was in the midst of its own renewal. Facing similar challenges of neglect, aging infrastructure, and low levels of public investment, City Heights was undergoing comprehensive community redevelopment spearheaded by another San Diego private family foundation, Price Charities. This plan emphasized large-scale physical renewal and economic development. Similar to the Jacobs Family Foundation, Price Charities had its detractors along with its supporters.

Fast forward six years and both City Heights and southeastern San Diego look physically different. Both communities now have urban villages that contain large grocery stores, nationally franchised restaurants, community facilities, and the ubiquitous Starbucks. These villages were completed in large measure due to the efforts of the two family foundations that worked in partnership with these neighborhoods. These physical accomplishments are only part of the story, though, and while they certainly give the neighborhoods the appearance of "successful" redevelopment, the outcomes are much more complex. The two foundations' best intentions did not always match the needs of the low-income residents that reside in the respective communities. The reasons are complex and challenging to evaluate but are critically important in this time of continued federal retrenchment and limited local resources. The landscape of local community development is on a trajectory of change and partnerships are critical.

Three generations after urban renewal and two generations after the demise of the War on Poverty, philanthropic entities, namely public and private foundations, have increasingly taken on the continuing challenge of revitalizing poor communities in our cities. Their admirable intentions—like those of federal and local governments—have encountered division, controversy, and sometimes protest. This book traces these community development efforts from initial intent through the complex path of implementation, presenting key findings that provide important lessons through an analysis of multiple case studies reflecting the broad scope of foundational engagement in community development.

We were introduced to these two San Diego neighborhoods, these two foundations, and each other, over ten years ago. Contacts we made opened doors to local schools, community stakeholders, public sector employees, and city hall. The Spanish-speaking fluency of one of us provided an opportunity for Spanish-speaking residents in City Heights to share their hope for change as they struggled to keep their children out of gangs. Professional relationships forged with staff and board members at both foundations provided opportunities to witness first hand the challenges and rewards of this unique type of work. One of the first questions we asked of each other was whether or not what we were observing in San Diego was unique or part of a larger trend. We wanted to know how many other family foundations were engaged in this type of deeply engaged place-based community revitalization. We knew from the academic literature that large foundations such as Ford had played a pivotal role in supporting community development over the second half of the twentieth century and on into the New Millennium, but the efforts in San Diego appeared different. Price Charities and the Jacobs Family Foundation had embedded themselves in their target neighborhoods and, rather than dictating policy from afar, staff members and often board members, too, were on the ground in the community on a daily basis partnering with networks of individual and organizational stakeholders. We asked ourselves if this was a unique model and, if so, how did one go about measuring impacts. These questions were the genesis for this project.

Philanthropic support for underserved communities has a long history and the levels and types of involvement have evolved in reaction to prevailing societal norms and federal political, economic, and social policy. Foundations in general are known to be risk averse, but at specific moments in history they have demonstrated the ability to ignite innovative approaches to community revitalization. Whether experimenting with programs that ultimately influenced federal policy, such as the Ford Foundation's Gray Areas program which led to federal Model Cities legislation, seeding grassroots systems change effort as exemplified by the Liberty Hill Foundation's support for multifaceted community organizing efforts in Los Angeles, or supporting community building for disenfranchised minority groups as illustrated by the Frothingham Fund and Slater Fund's investment in the Calhoun Industrial School for Blacks in Alabama in the nineteenth century, a small but growing number of foundations have shown the potential of the sector to challenge the status quo and strategically channel charitable giving in ways that can potentially transform business-as-usual in low income communities.

Foundation funding has catalyzed community development initiatives from Boston to San Diego, yet the role of foundations as key actors in revitalizing urban neighborhoods is largely under-theorized. The relationship between private foundations, underserved communities, public agencies, private interests, and community nonprofits gains salience as a declining economy and public sector fiscal crises have forced foundations engaged in community development to reexamine their capacity to fund scalable comprehensive community change. Significantly, this has led a cohort of foundations to reexamine their efforts in the larger context of systems change. Some foundations have assumed a more aggressive approach that has transformed their role from funder to policymaker and policy implementer. In numerous examples across the country, their efforts have sparked urban reinvestment and redevelopment. This is contributing to a proactive culture in certain segments of philanthropy that has significant implications for the future of local community development. Some of these private and public foundations are at the forefront of innovation and require further study as practitioners, academics, and public sector agencies consider new paradigms in community development.

This has been best illustrated by the increased philanthropic support for CCIs. CCIs emerged in the late 1980s as growing evidence revealed that the complex social, physical, and economic challenges of community development in low-income neighborhoods were interconnected and required a holistic response. Rather than the traditional project-oriented philanthropy, CCIs were envisioned as a new strategic approach to charitable investment by linking public and private resources along with community participation in a comprehensive manner targeted towards a specific geographic area. This ambitious approach has yielded mixed results and simultaneously points to the challenges and rewards of comprehensive community change. We situate CCIs at the center of our analysis.

We consider three key areas that arise from the role of private foundations in comprehensive community development. First, we analyze the scope and content of foundations' community development work by considering their qualitative and quantitative impacts. From a quantitative perspective, we identify the number of foundations engaged in community development work, the type of efforts they support, and the financial scale of dollars invested and communities served. Looking at their qualitative impact, we document and compare the ways in which foundations define community development work and the impact this has on their funding priorities. We situate this analysis within theories of systems change to understand their varying motives, approaches, and goals for underserved areas.

Second, we analyze the governance structures and approaches of foundations engaged in community development work. This includes consideration of the foundations' role in the community development plans and the varying degrees to which the foundations either lead the community development efforts or allow for the community to emerge and direct the planning process. We assess the extent to which foundations approach this work with clearly defined strategies and consideration for the sustainability of community development efforts. This raises questions about the degree to which foundations set policy and interact with the complex web of public, private, nonprofit, and community stakeholders.

Third, we consider issues of accountability. We evaluate varying degrees of transparency in philanthropic support for community development. As private entities, not elected by the populace to make policy decisions, we consider the types of checks and balances that are in place to monitor foundation accountability in community development.

Our approach is two-pronged. We surveyed the field and assembled the first comprehensive typology of foundations engaged in community development. Using the three primary criteria identified above, we were able to identify larger trends in the field. We complement the typology with the presentation of numerous case studies illustrative of the innovation occurring in foundation-driven community development. We take a closer look at two specific efforts from San Diego as a way to present and analyze the many nuances, complexities, and contradictions of CCIs.

Our analysis seeks to challenge theories of comprehensive community change that espouse a grand model for revitalizing underserved communities. While our case studies may appear narrow in their application to community development initiatives, we argue that the differing approaches to community development illustrate the importance of context in addressing the assets and needs of underserved communities; the challenge of defining and developing participation from stakeholders (including neighborhood-based nonprofits); the importance of evaluation of community development initiatives; and, most importantly, the issue of sustainability of comprehensive community change.

Our findings suggest that the relationships between community engagement, capacity building, and public–private collaboration are critical indicators of private foundations' effectiveness in catalyzing local community development. We suggest that the goal for private philanthropies is not the transfer of community development models from one underserved community to another; rather, it is a deeper understanding of different approaches to realizing significant community revitalization and the type of innovation that is possible at the local level.

Often the key questions raised in examining these types of public–private relationships are focused on results or outcomes (Kubisch, Auspos, Brown, and Dewar, 2010). Do these public–private initiatives achieve their goals of improving underserved communities and how is "improvement" defined and measured? The answer is complicated and contentious and, ultimately, it depends on whom you ask. For two of the family foundations included in our book, residents, nonprofits, foundation and city staff interviewed for this research would all agree that their respective communities have benefited in many ways from the engagement of these private foundations in community development efforts. These two foundations included in our research have raised the profile of their targeted areas, attracting new funding sources and capturing attention from city hall and the media. But clearly, as our research presents, context matters. The vision and philosophies of family foundations differ, as do the political, cultural, and demographic history of each community. These differences in approach were evident in the differing definitions of community development articulated by community stakeholders, foundations, nonprofit organizations, and city staff. Thus measuring success is difficult when a common metric has not been negotiated or agreed upon. And we must continue to ask whether success should be measured by physical outcomes alone. The process through which change occurs, and the mechanisms that are developed to support this process, are equally meaningful for certain stakeholders. Until we ascertain desired goals, it is difficult to develop theories of change for underserved communities targeted by public and private foundations.

These issues merit attention as more private foundations refocus their efforts towards a holistic place-based approach to philanthropy that may have a greater impact on underserved communities. The California Endowment's (CalEndow) recently announced ten-year funding commitment to 14 underserved communities in California (2009); the Kellogg Foundation's shift in philanthropic direction (Cohen, 2008); and the Local Initiatives Support Corporation's (LISC) Building Sustainable Communities program all provide examples of this change. Furthermore, recently completed research from the Aspen Institute indicates a growing trend in foundation-supported CCIs (Kubisch et al., 2010). All of these examples are united by their objective to improve underserved communities through a variety of community development initiatives, and all are challenged to develop a common definition of community development, a vision for the future of these communities, and to develop relationships based on trust with the variety of stakeholders in each of these communities.

The book is divided into two parts. Part I reviews the historical record of private and public foundations engaged in comprehensive community revitalization initiatives, surveys the different types of foundations involved in this work, presents a typology of these efforts, and concludes with a discussion on the merits of using systems change theory to understand the structure, context, and impact of philanthropic support for comprehensive community development. We include the history of both the large, mainline foundations such as the Ford Foundation and the Sage Foundation, along with the smaller, primarily family foundations that have engaged in neighborhood-based community development partnerships in collaboration with residents, government entities, and other private sources. The research indicates that their involvement has transcended funding support and in an increasing number of cases also includes policy formulation and implementation. These action-oriented foundations are often at the forefront of innovation in local community development and serve as important catalysts for neighborhood reinvestment and redevelopment. Many of these foundations also fall under the category of social justice philanthropy. This is a branch of philanthropy that emphasizes systems change and democratic grassroots processes that empower and enfranchise traditionally marginalized subsets of the population, particularly those that live in low-income urban neighborhoods. In this section we also explain how the devolution of federal support for community development has influenced philanthropic involvement in the field.

This historical investigation begins with the precursors to formalized philanthropy in the seventeenth century including informal networks of charities and then moves on to the first generation of foundation support in the settlement houses of the late nineteenth and early twentieth centuries. We then consider the impact of urban renewal and the War on Poverty, the decay of urban areas in the 1970s and 1980s, the creation of public–private partnerships that became prevalent in the 1990s, and new models that are currently emerging in the twenty-first century. Some of these newer, innovative foundations were born out of the disappointments of urban renewal and the rethinking of strategies for rebuilding urban communities that followed. Certain foundations committed to investing in underserved areas are also seeking higher returns for their philanthropic investments, narrowing their scope to specific areas or neighborhoods in a concerted effort to implement comprehensive change at a smaller scale. This new approach to community development is based on the assumption that concentrated interventions will have a greater impact than providing smaller, piecemeal support for numerous philanthropic projects in many locations.

Part I continues with an overview of the philanthropic sector and identifies the different types of foundations involved with community development efforts. Specific attention is given to CCIs and we provide an overview of the national trends and accomplishments of CCIs since they were first established in the late 1980s. Numerous case studies from across the country, including Dallas, Los Angeles, and New York, are incorporated into the discussion. This is synthesized into a comprehensive typology that identifies two primary models of philanthropic engagement in CCIs. First, we look at foundations as supporters of comprehensive community development. These foundations work with nonprofits, public entities, and other foundation partners to fund change within defined geographic areas. The lead foundation may provide the bulk of funding (often long term), but the staff and board rely on partners to work on the ground. The second category includes what we refer to as foundations as managing partners. Largely embedded in the communities they serve, these foundations focus on place as a significant unit of analysis and as a target for comprehensive change. They are committed to significant direct interaction and relationship building with community members and provide long-term funding commitments. They are flexible and entrepreneurial in their charitable endeavors and often, but not always, work off of a clearly articulated theory of change that encompasses their views on the ways targeted neighborhoods can be changed and made stronger. The typology includes data on governing principles, funding sources, programmatic priorities, and issues of accountability and transparency.

The first part of the book concludes with an argument supporting the value of using systems theory to frame our analysis of philanthropic support for community development. Systems theory offers a promising approach as it allows for the examination of systems as component parts that interact within a particular context and through those relationships can function as an entity or organism. Systems theory provides a framework that responds to the complexity of comprehensive neighborhood change as undertaken by CCIs, and it helps identify the key drivers of change for underserved communities. It focuses on communities as systems but, more importantly, how communities interact with other systems, including foundations, local government, the private sector, and nonprofits.

Part II sharpens the focus and presents two case studies based on a detailed exploration of the origin, evolution, and outcomes to date of two private family foundations in San Diego, Price Charities and the Jacobs Family Foundation. Both foundations share a similar mission dedicated to place-based, comprehensive community development. The Price Family Charitable Fund was established in 1983 and its operating foundation, Price Charities, was created in 2000. Price Charities' mission emphasizes large-scale physical and economic revitalization in the City Heights neighborhood. It has successfully developed hundreds of affordable housing units, improved educational infrastructure in the neighborhood, and built a comprehensive urban village containing retail, recreational, public safety, and educational institutions. Established during the same time period, the Jacobs Family Foundation was created in 1988 and its operating arm, JCNI, was created in 1995. The Jacobs Family Foundation is also focused on comprehensive community development, but resident empowerment, comprehensive asset building, and community ownership of the larger process is the cornerstone of Jacobs' approach. While it has improved the physical fabric of the community by developing a large retail center and community center, it emphasizes the thousands of residents that have been engaged in, and empowered by, the planning process.

Our comparative analysis illustrates that while each foundation's approach to community development differs, they share a number of characteristics and approaches. Both Price Charities and the Jacobs Family Foundation have national reputations, and their initiatives have been identified as examples of best practices by the Urban Land Institute, PolicyLink, the Aspen Institute, and others, yet their efforts have not been the subject of comprehensive research. The legal and financial structure of foundations requires relatively low levels of disclosure and foundations vary considerably in terms of the degree of self-reporting and public information sharing. Over the course of ten cumulative years of participatory research, we assembled the data necessary to tell the story of these foundations in what we believe is an accurate, fair, and critical fashion.

Utilizing a mixed-methods approach, we gathered and analyzed scores of material on Price Charities and its efforts in the City Heights neighborhood and the Jacobs Family Foundation and its operating arm, JCNI, in southeastern San Diego. Hundreds of hours of interviews with community stakeholders and attendance at countless community meetings, foundation-sponsored events, and public forums enabled us to identify the many nuances of comprehensive community development in these two neighborhoods. Archival materials and public documents added an additional layer of information. Through the course of our research we developed a genuine level of care for the well-being of the communities targeted for change. Our involvement in the neighborhoods led us to develop casual friendships with a range of stakeholders including foundation staff, board members, neighborhood residents, and nonprofit and public sector employees. We have made a concerted effort to present our findings as dispassionately and accurately as possible.

We want to see Price Charities and the Jacobs Family Foundation catalyze the community change desired by the residents of the two respective neighborhoods, but our findings have left us with unanswered questions. For one, we question whether or not neighborhood transformation occurs in a timely and cost-effective manner. Price Charities could argue that the answer is yes, as they point to the phenomenal physical change occurring in City Heights. But for the estimated 3,000 residents displaced due to new school construction and redevelopment projects, the answer may be different. Price Charities did not want to discuss displacement or the threat of gentrification as potential outcomes for their work, although later we were heartened to hear Price Charities' founder and chief benefactor, Sol Price, mention that this was an unintended consequence.

In the case of the Jacobs Family Foundation's work in southeastern San Diego, many stakeholders have grown impatient and expressed the desire to see more physical improvement. Despite the excitement evident in 2006 when Jacobs' announced plans to build its first affordable housing development, the housing has yet to materialize. In the meantime, the housing market has been destabilized by the financial crisis of 2008 and some stakeholders question whether or not Jacobs will be able to build the housing. Yet, despite these critiques, a core group of community residents have become more engaged and more knowledgable about the community development process. This has happened in City Heights, too. Some of the residents, mostly renters, have learned much through Price Charities' revitalization efforts and are becoming more vocal, experienced, and assertive as Price

Charities closes in on the twentieth anniversary of working with this community. Maybe this is one of the key lessons learned from this work—addressing decades of disinvestment will take decades of hard work.

Each of our case studies raises important questions about the effectiveness of comprehensive community development, the importance of context, the challenges in building community capacity, the role of foundations in these efforts, and the need to address the roots of poverty. Our research also suggests that efforts to develop a singular grand model for revitalizing underserved neighborhoods are, as they have been in the past, futile, and more attention must be paid to developing approaches for each underserved neighborhood that respond to its unique social, cultural, political, and economic conditions. These contextual conditions become more important as stakeholders seek to build change processes in poor neighborhoods that can be sustained after private and public funds disappear.

# 2

# THE ORIGINS OF COMMUNITY DEVELOPMENT PHILANTHROPY

The historical record reveals an inconsistent, yet substantive, legacy of community development philanthropy dating back hundreds of years to the first community building efforts of European colonists in the United States. It has taken different forms over the subsequent centuries and has demonstrated considerable variation, but its potential to catalyze community development has remained intact and is growing in importance as public resources for revitalizing distressed urban neighborhoods continue to erode. This chapter considers the history of philanthropic engagement in local community development initiatives in order to both demonstrate its longevity as well as better understand its many nuances and its capacity to endure. We begin with an exploration of definitions of community development in order to establish the parameters that frame our work. This is followed by a chronological look at the evolution of philanthropic support for local community development. Changes over time in societal norms regarding charity, social welfare, and self-sufficiency along with political ideology and economic conditions have impacted the scale and content of philanthropic involvement in community development. We identify five distinct periods in the history of philanthropic support for community development: the Colonial Era, the Progressive Era, the 1960s, the emergence of the New Right in the 1980s, and finally we end with trends in the New Millennium. Situating community development in a broader historical context illustrates the impact and potential of foundations to revitalize traditionally underserved neighborhoods.

Depending on the discipline or perspective, the evolution of community development is evident, but the literature is inconsistent in its definition of the term, and it describes a variety of processes and theories best understood through a historical lens. As illustrated in Figure 2.1, community development has been used to describe the settlement house movement and other Progressive Era programs from the late nineteenth and early twentieth centuries: urban renewal, New Deal programs aimed at revitalizing decaying urban centers, the work of the federal government through the Community Development Block Grants program (CDBG), and public–private partnerships aimed at bringing industry back into central business districts (O'Connor, 1996). While community development may not be clearly conceptualized and lacks specificity (Bhattacharyya, 1995), this vagueness also becomes one of its strengths because it encourages a range of acceptable possibilities for identifying participants, processes, and outcomes. Useful frameworks for establishing the components of the community development system are those that include a wide range of stakeholders from all sectors engaged in efforts that focus on place as well as people (Frisch and Servon, 2006).

Community development is recognized as broad efforts to improve quality of life by addressing asset building in five areas: social, human, physical, financial, and political capital (Ferguson and Dickens, 1999). Asset building includes the critical component of agency and the ability of people to conceptualize and contribute to the implementation of their own vision of change (Bhattacharyya, 1995). Individual and community agency play an increasingly important role in local community development, but local efforts should not be overemphasized at the expense of the broader challenges capitalism presents since the global economy impacts local communities. Some newer theories on community development and community building have been labeled as "romantic and nostalgic," and critics argue that the potential of civil society is given too much weight and overemphasizes local conditions without appropriate consideration of the role of capitalism and the state (DeFilippis, 2008). These newer approaches are much less confrontational and are focused on "moderate" strategies that do not challenge the root causes of community problems such as joblessness, poor housing conditions, low-quality education, and crime. Communities are products of larger social relationships and must turn outwards otherwise they risk creating successful organizations at the expense of the community itself. The challenge, therefore, is for local community development efforts to balance the needs of the community and stimulate local change within larger global forces if true asset transference and long-term community sustainability is to occur. The literature contains examples of efforts that achieved varying degrees of success in this regard (Heskin, 1991; Medoff and Sklar, 1994; von Hoffman, 2003). In this book local community development is defined as comprehensive asset building targeting a discrete geographic area of either one or several contiguous neighborhoods designed to improve quality of life, empower local stakeholders, and engage the public, private, and nonprofit sectors.

## Historical context

While the Progressive Era is commonly identified as the first period of notable charitable support for local community development in the U.S., philanthropy's roots are actually deeper and can be traced to the European colonists and the influence of ancient religious doctrines on charity. The practice of providing hospitality to strangers has been around for as long as humans have engaged in

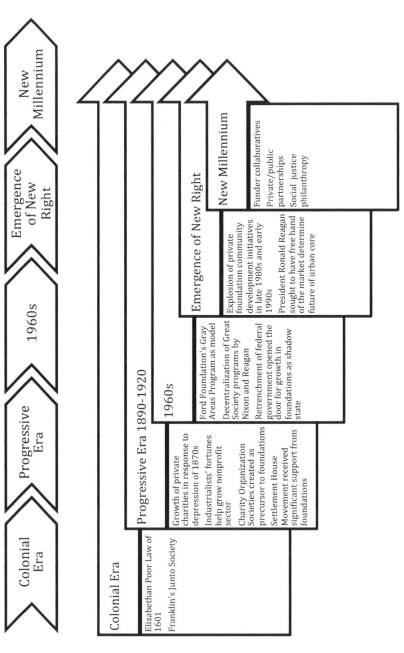

**FIGURE 2.1** History of U.S. philanthropic support for community development

Colonial Era | Progressive Era | 1960s | Emergence of New Right | New Millennium

Colonial Era

Elizabethan Poor Law of 1601

Franklin's Junto Society

Progressive Era 1890-1920

Growth of private charities in response to depression of 1870s

Industrialists' fortunes help grow nonprofit sector

Charity Organization Societies created as precursor to foundations

Settlement House Movement received significant support from foundations

1960s

Ford Foundation's Gray Areas Program as model

Decentralization of Great Society programs by Nixon and Reagan

Retrenchment of federal government opened the door for growth in foundations as shadow state

Emergence of New Right

Explosion of private foundation community development initiatives in late 1980s and early 1990s

President Ronald Reagan sought to have free hand of the market determine future of urban core

New Millennium

Funder collaboratives

Private/public partnerships

Social justice philanthropy

social interaction. The ancient Greeks and Romans discussed the role of charity in society and the words *charity* and *philanthropy* are of Greek and Latin origin. Ancient Judeo-Christian religious doctrines are critical to early American theories on charity (Jagpal, 2009). The Old Testament addresses the concept of *tzedakah* which encompasses the duty of giving and the right of those in need to receive assistance (Trattner, 1999). Christianity carried on this tradition through its emphasis on good deeds and the New Testament contains many explicit references to charity and the belief that society has a responsibility to assist those in need, eschewing the criminalization of poverty. While there were several early foreign antecedents in France and Germany (Watson, 1971), this Judeo-Christian ethic influenced English poor relief legislation in the Middle Ages and this, in turn, served as a main influence in Colonial American charitable policies. Between 1349 and 1601 a series of measures in Britain were established to codify and formalize the ways in which the British government provided assistance to those in need. Cumulatively, the measures served as the basis for the Elizabethan Poor Law of 1601 (Trattner, 1999).

The Elizabethan Poor Law of 1601 was the culmination of sixteenth-century poor relief efforts that established the parameters for state supported charity. It delineated individual and familial responsibilities as well as included the acknowledgment that the state had a responsibility to supplement efforts to relieve the needs and suffering of the deserving poor. The same year that the poor law was established, the British Parliament also enacted the Law of Charitable Uses that encouraged private philanthropy. Here we see private efforts complementing public policies, thereby creating the framework for an additional sector of institutions to provide resources and services for those in need (Trattner, 1999).

As the colonists engaged in community building in the United States, the English poor laws were used to frame their approach to charity and establish policies that promised state support for those unable to care for themselves or their families (Vale, 2000). This was a familiar model and despite their desire to break from British policies, the colonists were directly influenced by this legacy. Similar to the Judeo-Christian ethic that shaped the Poor Law, for most colonists a strong adherence to a belief in Christian duty motivated their assistance to those in need. John Winthrop's model of Christian charity and Cotton Mather's eighteenth-century *Essays to do Good* were premised on the belief that doing good was not a means of personal salvation but, rather, a responsibility to one's God. Mather, in particular, influenced philanthropic practice by calling for collaboration and group efforts to support charitable action that addressed both spiritual and physical needs. Among those influenced by Mather was Benjamin Franklin, whose Junto Society was used to combine public and private dollars for civic improvement projects such as street paving and lights, public safety, and a volunteer firefighting company (Bremner, 1988). Franklin's charitable approach of utilizing public and private sources was common for this time period.

As wealth increased by the eighteenth century, individuals and private groups provided an invaluable source of assistance for the poor. Religious groups also played a key role in distributing support for the needy (Fleishman, 2007). Trattner (1999) writes that the Quakers in particular invested a significant amount of time and resources into providing aid to those in need. In addition to religious institutions, numerous private organizations provided assistance: fraternal societies, nationality groups, social organizations, and charitable societies. Many of these charitable societies were organized to provide assistance to groups sharing a common nationality. These early forms of public assistance were done in partnership. Private philanthropy and public aid complemented one another and were dispensed in a cooperative fashion. The focus on local caretaking and mutual aid was initially the primary method of assistance. However, as the population increased and cities such as Boston and New York grew bigger, the problem of dependency became much more complicated and required a more systematic and codified approach (Trattner, 1999).

Embedded in these early Colonial charitable efforts were conflicts surrounding the determination of beneficiaries of charitable giving. Efforts to differentiate the worthy from the unworthy poor framed relief efforts and, more importantly, included a spatial dimension. Vale's (2000) history of public housing policies in Boston documents the Puritans' efforts to define "public neighbors" and shape public aid as a local responsibility. The challenge, however, was how to define local. The Puritans' "moral geography" guided charitable action; assistance was given to known members of the local community and excluded non-Christians, Native Americans, and new arrivals who were believed to require public support. Of particular note, when physical strategies were required to dispense aid in the form of almshouses and later houses of correction and industry, these institutions were spatially segregated from the center of Boston. Vale (2000) documents a progression of physical removal and replacement of these institutions that over the course of approximately 180 years took them from the edge of the Boston Commons to the West End to the South End and eventually an island in the middle of the harbor reserved for other similar public assistance institutions.

Whereas community-based philanthropy in the Colonial Era was influenced by the Judeo-Christian ethic of communal care that utilized contributions from religious and public institutions as well as private entities, by the mid part of the nineteenth century in the period immediately following the Civil War, we see changing attitudes about charitable support to benefit local community conditions. In the immediate aftermath of the war, communal care-taking impulses were strong in response to the concerns about wounded veterans as well as the women and their families who lost their male head of household during the war. State, local, and federal governmental agencies enacted a series of laws to provide resources for these segments of the population. The need to assist the millions of newly freed slaves also led to federal assistance (Trattner, 1999). However, this largess did not last long as the country recovered from the war and embarked on an aggressive industrialization and manufacturing campaign. The federal government simultaneously terminated most of its social welfare programming, leaving states and local governments responsible for many of these duties. It did not take long for most states and cities to significantly curtail their public welfare programs, too. Ameliorative measures subsequently came from the wealthy. This led to a growing group of private charities that were supported and administered by middle-class philanthropists (Dillick, 1953).

The severe depression of the 1870s contributed to the need for benevolence and by the end of the decade many cities experienced an explosion in private charity agencies. In Philadelphia in 1878, for example, 800 private charity agencies were in existence (Trattner, 1999). The lack of coordination among these organizations was a source of concern and gave rise to the charity organization movement, otherwise known as scientific charity (Dillick, 1953; Trattner, 1999). Charity organization societies (COSs) were established to organize and coordinate the dissemination of resources as well as to craft unified approaches to poverty relief and community improvement. The philosophy behind the movement identified poverty as a character defect as opposed to the result of larger structural problems. It was believed that individual character defects could be remedied through the socialization of the poor into mainstream society (Dillick, 1953). In theory, each city would develop its own registry and list everyone receiving public or private assistance in order to minimize duplication. This process would create greater efficiency at distributing public relief and allow for greater focus on the deserving poor. Home inspections by charity agents were also instituted to help develop a personal relationship between the client and the charity, and to help move the needy into solving their own problems. This approach was problematic on many fronts and was largely unsuccessful due to its large, unwieldy nature and the challenges of coordinating a cadre of charity agents (Katz, 1986; Trattner, 1999). However, many of the prominent COS supporters, such as Andrew Carnegie, eventually created their own private philanthropic foundations.

As the nineteenth century came to a close and the challenges of rapid industrialization, immigration, and population growth manifested themselves, the next stage in philanthropic support for community development took root. In the Progressive Era we see a differentiation between charity for individuals and larger community-based approaches utilized primarily by the settlement houses reformers. This was a pivotal moment in the nexus between philanthropy and community development. The history of Progressive Era reforms is well documented, but missing from this literature is the vantage point of foundations and their support for community development. Philanthropic entities have a long history of funding community development initiatives in blighted urban neighborhoods across the country and have their roots in a much earlier time period than previously explored (Dreier, 1997; Fleishman, 2007; Lubove, 1962; Traynor, 1995).

## Formalized philanthropy's evolution

The settlement house movement holds an important position in the history of local community development since this was the first significant attempt to coordinate holistic community improvement. Settlement house workers were particularly focused on "reviving the neighborhood in the city" and focused on the larger social and economic conditions that contributed to poverty and the effects that this had on local neighborhoods (Davis, 1967, p. 16). This was in direct contrast to the organized charity movement that sought to improve communities by focusing on the individual and their personal failings that caused poverty. Davis (1967), in fact, contrasts the differences between charity workers and settlement workers, noting that charity workers eschewed reform whereas the settlement workers approached community improvement with enthusiasm and less moral judgment. Others, such as the well-known college president and settlement house founder William Jewett Tucker, have contrasted the two efforts, noting that the settlement houses practiced a "higher philanthropy" as opposed to the "lower philanthropy" of charity organizations (as cited in Davis, 1967). The settlement house movement was complex, however, and, due to the class lines separating settlement house workers from the impoverished communities they served, some settlement workers were driven by moralistic impulses that often created conflict (Trolander, 1987).

The efforts of the settlement house movement have been well documented and analyzed from different perspectives including motivations for reform, religious influences, the role of gender, and the treatment of racial differences (Carson, 1990; Davis, 1967; Hayden, 1981; Lasch-Quinn, 1993; Lubove, 1962; Trolander, 1987; Wiebe, 1967). However, the direct link between philanthropy, community development, and settlement work has not been explicitly addressed. Settlement workers were involved in many neighborhood redevelopment efforts including housing reform, public playground advocacy, and sanitation and public health improvements because many settlement house workers believed that social reform required physical, neighborhood improvements (Davis, 1967).

One of the main sources of financial support for settlement house work was private philanthropy. Wealthy philanthropists funded settlement house efforts along with other community development projects (Dreier, 1997; Ehrenreich, 1985; Katz, 1986; Lubove, 1962). Philanthropists are probably best known for their support of housing reform during this time period and this includes the efforts of Edward Waller and Julius Rosenwald in Chicago, Robert Treat Paine in Boston, and Robert W. de Forest in New York (Dreier, 1997; Radford, 1996; Wright, 1981). Dreier (1997) thoroughly documents philanthropy's three-pronged involvement with the housing crisis during the Progressive Era, including efforts to change the behavior of the poor and address the most visible housing problems, improve housing conditions through the sponsorship of efforts such as model housing projects, and advocate for public policy reform and strengthening of the role of government in regulating housing conditions. Many of the prominent advocates for housing reform, such as Mary Kingsbury Simkhovitch and Jane Addams, were first exposed to poor housing conditions in the slums through their settlement work.

Philanthropic support for community development during the Progressive Era was uneven and largely found in urban areas populated by White, ethnic immigrants, thereby demonstrating a blind spot when it came to civil rights. While many settlement leaders were not ignorant of the problems that Black Americans confronted, they did make a clear distinction between immigrants and Blacks.

Most settlement houses were segregated and Black settlements were more often than not short on funds and found it more difficult to secure philanthropic support. Despite these obstacles, many settlement houses such as the Wharton Centre in Philadelphia offered a large range of activities to Blacks, including purchasing and renovating affordable housing to rent and providing low-interest loans to Black tenants to improve their rental properties. Some of the most innovative community development programming for the Black community was found in the South. The Calhoun Colored School and Social Settlement in Alabama, for example, educated the Black rural school population based on the industrial school model and established an innovative land bank that purchased and sold land to farmers. Critical to the success of the Calhoun School was the fundraising prowess of its director, Charlotte Thorn, a White well-connected northerner who successfully secured funding from the Slater Fund, the Rockefeller Foundation, and the Frothingham Fund (Ellis, 1984). Access to northern philanthropists was critical to Thorn's success, and other social settlements that tried to emulate this model failed due to their limited philanthropic connections. Georgia Washington, for example, founded the People's Village School in Alabama. Washington helped launch the Calhoun School but struggled to sustain the People's Village School because she was a southern Black woman who lacked access to the White philanthropists in the North (Lasch-Quinn, 1993).[1]

Many of the philanthropic entities that supported Progressive Era community development initiatives were family foundations (Dreier, 1997; Lubove, 1962; Vale, 2000; Ylvisaker, 1987). Many of these early foundations were cautious in their approach to philanthropy and, while motivated by social justice, they often supported conventional causes such as education since tax laws governing charitable donations were vague (Hall, 1987). Some, however, supported tenement reform and low-income housing policies (Lubove, 1962).

In the midst of the Progressive Era we see another pivotal milestone in philanthropy's evolution with the rise of modern foundations. This occurred in the early 1900s as large fortunes were accrued by industrialists such as Andrew Carnegie and John D. Rockefeller. These wealthy individuals established their foundations for different reasons: some had a sense of social/civic responsibility whereas others felt the need to develop more strategic methods to maintain and disseminate their large sums of money. Other wealthy individuals, it has been argued, set up their foundations to serve their own interests (Ostrander, 1999). While early foundations are often portrayed as working in an elite environment disengaged from the public sector and public participation, Jacobs (1999) argues that these early foundations had "competing visions of political economy and the public" (p. 102). The conditions of the time were ripe for the creation of these entities, as a "crisis of authority" took place as Protestantism, which had provided many services to uplift societies, was being challenged by the massive immigration of Catholics, Jews, and Orthodox Christians. Foundations were able to step in and provide funds outside of religious organizations and subsequently helped many nonprofits with their efforts (Hammack, 1999). While the emergence of the modern foundation was welcomed on many fronts, skepticism existed as well. The U.S. Congress' Walsh Commission reported in 1916 that a small group of wealthy families not only had control over most major industries, but they also (through their foundations) exerted control over education and social services and these were serving their business interests better than actual philanthropy (Hammack, 1999). Even though legislation did not immediately result from the Commission's work, it put the philanthropic sector on notice that the U.S. Congress had concerns about the size, power, and accountability of large foundations.

While there was a considerable amount of variation in the motivations and philanthropy of these new foundations, quite a few were important supporters of local community development. The Sage Foundation, established by Margaret Slocum Sage in 1907, was among the first family foundations to adopt a less cautious and more explicit public-policy oriented approach to community-based philanthropy. The foundation's mission encompassed social, political, and economic change via surveys of living conditions in working-class communities. However, the foundation focused its efforts on understanding the problems of distressed communities and did not initially provide direct assistance (Russell Sage Foundation, 2007). Sage's vision for the foundation (established after her well-known parsimonious husband died in 1906) was to move beyond charity and support the improvement of life for the working classes. As an illustration of the dire need for funds to improve distressed communities, in 1906 Mrs. Sage received approximately 60,000 personal solicitations for assistance (Jacobs, 1999).

The Twentieth Century Fund, founded in 1919 by Boston department store magnate Edward Filene, also had a mission compatible with local community improvement. Filene believed that foundations should create new institutions to redistribute power and seed new social movements. He believed in preventative action and creating synergy between professionals, social science expertise, and public policy (Jacobs, 1999).

Another significant milestone in foundation history took root during this same time period in the early twentieth century. Along with the establishment of large foundations, we see the emergence of smaller funds with a more explicit social justice focus. The following chapter discusses this type of philanthropy in more detail, but here we note the significance of this new approach and its impact on underserved communities. Two of the first foundations with an explicit social justice emphasis were the Rosenwald Fund and the Stern Fund. The Rosenwald Fund, established by Julius Rosenwald and in existence from 1917–1948, provided significant charitable support for civil rights efforts and programming to support the well-being of African Americans (Ostrander, 2005). Several decades after Rosenwald established his foundation, the Stern Fund was created by Julius' daughter and son-in-law, Edith and Edgar Stern. In operation from 1936–1986, the Stern Fund began emphasizing racial justice and systemic change in the early 1960s. In 1963 David Hunter was hired as the foundation's executive director. Hunter had previously been at the Ford Foundation and was there during a pivotal phase of its evolution. Starting in the late 1950s, the Ford Foundation's work represented a new phase in philanthropy's effort to be more socially relevant and influence policy. Ford served as a change agent and a "catalytic force" for social change (O'Connor, 1999, p. 172). The 1950s thus led to a shift in foundations' focus on urban problems, and the turbulent political climate of the 1960s brought another major change as the United States faced a number of crises.

## Setting the stage for increased foundation investment

The federal government began to shift responsibility for addressing poverty and urban ills to local public and private organizations during the Johnson administration as criticism mounted over the unclear impact of War on Poverty programs, the rising costs of the Vietnam War, and the apparently bleak future of American cities (Patterson, 2000). With the creation of the U.S. Department of Housing and Urban Development (HUD) as a cabinet-level agency in 1965, and the institution of the Model Cities program by Congress in 1966, community development efforts were clearly placed in the hands of municipal governments and mayors (Lemann, 1991). By combining bricks-and-mortar funding with services, President Johnson was responding to criticism of federal antipoverty measures that were perceived as inefficient, costly, and ultimately contributing to urban poverty, rather than solving it (O'Connor, 1999). Edward Banfield, the chairman of the Advisory Committee on Demonstration Program Development, as the Model Cities program was known, reported in a letter to the President:

> In the view of the task force, most city governments can be trusted to use federal funds in the manner Congress intends [and] it is necessary to allow them much more latitude because the alternative is waste and frustration and/or their replacement by vastly expanded federal-state bureaucracy.
>
> (as cited in Scruggs-Leftwich, 2006, p. 33)

The federal government's delegation of responsibility for urban disinvestment to municipalities opened the door even wider for private foundations to play a significant role in this arena. Private foundations, particularly the Ford Foundation, were already key players in developing and supporting the Model Cities program. The Ford Foundation's Gray Areas project served as a framework for the development of the Model Cities program, and representatives from private foundations served on both the Task Force and the Model Cities program. The seven-member Model Cities program included two Ford Foundation staff members and a Gray Areas project board member (Scruggs-Leftwich, 2006).

The Gray Areas program, and later the Model Cities program, were among the first efforts at developing a more comprehensive approach to urban disinvestment, and some argue that many of the public–private partnerships targeting underserved urban areas continue to model these efforts. The Gray Areas program was formally initiated in 1961 and had spent approximately $26.5 million by 1965 to develop community action agencies in Boston, Oakland, New Haven, Philadelphia, and

Washington, D.C. (Halpern, 1995; Marwell, 2007). But comprehensive community development efforts began a decade earlier when the Ford Foundation's Paul Ylvisaker, head of the foundation's Public Affairs programs, sought to respond to the fragmentation of services targeting the inner city and the development of programs for the urban poor by "professionals and elite community leadership," which led to a lack of "realistic understanding ... of the problems faced by the poor" (Hughes and Hughes, 2000, p. 330). In addition, Ylvisaker argued that nonprofits and public agencies targeting the inner city worked in organizational silos, some focusing on bricks-and-mortar projects and others on services, without knowledge of each other's efforts. In response, "the Gray Areas program sought to coordinate service programs among local bureaucracies in an effort to integrate low-income residents into urban society" (Green and Haines, 2012, p. 97).

This collaborative approach to addressing the structural and social problems of the urban core is a key contribution by private foundations to today's CCIs. In addition, the Ford Foundation pushed for the notion of community action. The Ford Foundation's Ylvisaker sought to transform the process of community development to more fully engage urban residents, as the targeted recipients of services, in the design and execution of neighborhood initiatives (Hughes and Hughes, 2000).

The Model Cities program sought to learn from the lessons of the Ford Foundation's Gray Areas project. Thus the Model Cities initiative sought to improve coordination of social services and add bricks-and-mortar projects as well as economic development funds to targeted underserved urban areas. This comprehensive approach to urban revitalization was at the core of a package of six bills President Lyndon Johnson sent to Congress on January 26, 1966. The bill called for a demonstration project in a small number of urban sites, as proposed by Leonard Duhl and Antonia Chayes of the National Institute of Mental Health, who argued the following:

> We believe there is a need to accelerate the impact of the varied human development programs by a dramatic demonstration of ongoing and newly conceived urban aids in one or more especially chosen cities. Such a demonstration would involve long-range and short-term planning both for city-wide renewal and a comprehensive program of human services. The city should be of typical size and present typical problems of urbanization. The selection of the cities could take place through procedures established by the White House. The recipients should be assured of Federal funds sufficient to develop a model program for urban America.
>
> (as cited in Bernstein, 1996, p. 461)

The seven-member Model Cities Task Force, which included private foundation representatives, estimated the cost of the program at $2.3 billion over five years. Local mayors were to fund 20 percent of the projects with the federal government contributing 80 percent. But the rising costs of the Vietnam War drastically altered these funding projections (Bernstein, 1996).

A heated battle ensued between the House and Senate as they considered this legislation. Conservative House members sought to block the Model Cities program, arguing that the "Demonstration Cities" programs would "pay for Negro demonstrations in the big cities" (Bernstein, 1996, p. 466). As the opposition gained momentum, President Johnson called on 22 corporate businessmen and philanthropists, including Henry Ford II and David Rockefeller, to successfully convince the House members of the merits of the bill and it subsequently passed by a vote of 178 to 141. But the cost of compromise included significant concession on the amount of implementation funds as well as the number and location of the model cities chosen. Instead of a handful of demonstration projects, 63 cities were chosen in the first round in November of 1967, and an additional 12 were added in March 1968. By the second year, the number of demonstration areas had increased to 150 without a proportionate increase in funding (Mossberger, 2010).

The stage was set for private foundations to take a more visible leadership role in community revitalization. The Model City Task Force members had set an extraordinary agenda for the demonstration projects:

> The demonstration projects … should increase the total supply of low-income and moderate-income housing by massive amounts, combine physical reconstruction with social programs and a sensitivity to human concerns, allow local governments to operate flexibly and unconstrained by existing administrative arrangements, and alter existing building regulations and labor practices. In keeping with the widely-held perception that discrimination kept African Americans locked into ghettos, the panel also called for greater civil rights in the provision of housing.
>
> (von Hoffman, 2011, p. 29)

But pork barrel politics and fear of oppositional community participation gutted the original budget and design of the Model Cities program. It instead became a source of federal funds for various public agencies providing education, public safety, health, and recreation services (Savage, 2004). In addition, HUD lacked the authority to organize and build collaboration among the entrenched agencies targeting the urban poor, a key point for Ford and other foundations interested in better organization of the myriad interventions targeting urban areas.

By the end of the 1960s, funding for the Model Cities program began to decline. Congress cut its lifespan from six years to two, and its funding allocation was reduced from $2.3 billion to $900 million thinly spread over 150 sites (King and Vile, 2006). The Model Cities program officially ended in 1973.

President Richard Nixon continued the decentralization of Great Society programs after his election in 1968, transferring numerous community development initiatives housed in the Office of Economy Opportunity into other agencies in an effort to curtail the type of community action fostered by the Gray Areas program (DeFilippis and Saegert, 2008; Silver, 2006). Nixon's laissez-faire philosophy of New Federalism reduced federal oversight, moved community development closer to a block-grant model, and provided greater decision-making authority to the states (DeFilippis and Saegert, 2008). Two important initiatives further localized federal spending on urban problems: revenue sharing enacted in 1972 and the establishment of the CDBG program in 1974. The CDBG program spurred a variety of urban projects since it provided maximum flexibility for communities receiving federal funding.

Although these changes to community development spending did lead to an increase in CDBG funding over the next decade, the communities targeted were no longer the most needy, and the allowable expenditures were considerably broadened (Hays, 1995; O'Connor, 1999). The increased federal emphasis on local determination of funding priorities for underserved neighborhoods did motivate community organizations to develop institutional capacity and explore partnerships with other nonprofits and private foundations.

The Reagan Revolution of the 1980s continued the shift to localized decision-making to more efficiently address urban problems. Conservative foundations, and their privately funded think-tanks such as the Heritage Foundation and the American Enterprise Institute, supported the "get government off our backs" message promoted by President Reagan. The continuing devolution from federal to local problem solving led to shifting oversight of CDBG funds to non-entitlement cities from HUD to state governments. As expected, state governments concerned with responding to a variety of constituencies funded a greater number of smaller projects across the state, minimizing the impact of federal dollars. An HUD report concluded that the result of the shift to state oversight meant that "the average number of recipients in each state increased by 75 percent, and the average grant per recipient declined from $485,000 to $219,000" (Nenno, 1983, p. 146). Such a shift eliminated large bricks-and-mortar projects that could effect lasting change in underserved urban neighborhoods. This period in time also experienced the rise of the shadow state, which is a term used to describe the growing role of nonprofits in taking responsibility for public services and performing functions of the state (Wolch, 1990). The retrenchment of the federal government opened the door for the voluntary sector to fill service gaps left by the departure of the public sector but also raised questions about accountability to constituents. As INCITE!'s 2009 anthology, *The Revolution Will Not Be Funded: Beyond the Non-Profit Industrial Complex* attests, foundations as corporate funders limit nonprofits' capacity for social change by flexing their political and financial clout as a shadow state (INCITE! is a national activist organization of radical feminists of color located in Redmond, Washington).

By the early 1990s, after President George Bush took office, the "reinventing government" movement was responding to calls for allowing private sector values to make the public sector more efficient, increase productivity, and reverse its "incompetent, wasteful and overbearing" ways (Roelofs, 2003, p. 77). As a result of these public initiatives, the Ford Foundation, the Rockefeller Foundation, and the Annie E. Casey Foundation, among others, pushed for increased collaboration among public, nonprofit, and private organizations to more comprehensively respond to disinvestment in some of the poorer areas of the U.S. While some argue that these foundations were developing private solutions to public problems, others contend that private foundations were, and continue to actively participate in, filling a void as a result of federal retrenchment.

The expectations of the devolution exercise were that by curtailing the role of the federal government in community development, local efforts would more efficiently respond to the needs of each underserved community. But during the two decades following the election of Richard Nixon in 1968, these policy initiatives did not appear to have the desired outcomes as both the number of high poverty areas and the number of people living in poverty areas nearly doubled (Jargowsky, 1997).

The late 1980s and early 1990s saw an explosion of private foundation initiatives and partnerships that explored innovative approaches to urban problems. According to the Foundation Center, between 1950 and 1979, approximately 1,500 foundations were established per decade in the U.S. (http://foundationcenter.org/findfunders/statistics/found_estab.html). By 1980, the number of large foundations more than doubled as the Reagan administration sought to allow the free hand of the market to determine the future of the urban core (Bratt, Stone, and Hartman, 2006). Suggesting a response to the growing needs of decaying urban neighborhoods, the decade between 1980 and 1989 saw the creation of approximately 4,500 large foundations, with 18.5 percent of these foundations holding assets of between $25 and $100 million, and 16 percent with assets of $100 million or more. The number of foundations only continued to increase as George Herbert Walker Bush took office as the 41st President of the United States. The decade between 1990 and 1999 saw the establishment of approximately 10,000 foundations (http://foundationcenter.org/findfunders/statistics/found_estab.html). This latter group is composed of smaller foundations, with 16.1 percent holding assets under $1 million; 55.1 percent holding assets of between $1 and $5 million; 13 percent holding assets of between $5 and $10 million; and 9.5 percent with assets of $10–25 million.[2]

As we discuss in this book, a cohort of these foundations are serving a valuable role in stimulating urban revitalization efforts. Also noteworthy, however, was the rise in "strategic conservative philanthropy" beginning in the 1990s that used sophisticated networking, research, and advocacy to advance a conservative agenda (Covington, 2005).

Important to an understanding of the role of philanthropy in community development is the growth in the number of private foundations, which include independent and family foundations, and grant-making public charities such as community foundations that pool funds from various philanthropies and community members. According to the Foundation Center, approximately one-third of the foundations created between 1990 and 1999 were independent foundations and 36 percent were community foundations. The number of independent foundations more than doubled from the previous decade. That growth in private foundations continued into the most recent decade, 2000–2009, when more than 8,500 large foundations were established (http://foundationcenter.org/findfunders/statistics/found_estab.html).

Foundations have a historical legacy of charitable support for community development. While funding has been uneven at times, philanthropic entities have demonstrated the potential to both fill in funding gaps left by the public and private sectors and take risks to initiate innovative new programs and policies. The landscape of philanthropy is complex. It is governed by ambiguous laws and regulations and consists of many different types of foundations. The next chapter provides an overview of the numerous types of foundations engaged in community development.

# 3

# THE INTERSECTION OF PHILANTHROPY AND COMMUNITY DEVELOPMENT

The types of community change efforts in which private foundations engage vary across many levels including scale of support, type of support, and the type of foundation providing the funding. The philanthropic world is complex and the role that foundations play in society is not well understood despite its many contributions to society (Dowie, 2001; Fleishman, 2007). This chapter provides a comprehensive overview of the landscape of philanthropy and provides a typology of foundations documenting the ways in which they operate and support local community development.

As charitable organizations continued to grow in numbers and size, and as donations to these entities increased, the Internal Revenue Service (IRS) provided a framework and structure to these entities through legislative statute. Under Section 501(c)(3) of the Internal Revenue Code, the IRS first defines a tax-exempt charitable organization as one that is:

> organized and operated exclusively for exempt purposes set forth in section 501(c)(3), and none of its earnings may inure to any private shareholder or individual. In addition, it may not be an action organization, i.e., it may not attempt to influence legislation as a substantial part of its activities and it may not participate in any campaign activity for or against political candidates.
>
> (www.irs.gov/charities/charitable/article/0,,id=96099,00.html)

According to the IRS, organizations that use the 501(c)(3) designation fall into two broad categories: public charities and private foundations (see Figure 3.1). The IRS does not explicitly define "private foundation," and instead argues that all 501(c)(3) organizations are private foundations except for those that engage in inherently public activity and obtain an exception from the IRS (Richardson and Reilly, 2003). The source of funding for charity work is a key variable in determining whether an organization is a charity or a private foundation. According to IRS operation requirements:

> Public charities receive a greater portion of their financial support from the general public or governmental units, and have greater interaction with the public. A private foundation, on the other hand, is typically controlled by members of a family or by a small group of individuals, and derives much of its support from a small number of sources and from investment income. Because they are less open to public scrutiny, private foundations are subject to various operating restrictions and to excise taxes for failure to comply with those restrictions.
>
> (http://www.irs.gov/Charities-&-Non-Profits/EO-Operational-Requirements:--Private-Foundations-and-Public-Charities)

The number of subcategories under these two umbrella terms varies according to the IRS, the Foundation Center, and the Council on Foundations. Public charities typically receive one-third of their support from many sources, including the general public, private foundations, government agencies, and corporations. Public charities such as museums, parent–teacher organizations, or art groups can also use fees collected for services or admissions fees to fund their charitable activities (see Figure 3.2).

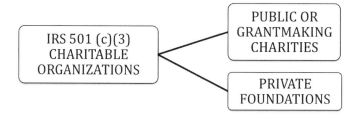

**FIGURE 3.1** Internal Revenue Service (IRS) foundation status classification

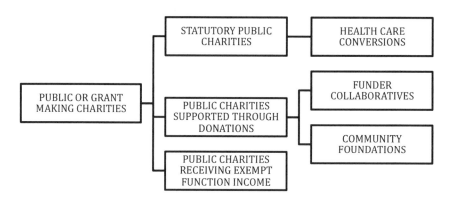

**FIGURE 3.2** Subcategories of public charities or grant-making charities

Statutory public charities, such as health care conversions and public charities supported through donations such as community foundations and funder collaboratives, are philanthropic efforts that are evident in place-based community development initiatives targeting the urban poor. This chapter takes a closer look at these specific forms of charitable giving beginning with health care conversions.

## Health care conversions

Also known as New Health Foundation Initiatives, health care conversions are foundations established from proceeds from the conversion of a nonprofit health care organization into a for-profit entity. Conversion of hospitals from nonprofit to for-profit corporations comprise 75 percent of health care conversions, but this group typically results in smaller foundations with median assets of approximately $41 million (Williams and Brelvi, 2000). Conversions resulting from health plans and health systems result in much larger foundations with a median endowment of $106 million from health plans and approximately $140 million from health care systems (Williams and Brelvi, 2000).

New health foundations largely focus their grant-making on health care issues within a specific geographic area and are increasingly engaging in community development programs as they relate to the overall well-being of families. The California Endowment (CalEndow), established in 1996, is at the forefront of these comprehensive community development efforts arguing that good health happens in healthy communities. It was created as a result of Blue Cross of California's creation of a for-profit corporation, the WellPoint Health Network. In 2010, CalEndow launched a ten-year Building Healthy Communities Initiative that targets 14 underserved communities in California. Arguing that place matters in the well-being of families, CalEndow has committed $1 billion to its CCI.

CalEndow has identified ten outcomes for a healthy community that will serve as a roadmap for improvement, as well as help measure success as the initiatives are implemented in each underserved neighborhood. These outcomes go beyond health conditions, encompassing every facet of community life, including education, housing, neighborhood safety, environmental health, employment, and access to healthy foods (California Endowment, 2010).

A growing number of foundations are expanding their health care missions to include economic and community development. Grantmakers in Health, a nonprofit launched in 1982 to foster collaboration among health-related grant makers, recently convened a strategy session in Washington, D.C. highlighting the importance of place for health-based initiatives. It argued that:

> Place matters in the lives of children. They and their families are generally only as safe, healthy, and productive as the communities in which they live, work, and play. Knowing this, there is more focus on mitigating negative influences on people's health and well-being by improving community conditions. By

addressing the social, economic, and environmental factors that shape out-comes for children and families, funders may find opportunities to support healthy child development.

(Grantmakers in Health, 2011, p. 2)

Using the well-known Harlem Children's Zone (HCZ) as an example of effective child-focused, place-based neighborhood improvement, other health care foundations are examining the potential of comprehensive community development partnerships (Orszag, Barnes, Carrion, and Summers, 2009). The HCZ encompasses a 97-block area in Harlem, New York, in which numerous nonprofits collaborate to support children's educational, health, and social development from birth to college (Smedley, 2008). Highlighting the complexity of holistic community change, efforts by the Obama administration to expand the HCZ to 21 communities has come under fire after a Brookings Institution study presented evidence that providing parenting classes, health services, nutritional programs, and other wrap-around social services fails to have appreciable effects on student achievement.[1] Critics also argue that few communities have access to the type of funding needed to effectively implement such a model. HCZ's assets in 2009 were $200 million with an operating budget of $84 million (Otterman, 2010).

A focus on children's health has also led to the use of comprehensive community initiatives by foundations. Realizing that place matters, health care foundations such as The Alleghany Foundation in Covington, Virginia, funded economic development studies on regional cooperation to attract industry to the area; it also provides funds for the removal of blighted property and historic preservation. Another example is the Birmingham Foundation, created from the sale of a private hospital in 1996 that now targets 14 underserved communities in the South Pittsburgh area for community development initiatives. The Byerly Foundation was formed in 1995 from proceeds of the sale of a hospital in Hartsville, North Carolina. It is actively engaged in the update of a comprehensive plan for the city of Hartsville and is serving as a funder and catalyst for the removal of the railroad from the center of town, paving the way for Hartsville's redevelopment.[2]

Communities across the U.S. may just be starting to feel the impact of health care conversion foundations. Baker (2001) argues that less than 21 percent of the 525 hospitals converting from nonprofit to for-profit ownership have established foundations as required by law. The sector saw a sharp increase in the creation of conversion foundations during the mid-1980s to late 1990s with approximately 60 percent formed between 1994 and 1999, and an additional 10 percent since 1999 with more than half located in ten states (Garigan, 2004; Shiroma, 2001).

## Community foundations

As a 501(c)(3) tax-exempt organization, a community foundation is a public charity created to attract large contributions for the benefit of a specific geographic area or community (IRS Reg. 1.170A-9[e][11][i]). Funds may be held by the community foundation, or by banks and trusts that distribute net assets to the community foundation from bequests or estates.

A critical issue for a community foundation to retain its tax-exempt status is the 33⅓ percent support test. The organization must receive more than one-third of its total funding in each taxable year from the general public in the form of "gifts, grants, contributions, membership fees" (IRC 509 [a][2]). These contributions include bequests, legacies, property, and transfers from private foundations.

Unlike private foundations that are free to develop their own criteria for board membership, including limiting board seats to family members (in the case of family foundations), community foundation boards have less flexibility according to federal statute. Not only must community foundations show a history of broad support from the community they serve, the governing body must also represent the public interest. In addition, the board of a community foundation must be independent, non-sectarian and not appointed by a single outside entity (Council on Foundations, 2008).

Community foundations have a long history in the U.S., with the first instituted in 1914. Some community foundations began as private foundations as is the case with the Brooklyn Community Foundation. First inaugurated in 1998 with a gift of stock valued at more than $56 million from the Independence Community Bank, the Independent Community Foundation focused on providing assistance to low-income residents of Brooklyn's 70 distinct neighborhoods. Recognizing that additional resources were needed to respond to the diverse needs of its targeted residents, more than one-third of which are foreign-born, the foundation transferred its endowment to create the Brooklyn Community Foundation in 2009.

The geographic areas targeted by community foundations vary, with many targeting counties as their service areas. The Midwest region has the greatest number of community foundations. In fact, Michigan, Ohio, and Indiana account for more than one-third of all community foundations based in the U.S. with 64, 78, and 79 respectively. California also has one of the highest concentrations of community foundations with 70 in the state (Council on Foundations, n.d.). Bernholz, Fulton, and Kasper (2005) argue that changes in tax laws spurred the growth of community foundations beyond cities, leading to dramatic growth in the Midwest. Many of these community foundations also have strong connections to community development work. The devolution of local policymaking and local support for service provision has positioned community foundations to play an increasingly important role in community development (Graddy and Morgan, 2006).

A number of challenges face community foundations in the twenty-first century. In their report, *On the Brink of a New Promise: The Future of U.S. Community*

*Foundations*, Bernholz et al. (2005) write that there are three key changes that community foundations must address. The first includes shifting their focus from "institution-building" and operational efficiency outward to the communities they serve as they redefine their purpose. They contend that many of the unique services community foundations provide are now available elsewhere. In addition, the communities they serve are changing rapidly and community foundations must give serious thought to their mission and target population.

Another key change community foundations must make includes moving beyond their traditional fiscal role. Initially created to manage the assets of a variety of donors to benefit a geographic area, community foundations can serve as effective leaders in developing strategic solutions, brokering collaborations, and building new knowledge in ways that respond to the specific needs of its community (Bernholz et al., 2005).

The third change promoted by Bernholz et al. (2005) addresses the need for community foundations to develop strategic and coordinated relationships with other foundations and funding sources, rather than competing against them. Community foundations must adapt to new contexts in which partnerships are the norm rather than the exception, as limited resources impact the foundations' work in an increasingly fast-paced, social, cultural, and economic environment.

## Funder collaboratives

Challenged by the complex, and often expensive, interventions needed by under-served, urban neighborhoods, foundations are also forming funding collaboratives to pool resources, information, and know-how. One of the most notable collaboratives is Living Cities, formed in 1991 as the National Community Development Initiative (NCDI), a collective comprised of 22 foundations, banks, financial institutions, HUD, and private corporations. The LISC and the Enterprise Foundation serve as intermediaries, working directly with CDCs in targeted low-income neighborhoods. NCDI's mission is bold and a clear departure from most traditional approaches to philanthropy. It emphasizes collaboration, innovation, leadership, and impacts and articulates two of these goals as follows:

- Innovation: We take risks, catalyze fresh thinking, and test new approaches in order to creatively disrupt the status quo, change broken systems, and provide opportunities for all;
- Impact: We are committed to making material improvements in the lives of low-income people, cities, and the systems that affect them. We hold ourselves accountable for evaluating our effectiveness and are intentionally self-reflective as we strive to continuously improve, adapt, and inform future innovation.

(www.livingcities.org/about/values)

Funder collaboratives go beyond pooling resources. As Elwood Hopkins (2005) of the Los Angeles Urban Funders (LAUF) states, "It entails pooling knowledge across institutions; facilitating the formation of groupings; networks, or alliances to do things collectively; reducing duplication of effort; and optimizing collective economies of scale" (p. 23). A growing number of funder collaboratives are focusing their resources on geographically defined communities in need, including the Detroit Funders Collaborative, the Philadelphia Neighborhood Development Collaborative, the Baltimore Neighborhood Collaborative, the Trenton Funders Collaborative, the East Bay Funders, LAUF, the Long Beach Funders, and the San Diego Neighborhood Funders.

The Surdna Foundation's Comprehensive Community Revitalization Program (CCRP) was one of the early funder collaboratives, operating from 1992–1998. The Surdna Foundation made an initial grant of $3 million, recruiting other foundations and corporations by focusing on place-based change via a "pragmatic approach." Four CDCs in four South Bronx neighborhoods identified neighborhood needs and solutions. Annie E. Casey, Chase Bank, Citigroup, Edna McConnell Clark, LISC, New York Department of Health, the Open Society Institute, Seedco, the Pew Trust, the Rockefeller Foundation, Uris Brothers Foundation, and the Wells Fargo Foundation all joined the collaborative, contributing $9.4 million; the four targeted CDCs raised an additional $10 million. This collaboration in New York served as a catalyst for the creation of Chicago's New Communities Program (NCP) with $47 million funding from the MacArthur Foundation. The ten-year NCP in Chicago started in 2002 and is managed by LISC Chicago. It engaged 16 Chicago neighborhoods and 14 local community organizations. In a preliminary evaluation of four lead agencies involved in this effort, Chaskin and Karlström (2012) argue that LISC's role as a broker for needed technical and financial resources was a key variable in developing collaborative relationships, but NCP has yet to achieve systemic change for achieving improved quality of life for disadvantaged residents.

Funder collaborations can be particularly effective at directing and funding comprehensive community development in low-income communities by spreading the risk of funding efforts that individual foundations typically avoid. Philanthropy is traditionally risk-averse, and comprehensive community change is complicated and does not occur in short intervals of time. By minimizing risk, funder collaboratives blend funding streams and build upon the expertise of the individual foundations to essentially deconstruct the challenges of complex neighborhood problems. This approach allows for a response that is thoughtful, multifaceted, and based on each foundation's knowledge and prior experiences. The availability of combined, sustained funding streams provide more resources for struggling neighborhoods and ensure a more consistent source of funds over a longer period that could ultimately bring about marked social change. Successful collaboratives share many of the same elements including clear values, goals, methods, trust, and accountability, equal voice between all funding participants, and clear expectations about participants' decision-making authority (Hamilton, 2002).

As of the mid-2000s, approximately 40 funder collaboratives were in operation and the number appears to be growing (Hopkins, 2005; Sharp, 2002). They vary considerably in terms of organizational structure, mission, and geographic target area and are still a very small proportion of the total number of foundations (Hopkins, 2005). They also have some identifiable disadvantages including barriers to collaboration based on funder concerns about time commitments, differences in mission, the silo culture of large foundations, pride of ownership, and lack of staff to manage the collaboratives. True collaboration is also hard to find and some efforts may be collaborative in name only or superficially collaborative (Sharp, 2002). A detailed example of funder collaboratives is discussed in Chapter 4, and the following section elaborates on the characteristics and function of private foundations.

## Private foundations

Private foundations devote the majority of their assets to the "active conduct of its exempt status" but, most importantly, derive their resources from private money, including from a family, individual, or a corporation (Foundation Center, 2011). In order to retain their tax-exempt status, five major restrictions are placed on foundations. According to Richardson and Reilly (2003) it is far more advantageous to operate a public charity, due to these restrictions on private foundations. This includes adhering to the 5 percent rule. Every year, the foundation must distribute 5 percent of the aggregate fair market value of all investment assets of the organization for charitable purposes. Additionally, they must not engage in self-dealing with disqualified persons, where disqualified persons are defined as a person who owns more than 35 percent of profit interest or holds voting power. They must also ensure that their holdings maintain a clear separation between the non-profit and for-profit entities. Further restrictions focus on ensuring foundations' grants or expenditures are used for charitable purposes and that the foundation's private investments mitigate risk and avoid jeopardizing their charitable work.

Private foundations engaged in community development efforts are increasingly hands-on, meaning that the foundation is significantly involved in efforts to revitalize the targeted underserved community. The IRS classifies these types of organizations as private operating foundations. These private foundations must distribute 85 percent of their adjusted net income directly to further their exempt activities. The foundation engages in providing grants to other charities or nonprofits without the assistance of an intervening organization; it maintains a staff of "researchers or other personnel who supervise and direct these activities on a continuing basis," and a specific purpose of the foundation is "relief of the poor or distressed, and its activities provide such relief" (IRS Reg. 53.4942[b]-1[d]). The foundation may also make grants to individuals to encourage involvement in programs of interest to the foundation's goals for the targeted community.

For donors, the difference between a private foundation and a private operating foundation is significant. Contributions to private operating foundations are deductible up to 50 percent of the donor's adjusted gross income (IRS Section 4942 [j][3]), whereas contributions to all other private foundations are deductible to only 30 percent of the donor's adjusted gross income. Private foundations are further subdivided into three categories, as Figure 3.3 illustrates.

Independent foundations derive their resources from charitable endowments that originated from one family or a handful of individuals (Council on Foundations, 2010). Unlike family foundations, independent foundations are not governed by the benefactor or the benefactor's family, and are focused primarily on grant-making. These types of private non-operating foundations do not solicit donations or seek public support. Some independent foundations began as family foundations.

Corporate-sponsored foundations are those involved in charity activities that may strategically assist the parent corporation's business activities. Corporate foundations may contribute products, cash grants, employee volunteers, or in-kind services such as consulting to nonprofits. Corporate philanthropies are typically classified as non-operating private foundations because they are primarily concerned with grant-making, although there are corporate foundations that do take a more active role in administering and evaluating their charitable programs.

As an example of private operating foundations, family foundations derive their resources from members of a single family and continue to play an important role in the redevelopment of urban neighborhoods. According to the Council on Foundations (2010), more than half of all private foundations are family foundations, totaling approximately 40,000 organizations in 2010. Although three out of five family foundations hold assets of less than $1 million, family foundations donated approximately $21.1 billion in 2008, which comprised 62 percent of all foundation giving (Council on Foundations, 2010).

The focus of this book is on philanthropic organizations engaged in community development change efforts in underserved neighborhoods. According to the Foundation Center, "between 1975 and 2010, growth in giving by independent and community foundations far outpaced increases from other sources" (2010).[3] In examining the category of independent foundations more closely, the importance of family foundations for improving the quality of life of economically disadvantaged

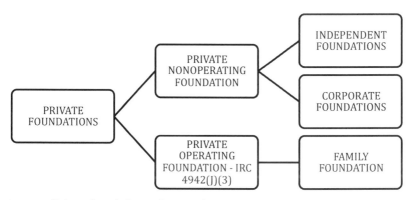

**FIGURE 3.3** Private foundations subcategories

communities becomes evident (Foundation Center, 2011).[4] An analysis by the Foundation Center presents a compelling case for the importance of family foundations in addressing the types of urban problems that are targeted by CCIs. Approximately 35 percent of the $20.6 billion granted by family foundations in 2010 went to the economically disadvantaged and nearly 60 percent of grant dollars by family foundations was directed at programmatic activities. The impact of family foundation dollars on the urban poor may be in its infancy as one-third of family foundations were established in the 2000s, and these institutions are just starting to mature (Foundation Center, 2012).[5]

The literature on foundations includes other terms used to identify various types of philanthropic efforts that engage private foundations, many of which are focused on community development activities. The terminology overlaps at times and the following definitions clarify the lexicon:

> *Checkbook philanthropy* is the traditional model of giving in which corporate CEOs or wealthy philanthropists write a sizeable check to a worthy cause without expectations of involvement, or assessment of the impact made by their contribution.

> *Place-based philanthropy* is used to describe community development programs in clearly identified geographic areas with physical boundaries. Sometimes referred to as embedded philanthropy, this approach involves "intimate, active engagement in community change, specific to a local community. Embedded philanthropists make a long-term commitment to living and working in a community or neighborhood … often providing direct services and technical assistance" (www.ncfp.org/resources/ask_the_center/embedded_philanthropy).

> *Place-based vs. people-based philanthropy* contrasts those foundations that focus on bricks-and-mortar projects to catalyze physical change in underserved communities with other foundations that focus on people in an underserved area and may direct their philanthropic resources towards increasing human capital such as education. Physical boundaries for the target area of this latter approach are more flexible.

> *Embedded philanthropy* is sometimes used interchangeably with place-based philanthropy. It refers to a foundation that embeds itself in a community, with staff actively engaged with residents on a day-to-day basis to effect community-wide change.

> *Venture philanthropy* describes entrepreneurial philanthropists, many of whom made millions during the dot-com boom days, who expect to actively engage with the nonprofits or communities in need, providing technical as well as management assistance.

> *New scientific philanthropy* encompasses venture philanthropy ideals but also seeks to apply business models to philanthropic giving. It has also been referred

to as "philanthrocapitalism" by Edwards (2008) who argues that this approach is grounded in a belief that methods drawn from the business world can effectively transform society when applied to public sectors.

*Creative philanthropy* is an approach espoused by Anheier and Leat (2006), who argue that foundations are products of their historical conditions and, as a result, their approaches reflect societal norms and values. But as communities face uncertain conditions in the twenty-first century, foundations need to respond with creativity by fostering sustainable change, encouraging constructive conversation with key stakeholders, and changing the focus of public discourse to examine new approaches to old problems. These creative philanthropic efforts are also more likely to involve collaborations with other foundations and receive funding for ten years or more.

An emphasis on equity and social justice is an important component of several of these types of philanthropic efforts, and the next section summarizes the common attributes of social justice philanthropy.

## Social justice philanthropy

One other category of philanthropy critical to the discussion on the types of foundation-supported models for community development is social justice philanthropy, also referred to as social change philanthropy, responsive philanthropy, and/or social movement philanthropy. This branch of philanthropy strives to change institutions and defines issues based on community priorities, particularly communities that have been traditionally disenfranchised. It emphasizes democratic civic participation based on direct citizen engagement driven by grassroots organizing (Faber and McCarthy, 2005). Progressive social change and egalitarian redistribution of power and resources is a critical component of this approach (Ostrander, 2005). Core principles include prioritizing a focus on the root causes of inequity and pursuing structural and systemic change based on inclusive, collective action, and channeling philanthropic dollars to nonprofit organizations to increase opportunities for those with the least amount of resources (Foundation Center, 2011; Jagpal, 2009; National Network of Grantmakers as cited in Faber and McCarthy, 2005). It is also characterized by an emphasis on transparency and increased funding for marginalized communities (Jagpal, 2009). Some look to John Rawls' *A Theory of Justice* as providing the theoretical foundation for this philanthropic approach. His principles of equal rights and distributive justice leading to a fair and equal welfare state is in alignment with the goals and objectives of social justice philanthropy (Jagpal, 2009; Rawls, 1971).

Social change philanthropy began in the early 1950s with the Field Foundation, Emil Schwarzhaupt Foundation, and the Wiebolt Foundation (Dreier, 1997). The Field Foundation funded the National Association for the Advancement of Colored People (NAACP) and the Schwarzhaupt and Wiebolt Foundations supported Saul Alinsky's work and the Highlander Center (Jenkins and Halcli,

1999). By the end of the 1950s, nine additional foundations emphasizing social change allocated funding for community organizing, civil rights, and voter registration efforts. By the 1960s some of the mainstream foundations including Ford, Carnegie, Rockefeller, Sloan, and Lilly provided support for social change philanthropy (Dreier, 1997). The involvement of large, mainline foundations is partially responsible for the expansion of this approach during this time period as many of them financed community organizing efforts.

In addition to the involvement of large foundations, smaller family foundations also emerged as supporters of social change initiatives (Jenkins and Halcli, 1999). Among the earliest and most prominent foundations with a social justice emphasis were the Rosenwald Fund and the Stern Fund. The Rosenwald Fund was in existence from 1917–1948. Its founder, Julius Rosenwald, accrued his fortune from Sears, Roebuck and sought for the foundation to expend all of its assets within 25 years of his death. Rosenwald was influenced by the work of Booker T. Washington and subsequently made the well-being of African Americans the primary focus of the foundation. Subsequently the foundation established the Rosenwald Fellows program to provide funding for separate educational and training facilities for African Americans interested in careers in education, health, and medical services. The foundation also supported civil rights organizations that worked to dismantle segregationist policies. The efficacy of Rosenwald's foundation has been debated. Some argue that his support for separate organizations for African Americans continued to subjugate this group, whereas others defend his impact and point to his support for the Highlander Center that trained union organizers in the South in the 1930s (Ostrander, 2005).

One of the more significant legacies of the Rosenwald Fund is its clear connection to, and influence on, the Stern Fund. The Stern Fund was established in 1936 by Julius' daughter and son-in-law, Edith and Edgar Stern, as a one-generation foundation. It adopted the same model as the Rosenwald Fund but its funding priorities shifted after Edgar's death, who preferred more traditional avenues of philanthropy such as supporting cultural institutions and universities. When the fund's new executive director, David Hunter, arrived at Stern in 1963 (from the Ford Foundation), Edith dictated a change in funding priorities with a shift to racial justice and a desire to fund systemic change. Most of its grants, though, were given to national organizations such as the National Organization of Women, Students for a Democratic Society, and the National Congress of Neighborhood Women before the Stern Fund closed its doors in 1986 (Ostrander, 2005).

Social justice philanthropy shifted its emphasis in the 1950s and early 1960s from focusing almost exclusively on civil rights, to a more expansive definition of civil rights encompassing other groups such as women, children, and the disabled by the late 1960s and 1970s. Concurrent with the broader definition of rights and the growth of middle-class reform movements, social change philanthropies became supporters of environmental organizations and organizations that supported political and social rights, particularly those working in low-income communities (Jenkins and Halcli, 1999).

The 1970s experienced the emergence of new alternative social change foundations. A new social justice model that gained traction was that of the foundation supported by small, individual contributors. The first effort was the Agape Foundation created in 1970 in San Francisco by a group of peace activists. The foundation was supported by individual donors along with the proceeds from benefit concerts by Joan Baez and Gordon Lightfoot. Its model for effecting change through nonviolence and social protest was then adopted by seven additional foundations in the 1970s including the Vanguard Foundation in San Francisco, the Haymarket People's Fund in Boston, and Liberty Hill in Santa Monica. These alternative charities also shared the same funding model (Jenkins and Halcli, 1999). The Haymarket Fund, for example, has funding boards comprised completely of community activists and supports a range of movement issues including racism, workers' rights, housing and homelessness, and environmental and health issues. Ostrander (2005) points to Haymarket's decision-making process as a valuable model that also ensures much more accountability. By 1979 the number of these foundations increased to the extent that they created a technical assistance center, the Funding Exchange, to support their efforts (Jenkins and Halcli, 1999). The Funding Exchange now has 16 member foundations (2012).[6]

By the 1980s social justice philanthropy grew in terms of active foundations and funding priorities. By 1990, 146 social change foundations were identified and had invested close to $88.1 million in social change efforts. The overall majority of these foundations, 61 percent, were family foundations. With the ascendancy of the "New Right" during the Reagan and Bush presidencies of the 1980s, social change philanthropy experienced growth with a significant amount of grants supporting minority groups and community organizing in both rural and urban communities (Jenkins and Halcli, 1999).

Despite its tangible impact on its beneficiary communities and stakeholders, social change philanthropy is a small percentage of overall philanthropic giving. Even though the absolute number of social justice foundations increased in the 1970s, adjusting for inflation, we see that funding levels declined. Between 1953 and 1980 only 131 out of 22,000 grant giving foundations supported social movement projects (Jenkins, 1989). In 2009, social justice grant-making accounted for 14.2 percent of the grants awarded by the largest foundations. The majority of the grant dollars were allocated to economic and community development (29 percent), health care access and affordability (17 percent) and human rights and civil liberties (13 percent) (Foundation Center, 2011).

Over its six decades of existence, social justice philanthropy has ebbed and flowed. During the first half of the 2000s, social justice philanthropy was on an upswing and was growing faster than overall giving, due in part to optimism about the Obama administration's agenda. However, when the global financial crisis hit in 2008, philanthropy in general, and social justice philanthropy in particular, were severely impacted. The assets of U.S. foundations declined 17.2 percent in 2008. Between 2008 and 2009 social justice philanthropy declined at a comparable rate from $3.7 billion to $3.1 billion (Gould, 2011).

A study completed by the Foundation Center (2011) identified challenges that social justice grant-making will encounter through 2015. It concluded that unless the field experiences five years of above-average returns on its investments, social justice grant-making will not return to pre-2008 levels. Since small foundations (less than $50 million in assets) face greater challenges in recovering from the financial crisis, social justice change efforts will suffer since nonprofits engaged in social justice work rely heavily on these small foundations for funding support. Gould (2011) adds that an additional challenge is the strategy of some foundations to reduce their grant-making in order to maintain their endowments, whereas others are altering their grant review processes and making them more selective by denying unsolicited proposals.

Given its small overall share of philanthropic giving, questions have been raised about the efficacy and impact of social justice philanthropy. Faber and McCarthy (2005) argue that as a result of its community organizing efforts and grassroots democracy, social justice philanthropy has the potential to catalyze needed change. In addition, larger mainline foundations can partner with social justice philanthropies to more explicitly incorporate social justice language into foundation programming, serving as "institutional entrepreneurs" by legitimizing grant-making of this nature (Suarez, 2012, p. 260).

Others have advocated for social justice philanthropy to depart from a fractured approach to funding and instead organize coalitions and focus on larger movement building (Dreier, 1997; Dreier, 2002). Foundations are also called to play a greater leadership role in these efforts and invest in civic capacity (Auspos, Brown, Kubisch, and Sutton, 2009). A significant challenge, however, is measuring and quantifying the impact of social justice philanthropy. The National Committee for Responsive Philanthropy (NCRP), a nonprofit independent watchdog group based in Washington, D.C., answered this challenge through recently proposed criteria for grant makers to evaluate their work, a program named *Philanthropy at its Best*. Based on the premise that foundation assets should be viewed to a certain extent as public dollars since donors receive large tax subsidies, this evaluation framework focuses on values, effectiveness, ethics, and commitment, and defines specific benchmarks in each of the four categories (Jagpal, 2009).[7]

The NCRP also supports efforts to quantify and monetize the impact of social justice philanthropy. In a study of the policy impacts of 15 community organizations in Los Angeles County that received funding from foundations, the NCRP found that these groups collectively gained over $6.9 billion for marginalized communities in Los Angeles over a five-year period. For every one dollar invested in advocacy, organizing, and civic engagement (a total of $75.5 million), the target communities realized $91 in benefits. Philanthropic sources provided the capital necessary to attain these goals and contributed $58 million (77 percent) of the seed funding for these efforts (Ranghelli and Craig, 2010). These findings suggest that the broader impact of targeted philanthropic entities can yield a significant return on investment and measurable accumulated benefits.

## Challenges in philanthropic giving

The literature demonstrates that foundation partnerships engaged in community development initiatives offer potential to stimulate community change. But the legal and financial structures of foundations contain challenges to the viability of these efforts. For example, foundations that support community development differ on the types of funding mechanisms used. Research indicates that "managed pooled funds, co-funding arrangements, grants coordination systems … and temporary joint ventures" are all tools used by private foundations, along with contributions of stock by the parent company, as in the case of Price Charities (Hopkins, 2005, p. 20). One of the challenges faced by foundations, particularly private foundations in which the parent company is still active, is the clear separation of nonprofit and for-profit funding. In addition, although all 501(c)(3) organizations must file annual 990 forms with the IRS in order to retain their nonprofit status, tracking their sources of funding and the expenditure on community development projects can be difficult. As the Foundation Center (2009) attests, only 13 percent of approximately 12,000 surveyed foundations issue an annual report, and approximately 28 percent maintain a website. The lack of access to information makes it difficult to quantify philanthropy's impact on community development, as well as the sources of funding used to realize complex neighborhood projects. An additional challenge stems from the ways in which foundations define and report their activities. Community development is not one of the main categories used to measure charitable giving and it overlaps with many commonly used categories including poverty, social justice, and underserved communities.

The NCRP issued a report highlighting the challenges faced by the general public in accessing information that can help determine whether foundations are appropriately utilizing taxpayer subsidies (Jagpal, 2009). Focusing on ethics, effectiveness, and commitment as values that the charity sector espouses, the report called for greater transparency as a new round of U.S. Congressional hearings begins in response to concerns over the federal government's capacity to monitor this growing sector (Perry, 2012).

The IRS, the agency charged with processing applications for new tax-exempt charities and monitoring their effectiveness, is woefully underfunded according to the United States General Accounting Office (GAO) (2002). Its analysis, conducted after public concerns over charities that misused funds donated to 9/11 victims, indicates that the IRS is overwhelmed as applications for new tax-exempt foundations have increased by 9 percent, while the number of IRS staff charged with overseeing this sector was reduced by 15 percent. In addition, as a result of changes in IRS requirements adopted in 2006, there were approximately 400,000 registered nonprofits that had failed to file the appropriate reporting forms and were threatened with the loss of their nonprofit status (Strom, 2010). The final total number of organizations that received revocation of their 501(c)(3) charitable status is estimated at 275,000 and the majority were social service organizations (Blackwood and Roeger, 2011).

Critics of the tax subsidy for charitable foundations argue that charitable deductions privilege the wealthy by providing taxpayer subsidies for donations. An Urban Institute study estimated that the potential taxable income from charities could potentially total $25.4 billion in 2002, equal to a loss of $10.1 billion for the U.S. government (Pew Charitable Trust, 2010).

Proponents of the federal subsidy argue that the types of goods and services provided by the nonprofit sector, including foundations, are those that the market cannot, or is not willing to, provide. Thus government can provide incentives, such as allowing a tax deduction for charitable giving, to encourage individuals and institutions to provide needed services. By the mid-1980s, foundations sought to maximize these governmental incentives by collaborating with the private sector towards a more comprehensive, place-based model for community change. A particularly innovative approach to comprehensive community development that aims to diversify funding streams is the Living Cities' Integration Initiative. Five sites will receive $85 million from 2011 to 2013 in the form of flexible debt, grants, and commercial debt. The goal is to provide opportunities and incentives for private markets to work to improve the lives of low-income people through the use of Living Cities' members as intermediaries. Living Cities as a foundation collaborative thus facilitates the public, private, and nonprofit partnerships needed to successfully address complex urban problems. This strategy is evident in the structuring of community financial assistance through flexible and commercial debt. The goal is for low-income communities to use these financing tools to establish long-term relationships with private funding institutions, and for the institutions to realize the opportunities available in underserved communities. But as our research indicates, funding is not the only important variable that can impact outcomes. Community context also plays a major role in the development of a CCI. The diversity of approaches to the development of CCIs merit attention and we present a typology that aims to illuminate the range of models utilized to generate neighborhood change (Chapter 4).

# 4

# TYPOLOGY OF COMPREHENSIVE COMMUNITY INITIATIVES

One of the lessons learned from the Great Society programs in the early 1960s, including the War on Poverty and the private philanthropic response in the 1980s, is that poverty is a complex issue that demands multifaceted resources. CCIs respond by linking public and private resources while providing an infrastructure for a more holistic response to entrenched social problems. CCIs merge philanthropic resources and expertise with community development through comprehensive planning strategies that can show the effects of a focused approach to change in a manageable geographic area (Pitcoff, 1997). Although we know much about the structural, economic, and social characteristics of underserved neighborhoods, remedying the complex interplay of conditions through a grand model for comprehensive redevelopment is an elusive goal. Yet as Turnham and Bonjorni (2004) argue, developing a classification system for CCIs may help identify context-based best practices and the tools that work best in different types of neighborhoods.

We move the field in this direction by providing a typology of public and private foundations engaged in comprehensive community development in low-income neighborhoods in the U.S. Defining comprehensive community initiatives is challenging as they vary in their form, content, funding, and underlying beliefs and values. The focus of this work is on place-based comprehensive community initiatives in which private and public foundations are actively engaged. Key elements of our definition and criteria for inclusion include:

> *Place-based:* These are comprehensive initiatives that engage in improving neighborhood(s) or communities within a clearly specified geographic area. This approach acknowledges that place impacts the well-being of families and future outcomes for their children (Dreier, Mollenkopf, and Swanstrom, 2001).

*Comprehensive:* This ensures the provision of two or more services, or if those services are not available, providing the resources necessary to refer clients to the appropriate service provider (Hayes, Lipoff, and Danegger, 1995). A comprehensive approach may involve coordinating efforts from numerous service providers and funders to deliver a unified plan that improves people's overall quality of life (Morikawa and Berardino, 2010). This approach means working across professional and institutional domains to best respond to the needs of families.

*Funding includes a mix of public and private sources:* Comprehensive community initiatives often include financial resources from private foundations, local and state agencies, nonprofits, and private industry.

*Community-based decision-making:* Many of these initiatives work in collaboration with residents to plan and guide the redevelopment work. Community capacity building is a prominent goal in many CCIs, implemented through efforts to build community "cohesion, generating public leverage and promoting accountability on the part of the organizations working in the community" (Morikawa and Berardino, 2010, p. 8).

*Committed to community change:* CCIs aim to develop the networks, organizations, and neighborhood leadership necessary to sustain the community change efforts long after the CCI ceases to exist (Brown and Fiester, 2007).

Although CCIs intuitively offer holistic approaches to addressing the complexity of issues impacting the urban poor, they are difficult to design, implement, and evaluate because they aim for effective synergy between three independent systems operating in an underserved neighborhood: the social, economic, and physical spheres; they strive to be inclusive and work to engage residents as partners but recognize that the resources the poor need are often outside the community; they seek to engage the private sector in developing a mix of funding sources; and they recognize that changing a landscape that declined over decades of neglect will require an equally long commitment to resolve (Kubisch, Weiss, Schorr, and Connell, 1995).

Pitcoff (1997) argues that a key element in CCIs is the relationship between the foundation providing the funding and the community organizations leading the effort on the ground. Private foundations were at the forefront of community development initiatives in low-income areas and were among the first institutions to fund CCIs, taking an active role in the revitalization of urban areas, as well as providing investment in these risky neighborhoods for longer periods of time (7–10 years). The power (financial, political, and informational) foundations wield creates a decision-making dynamic in low-income neighborhoods that can be challenging for local stakeholders. Foundations, particularly those that are research driven, may have specific expectations of the work to be done, which may differ from the neighborhood's goals. This tension highlights the careful negotiations that CCIs engage in to achieve common goals with residents for improving distressed urban communities.

The focus of this book is community change efforts that are place-based, comprehensive, engage public and private partnerships, and are committed to community engagement. Although there is no firm definition of CCIs or "place-based strategy" in the literature, there are key aspects within which CCIs operate: their operational logic and structure is collaborative and comprehensive; the sources of funding and where they focus their expenditures is a geographically narrow area; their governing principles clearly guide their work; and their programmatic dimensions are broad as they strive to address each element needed for a healthy community. Additionally, the type of leadership structure CCIs create to govern change in their target community illustrates the challenges of working to include the variety of stakeholders engaged in improving underserved communities: public, private, and nonprofit organizations, neighborhood groups, neighborhood residents, investors, corporate interests, other foundations, and research institutions. These are the aspects that we use to develop our typology, found in the Appendix.

Some CCIs focus on several sites at once in an effort to develop a comprehensive and integrated working model (Chaskin, Danoskho, and Joseph, 1997). This is the strategy used by the Ford Foundation's Neighborhood and Family Initiative (NFI) launched in 1990 and lasting ten years. Four neighborhoods were chosen in Detroit, Hartford, Milwaukee, and Memphis. The principle for this CCI's structure was developing links between the four sites to allow for comparisons but also for the development of a "relatively coherent, multi-site 'demonstration' project" (Chaskin et al., 1997, p. 3).

Other comprehensive efforts focus on one neighborhood or a more geographically specific area, such as Price Charities' focus on City Heights, a densely populated urban neighborhood of approximately 81,000 residents in San Diego (U.S. Census Bureau, 2010); or the Riley Foundation's efforts on Dudley Street in Boston which led to the creation of the Dudley Street Neighborhood Initiative (DSNI).

The role foundations play within CCIs also differs widely, leading to a variety of governance structures. Price Charities embedded itself in City Heights, with its staff actively involved in education, housing, social service, and capacity-building initiatives. Price Charities manages its own programs in partnership with small and large nonprofits including those serving refugee communities. On the other hand, CalEndow does not fund programs directly but instead works through host agencies that develop community collaboratives within the target community. The Ford Foundation's NFI presents another approach by relying on community foundations as intermediaries between the foundation and the community to help create governing boards for each local initiative. The expectation was that since the community foundations had long-standing relationships with local organizations they were better equipped to develop collaborative boards that could determine needs for technical assistance, allocate funding, and track and evaluate sites based on their own missions and circumstances. The Ford Foundation staff provided oversight through visits to each site and annual cross-site meetings for the local initiative leaders.

Many of the ground-breaking CCIs were established by foundations in the 1980s and early 1990s—the DSNI (1984), the Annie E. Casey Foundation's

New Futures Initiative (1987), the Ford Foundation's NFI (1990), the Enterprise Foundation's Community Building in Partnership (CBP) in Baltimore (1990), and the Surdna Foundation's CCRP (1992) fall into this category. But the scope, the funding commitment, the length of support, and the innovative efforts at partnerships that each of the foundations introduced differ, and some have built on the lessons learned from earlier efforts. The context for the newest iterations of these place-based initiatives has changed significantly: private foundations' resources were diminished by the longest recession in the U.S. history; joblessness and high foreclosure rates are impacting some formerly healthy communities and have a disproportional effect on already struggling areas; state and local governments face budget deficits that are forcing new types of partnerships; and the Obama administration is pushing for more place-based policymaking, bringing heightened attention to this approach to community change (Cytron, 2010).

To begin to elucidate a typology of CCIs, we developed an analysis of foundations engaged in community development using membership lists from the Foundation Center, the Council on Foundations, foundation annual reports, individual private foundation websites, IRS 990 forms found through GuideStar.com, as well as a global search through the literature. Approximately 60 foundations engaged in comprehensive community change were identified and listed in a matrix identifying a variety of criteria including geographical focus, funding priorities, assets, theories of change, and types of community development activities. A new matrix was created that summarized each initiative's governing principles, sources of funding, program dimensions and outcomes, and accountability (see Appendix).[2] Each of these dimensions was identified after a thorough search of the literature, paying particular attention to numerous reports including those by the Aspen Institute Roundtable on CCIs, the University of Chicago's Chapin Hall, the Foundation Center, and records from the IRS.

An analysis of each foundation initiative across the four categories presented a number of notable differences and similarities that were identified and analyzed, resulting in the initial stages of categorization. Clearly these initiatives could be categorized by assets, by programmatic focus, by size of the targeted community and its characteristics, and by values/mission statements. But none of these categories provide a complete explanation to our research question. We know that CCIs' theory of change is to transform underserved communities, but their approach to effecting change differs. The typology was created to help us ascertain the assumptions that undergird each CCI's approach to change and better understand how each CCI's logic impacts the work that they do.

## Categorizing community change initiatives

The number and types of approaches to comprehensive community change are broad and ever changing, yet these initiatives do share a number of common tenets. At the core is the belief that place-based change is crucial to stabilizing and transforming underserved neighborhoods. In addition, most foundations engaged in CCIs seek to impact change through a range of activities, including but not limited to coordination of social service and through mutually reinforced change across numerous levels including neighborhoods, families, individuals, educational institutions, nonprofit organizations, and health care providers (Sviridoff and Ryan, 1996).

Yet Hopkins (2010, p. 18) argues that before determining the type of intervention needed for community-wide change, funders and neighborhood stakeholders must step back and begin by understanding the type of neighborhood the initiative is targeting:

> The toolbox of community development instruments has grown incredibly diverse, ranging from affordable housing production to individual development accounts and family asset-building programs, yet not every strategy is the right tool for every neighborhood. And yet nonprofits and funders often choose strategies on the basis of a nonprofit's core competencies or a funder's interest—completely separate from a holistic understanding of the neighborhood, its possible trajectory, and what is really needed.

Focusing on economic conditions as a linchpin for transformational change, Hopkins (2010) developed a typology of neighborhoods that can help guide the type of interventions needed, thus assisting CCI architects and community partners in developing a joint understanding of "the problem" with residents and other neighborhood stakeholders. His neighborhood typology responds to the context of each community by using quantitative and qualitative approaches to address a series of questions in six broad categories: degree of assimilation of residents into the mainstream economy; stabilization levels of the neighborhood; land value conditions; availability of a competitive labor pool; capital flow in and out of the neighborhood; and political economy.

We engage in a similar process at the other end of the spectrum by categorizing the types of community change initiatives targeting underserved neighborhoods. This approach is timely as the first CCI approaches 26 years of operation, and foundations are increasingly focused on lessons learned from these efforts that can propel the field forward. To understand the theory behind these initiatives, an examination of the assumptions CCIs make about their work and the neighborhoods they target is warranted, since as Kubisch et al. (2010, p. 10) argue, to date the results are mixed:

> Despite these accomplishments at the programmatic, community and system levels, most of the CCIs have not produced the degree of community transformation envisioned by their designers. For example, few, if any, were able to demonstrate widespread changes in child and family well-being or reductions in the neighborhood poverty rate. The reasons for this can be attributed both to "theory failure" and "implementation failure."

We construct our typology by closely examining the common elements of major CCIs (those evident in the literature) and the assumptions that surface from their mission statements and other information available on annual reports, websites, and ancillary literature. The common elements and, as stated earlier, the criteria for inclusion in this volume, include: place-based, collaborative, comprehensive, using public and private funds, and committed to community change.

## Common elements in foundation-led CCIs

### Place-based change

There are a number of similarities among the foundations engaged in comprehensive community initiatives. Many are interested in place-based change as a model that can be replicated elsewhere, and thus lead to policy-level change. The Piton Foundation, engaged in place-based change in Denver, Colorado, states:

> Comprehensive change requires both high-level policy and system reform as well as place-based, ground level efforts and results. Piton will continue to invest in both. At the policy level, Piton will support legislative and institutional reforms that lead to better outcomes for all children. On the ground, Piton will focus its efforts on the 14-mile long Children's Corridor, where new ideas can be tested and evaluated.
>
> (www.denverchildrenscorridor.org/why)

CalEndow, engaged in 14 communities across California, is more explicit in its goals to effect comprehensive change by arguing that the sites chosen provide opportunities for developing effective models that can spur policy changes.

The scale of neighborhood change provides an effective testing ground for innovative approaches through comprehensive community efforts. In addition, a place-based approach to transformational change "shift[s] the attribution of responsibility away from specific individuals and groups (e.g., the racialization of social problems) and *makes it easier to think about how 'place' advantages and disadvantages community residents*".[1] Foundations and community groups engaged in place-based change thus seek to bring together the physical and social ecologies of neighborhoods, including the norms, values, structures, and processes that work in a symbiotic way to produce community outcomes (Gilliam, 2011).

### Collaboration

Collaboration is raised by most CCIs as a key element in response to a perception that public agencies operate in organizational silos, engage in a narrow view of their work, and at best ignore, at worst work against, other units within and outside the organization. Public agencies serving the poor are also perceived to be distant geographically and culturally from their urban clients, and more interested in punitive rather than preventive work to ameliorate neighborhood conditions. Many foundations engaged in CCIs see collaboration as integral to effecting sustainable neighborhood change. The Annie E. Casey's New Futures Initiative (1987–1994) argues in its reflection of its comprehensive change efforts that systems change is needed, one requiring "pooling of funding and program boundaries; decentralization of resource and policy decisions; development of collaborative governing bodies empowered to make decisions across youth-serving systems" (Annie E. Casey Foundation, 1995, p. xi).

Collaboration is expected to create synergy between housing, economic, and human capital resulting in comprehensive change as exemplified by the Ford Foundation's NFI. Ford provided $3 million to each of four cities for operations and programs targeting neighborhoods, plus dedicated support for evaluation and a $3 million investment fund for development projects (Turnham and Bonjorni, 2004). Ford emphasized building on existing resident participation as integral to building effective collaborations in underserved neighborhoods. Thus a key element for choosing neighborhoods in Detroit, Memphis, Milwaukee, and Hartford was the foundation's belief that those cities possessed a variety of assets, including active residents and nonprofits, on which to build a comprehensive change initiative.

To institutionalize collaboration, CCIs may require the creation of community collaboratives in each targeted neighborhood or city. Composed of residents, business owners, and professionals, the collaboratives are charged with identifying neighborhood needs, developing strategies to address needs, and overseeing implementation. The Ford Foundation's belief in collaboration extends beyond individuals to organizations and sites. Thus Ford created a Cross-Site Council and held several cross-site sharing conferences for NFI participants. The foundation contracted with the Center for Community Change (CCC) to provide technical assistance to the four NFI sites, and to facilitate cross-site learning and communication.

The type of collaborative created matters to the success of the CCI (Chaskin et al., 2001). The evaluation of the Ford Foundation's NFI suggests that comprehensive community initiatives that were led by strong and experienced nonprofit agencies were more successful at launching efficient programs and building organizational capacity than those CCIs led by informal collaboratives (Chaskin et al., 2001). The informal collaboratives appeared to flounder as differing community interests clashed and consensus on the type of change, and the strategies needed to effect change, were more difficult to achieve.

## Program strategies

CCIs may initially focus on one programmatic area, broadening their approach as community input and buy-in occurs. The programmatic area may be one in which the foundation or key partners in the CCI has experience; or it may be an area readily identified as needed by the community. Some CCIs may focus on specific populations, with families and children as frequently targeted groups, as evident in the initiatives by the Annie E. Casey Foundation. Others, such as Price Charities in San Diego and the Pew Charitable Trust Initiative in Philadelphia, may focus on physical change, believing that infrastructure transformations can spur social transformations. Others, such as the Edna McConnell Clark Foundation's Neighborhood Partners Initiative (NPI) in New York follow Robert Putnam's (2000) approach to reversing neighborhood decline by focusing on strengthening neighborhood networks, and linking underserved areas with resources outside the neighborhood.

While foundations engaged in CCIs may have much in common, they also vary on a number of levels. They differ by the structure used to develop and manage community change, whether it is a multi-site effort or embedded in one community, the geography and size of the area targeted, and their approach to community engagement and decision-making. These key differences between foundations engaged in CCIs assist in the development of a typology that can be used to determine the needs of underserved communities and the appropriate intervention that can best respond to those needs.

## Differences in foundation-led CCIs

### Structure

Foundations engaged in CCIs may use intermediaries to help them choose the target neighborhood and to develop a governance structure, or they may embed themselves in the targeted community, using foundation staff to interact actively with nonprofits and residents. Or they may use a combination of these techniques.

Private foundations may use community foundations as fiscal agents in targeted cities, as well as on-the-ground experts that can assist in hiring local staff, identifying potential target neighborhoods, and developing governance structures such as collaboratives that are representative of the residents, as well as that neighborhood's nonprofit community. This is the approach used by the Ford Foundation for its NFI in its four targeted neighborhoods. The foundation made a ten-year funding commitment, with the community foundation in each city administering the funds.

The success of this approach may depend on the community foundation's capacity to help guide the community change and provide the technical assistance community organizations need. But as the William and Flora Hewlett Foundation discovered, this approach may also depend on the strength of the connections the community foundation has developed in underserved communities. The evaluators of Hewlett's Neighborhood Improvement Initiative (NII) in the Bay Area state:

> Hewlett staff assumed that NII's partnering community foundations already possessed deep relationships with the target neighborhoods, the reporting and

financial management capacities required by an initiative like NII, and a track record of strategic and proactive work. As we have seen, those assumptions proved to be only partially accurate. As in the Ford Foundation's Neighborhood and Family Initiative, for instance, NII's community foundation intermediaries tended to have some connections with most local constituencies but not the deep relationships beyond neighborhood gatekeepers that Hewlett had hoped for.

(Brown and Fiester, 2007, p. 27)

Other large-scale CCIs rely on foundation staff to internally manage the initiative, as was the case with the Annie E. Casey Foundation's Rebuilding Communities (1993–2001) and its Making Connections Initiatives (1999–2009), as well as the Edna McConnell Clark Foundation's NPI (1996–2003). In the case of the Edna McConnell Clark Foundation's efforts in Central Harlem and South Bronx, staff worked closely with five targeted neighborhood organizations operating under the belief that embedded staff can help effect change in needy communities. By strengthening the organizational capacity of two multi-service agencies, an organizing group (ACORN), and two CDCs, the foundation sought to improve the existing community assets to stimulate and sustain concrete change.

Smaller foundations such as Price Charities and JCNI opt for hands-on collaboration between foundation staff, residents, and nonprofits to develop and sustain effective change. Price Charities developed a structure that encompasses a partnership with the local school district to operate three schools in the targeted neighborhood, in addition to an active physical redevelopment program in partnership with the city of San Diego.

Price Charities hired staff to oversee each programmatic area and work closely with interested residents and the thick web of nonprofits operating in City Heights. As foundation staff turnover occurred and residents' interest ebbed and flowed, the CCI's structure has evolved and changed. Most recently, Price Charities sought to refocus its efforts on physical redevelopment, contracting out the management of its apartment buildings and examining the potential for increased collaboration between parent leaders across school sites. The staff also works closely with a community collaborative formed in the late 1980s comprised of schools, businesses, nonprofit organizations, government agencies, youth, parents, ethnic and cultural groups, civic associations, and faith-based institutions. Structurally, Price Charities' CCI exists as a program within the foundation.

In contrast, the Jacobs Family Foundation established an operating foundation, JCNI, which structured an approach that was based on an equal partnership between foundation staff and neighborhood residents and stakeholders. Fundamental to Jacobs' mission of resident ownership of community change was building the capacity of the community to participate in the planning and implementation of the neighborhood's comprehensive change. While hundreds, perhaps even thousands, of residents had the opportunity to contribute to the efforts, one of the consequences was a lengthy delay in implementation due to the challenges of managing such a large number of participants. Recently Jacobs acknowledged that it did not have the capacity, in terms of both staff and resources, to do all of the work itself and has embarked on building institutional partnerships and expanding its model of collaboration.

Regardless of the structure of the partnership—whether embedded, using intermediaries, or as a program within a foundation—clear communication between all stakeholders and agreement on roles and mission are clearly needed, as the evaluators of the William and Flora Hewlett Foundation's NII discovered. Hewlett staff expressed frustration with the community foundations' difficulties in retaining key staff, deficiencies in providing needed technical assistance to sites, lack of timely financial reports, and inadequate collaboration on the evaluation of the initiative (Brown and Fiester, 2007). The community foundations' staff countered that Hewlett shirked its responsibilities by expecting the community foundations to do the groundwork as well as administer the grant, and that priorities kept changing, thwarting effective community change (Brown and Fiester, 2007).

### Multi-sites or single location

It is apparent that the larger, more established private foundations often seek to develop initiatives in multiple sites across the country. The Annie E. Casey Foundation's New Futures Initiative (1987–1994) invited ten communities to apply for grants and five were chosen: Dayton, Ohio; Lawrence, Kansas; Little Rock, Arkansas; Pittsburgh, Pennsylvania; and Savannah, Georgia. Each received from $5–$12.5 million over five years to improve the lives of disadvantaged youth. Three years later, the Ford Foundation's NFI kicked off in four neighborhoods in four cities. Its focus was creating synergy between housing, economic, and human capital to achieve comprehensive change. The Pew Charitable Trust also used this multi-site approach through its Neighborhood Preservation Initiative (1993–1996) that funded nine neighborhoods through each city's community foundations. The nine foundations received three-year grants totaling $6.6 million to help identify target neighborhoods, assist in forming governance collaboratives, and provide technical and other assistance to lead community organizations. Communities could each receive $800,000 over three years with an expected 50 percent local match (Turnham and Bonjorni, 2004).

The goal of developing CCIs in multiple sites is to develop a set of best practices in multiple contexts, develop learning communities between sites, and move the field towards finding strategies for influencing state and national policy on the needs of underserved communities. But as Brown and Fiester (2007) found in their analysis of Hewlett's NII, context is a powerful intervening factor. Stakeholders were in agreement that there was a lack of coherence across sites as each site developed its own programs to fit each community's cultural, economic, and social conditions, an issue that frustrated neighborhood representatives who chafed at Hewlett's efforts to engage in cross-site learning. Hewlett staff acknowledged to the initiative evaluators that each site "needed different things" (Brown and Fiester, 2007, p. 36).

The Annie E. Casey Foundation came to the same realization in its Rebuilding Communities Initiative (RCI). Staff working with residents in North Philadelphia realized that political dynamics, cultural differences, historical conditions, and community values differ across sites and technical assistance could not address all of these conditions (Pitcoff, 1997).

## *Size and geography of targeted area*

CCIs may target a neighborhood, a county, a city, or an area that shares socio-economic conditions, such as the Piton Foundation's Children's Corridor. The foundation's initiative is modeled after the HCZ and encompasses the approximately 50,000 children living in poverty in a 40-square mile strip from Denver to Aurora, Colorado. Encompassing 14 neighborhoods with low-performing schools, the Piton Foundation's goal is for every child in the Children's Corridor to graduate from high school and have access to a health care community that stays with them from birth through to adulthood.

Many foundations choose to engage with cities, working in partnership with community foundations or local elected officials to help identify targeted neighborhoods. The Annie E. Casey Foundation followed this approach in its New Futures Initiative (1987–1994). Ten cities were invited to apply and five were selected; each one received five-year grants that ranged from $7.5 million to $12.5 million, depending on the size of the city. Each city was expected to create new local governance bodies called collaboratives, made up of elected officials, business people, public administrators from a wide range of agencies and organizations, parents, and community representatives. The goal of Casey's place-based initiative was to address the perceived inefficiency of service delivery to the poor. Arguing that systems change is needed, Casey sought to work with cities to pool funding and cross program boundaries to create new systems in collaboration with residents of underserved neighborhoods. The foundation shifted its approach for its RCI (1993–2001), funding lead agencies in five cities, rather than the cities themselves, as was done in the New Futures Initiative. The agencies were chosen based on the nonprofit's standing in their community and their ability to lead community-driven change efforts.

The Kresge Family Foundation has also focused on city-wide, place-based change. The foundation has invested approximately $100 million to transform Detroit, including $26 million for the Neighborhood of Choice Program. But their partnership with the city has struggled, as reported in a *Wall Street Journal* article:

> Kresge stopped funding Detroit Works at the start of the year after disagreements with City Hall over the role of outside consultants. The foundation also is rethinking its support for the rail line amid a separate spat with city officials … That foundation-knows-best attitude exasperates Mayor Dave Bing and City Hall officials, who have sought to reassure Detroiters that their voices, not outsiders, will guide efforts to rebuild the city.
>
> (Dolan, 2011)

These city-wide efforts are challenged by city and neighborhood politics, funding concerns, and decision-making strategies. Newer iterations of CCIs offer a more focused approach, suggesting a more manageable project. In fact, the geographic boundaries of CCIs appear to be shrinking, with a growing number of private foundations targeting CCIs for specific neighborhoods (e.g., California Endowment, 2009; LISC Chicago, 2009; MacArthur Foundation, 2007). The Kellogg Foundation, founded in 1930, is an example of this shift (Cohen, 2008). It evolved from primarily supporting programs in its hometown of Battle Creek, Michigan, to extensive philanthropic initiatives in Africa and Latin America. Shortly after the board re-evaluated its international and national goals in 2007, it refocused its commitment to its hometown through comprehensive community change:

> Building on nearly 80 years of experience, the new framework recognizes that success for vulnerable children depends on an intricate weave of elements. Our programming emphases on Education and Learning; Food, Health and Well-Being; and Family Economic Security all play interconnected roles in creating an environment in which vulnerable children are protected, nurtured, equipped and stimulated to succeed.
>
> (www.wkkf.org/who-we-are/our-history.aspx)

The MacArthur Foundation, with assets of more than $6 billion and a global philanthropic portfolio, has also recommitted to place-based community change through its Chicago NCP launched in 2010. The ten-year, $47 million initiative, managed by LISC, emphasizes a relational approach to community change by building collaborations in 16 underserved Chicago neighborhoods as a platform for broad and sustained improvement, even as local conditions change.

CalEndow, a nonprofit foundation created from the conversion of Blue Cross into a for-profit corporation, similarly repositioned itself in 2010 to focus on place-based change. Its $1 billion, ten-year Healthy Communities Initiative targets 14 underserved neighborhoods across the Golden State:

> The research is undeniable: Our health is linked to employment, education, economic opportunity, housing, the environment and more. These interrelated problems require interrelated solutions. So we're working across all

systems that impact community health—schools, human services, economic development, transportation, and land use.

(http://calendow.org/healthycommunities/pdfs/BHC_Overview.pdf)

The Endowment's goal is also to effect policy and systems change to ensure that the improvements made by the targeted communities are sustainable. There are many other examples of CCIs focused on neighborhoods, including the Riley Foundation's groundbreaking efforts to improve the 1.5-square mile Dudley area of the Roxbury/North Dorchester neighborhoods, close to downtown Boston (Medoff and Sklar, 1994); the Enterprise Foundation's CBP targeting the Sandtown-Winchester area in Baltimore—a 72-block neighborhood that is primarily residential, with a commercial corridor on Pennsylvania Avenue; and the C.F. Foundation's efforts to effect change in the largely Vietnamese East Lake neighborhood in Atlanta.

A telling example of the potential and challenges of this focus on neighborhood change is the NPI (1996–2003) by the Edna McConnell Clark Foundation. As a learning organization, the Edna McConnell Clark Foundation shifted its focus in 1995 as homeless residents of the South Bronx identified pressing issues. The foundation's new strategy, New York Neighborhoods, incorporated placed-based areas of concern such as a lack of affordable housing, little economic opportunity, poor neighborhood conditions, and public safety. The New York Neighborhoods' place-based strategy gave birth in 1996 to the NPI. This seven-year project supported five lead agencies working within three-to-ten block neighborhoods in two communities located in some of the poorest sections of the Bronx. The foundation's belief was that a block-by-block approach within a small geographic area can develop momentum for community-wide change.

These neighborhood-focused CCIs have also faced a number of challenges. The Edna McConnell Clark NPI faced questions around the role of the foundation in managing place-based change, for example: when to allow residents and community leaders to take the lead; when shared decision-making should occur; and, if an intervention was needed, how does a foundation influence the process without highlighting the power imbalance that exists between the foundation and the community? The Edna McConnell Clark Foundation responded by framing its work as a learning enterprise, allowing for flexibility in the approaches needed to partner with residents and other stakeholders. As Brown, Branch, and Lee (1998, p. 54) state in their evaluation of the NPI's start-up period:

> Part of the genius of managing initiatives such as NPI may have to do with knowing when to push and when to let things evolve, when to recognize and support organic growth and when to insert an artificial stimulus to help a site take a new direction.

## Community partnerships and capacity building

Foundations may differ in their collaboration with existing organizations, but a common theme across initiatives is that institutionalizing partnerships and leadership structures takes many years (Turnham and Bonjorni, 2004). Thus some CCIs, such as the CCRP led by the Surdna Foundation in Brooklyn, focused on neighborhood-based organizations. CCRP board member Anita Miller explains their reasoning:

> They are genuinely community-based, with community-wide improvement as their mission. Their capabilities, their leadership and their credibility are well established. In contrast to other organizations, they have the responsibility for the long-term viability of many millions of dollars of real estate which they likely manage, and perhaps own. As a result, they interact with hundreds, even thousands of community residents. And, having built a basic organizational infrastructure, they now have the potential to spearhead wider efforts aimed at improving the quality of community life.
>
> (as cited in Miller and Burns, 2006, p. 1)

The CCRP reduced its learning curve by focusing on capacity building of organizations firmly rooted in the targeted communities; those that were knowledgable about community culture, politics, and history. This approach does raise concerns over the need to build capacity for local community organizations to take on the broader and more complex work of a CCI, and the fine line between oversight and collaborative decision-making that may highlight the power differential between foundations and local community groups (see Table 4.1).

Foundations engaged in CCIs may also turn to local community foundations as intermediaries, if local neighborhood organizations lack the capacity, or the redevelopment model calls for technical expertise to which community foundations can respond. But again, evidence indicates that this model may not fit every community. In the case of the Ford Foundation's NFI (1990–2000) each of the four sites had a community foundation that helped select target neighborhoods within each city, hired staff directors, and created community collaboratives in each of the four neighborhoods, as local governing structure.[4] Each community foundation also managed the initiative's funding as the fiscal agent for the CCI. The sites differed in their adoption of this governance structure with some neighborhoods seeking independence from the community foundation, while other sites worked well within the foundation structure. An example of a community that sought independence from the community foundation structure was the 14 neighborhoods engaged with the Piton Foundation's Children's Corridor. The foundation discovered that residents did not always view nonprofit leaders as being in a position to adequately understand the community and best represent its needs, highlighting the need for community foundations to not lose sight of on-the-ground work with nonprofits and community stakeholders (Brown, Chaskin, Richman, and Weber, 2006).

**TABLE 4.1** Potential and concerns of private foundations engaged in CCIs in the U.S.

| Potential of private foundation | Concerns about private foundations |
| --- | --- |
| Sensitivity and flexibility | Structural inability to expand the scope and outreach of programs and little replicability across sites |
| May enable capacity building of civic society | Foundation tax breaks eliminate potential funding for effecting community change |
| Not fixed to volatile political cycles or public budgeting rules | Accountability and transparency in funding, board composition, outcomes, and decision-making process for programs within initiatives |
| Innovative and risk-taking due to independence | Poor or little evaluation of results; little adoption of best practices in this area |
| Longer financial commitment than traditional donors | May take a technocratic or isolated approach to development without sustainable results |
| Opportunity to work with local actors for more contextually appropriate solutions | Unclear and complicated organizational structure |
| High-profile personalities attract media attention and public support | Uneven balances of power in decision-making and target setting between foundation headquarters and field offices/operations |
| | Risk averse due to desire to see measurable outcomes |

Adapted from Srivastava and Oh, 2010.

Allowing each target community to develop its own governance structure may also present differing outcomes, as was the case with the Annie E. Casey's Rebuilding Communities Initiative (RCI). Germantown Settlement is a nonprofit human service agency in Northwest Philadelphia that responds to the needs of approximately 200,000 low-to-moderate income residents. Settlement programs include a mature adult center, a charter middle school, a family center, and HIV/AIDS education and outreach programs, as well as collaboration with the Germantown CDC on housing projects. As it engaged with Annie E. Casey, the Germantown Settlement had to establish a plan and structure for the RCI that would be integrated with its existing work while expanding its mission. One proposal was to allow Germantown Settlement to act as the fiscal agent for the initiative, providing space and staff support, but resident leaders chose instead to create a new entity, the Germantown Community Collaborative Board (GCCB), to govern the process. But not all RCI sites chose this approach. The DSNI in Boston chose to integrate the RCI project into the existing organization, using Annie E.

Casey Foundation's resources to expand its board, enhance its responsiveness to residents, and broaden its effectiveness. The Annie E. Casey Foundation initially resisted this approach but after DSNI staff members and resident leaders showed that their organization's structure could effectively lead the RCI process, Casey supported their choice.

Ultimately, the work that must be done to effect community change requires a careful balance of collaboration and capacity building for both the community and the public–private partners. As Joan Walsh, a journalist and nonprofit consultant who researched effective community building efforts for the Rockefeller Foundation suggests, a key element to community change involves planning-while-doing. She explains that in an effort to be truly comprehensive, CCIs engage in endless planning sessions that frustrate stakeholders as their communities continue to decay, thus what is needed is a balance of responsiveness, planning, and joint oversight engaging foundations and stakeholders (Walsh, 1996).

The potential of private foundations to effect comprehensive change is indisputable, but it must be tempered with concerns raised by neighborhood stakeholders and critics who argue that the lack of accountability and transparency by foundations demands scrutiny. Achieving a balance between the potential and concerns is the challenge faced by private foundations engaged in community change in the twenty-first century. Srivastava and Oh (2010) offer a promising approach through their work in international philanthropy by presenting a promising framework for examining the dichotomous nature of these efforts (see Table 4.1).

To begin comprehensive community improvements and ensure that the challenges of foundation involvement are addressed, a clear understanding of the initiative's theory of change is needed. It must be clearly articulated by all stakeholders in order to provide a roadmap, as Kubisch et al. (2010, p. 11) explain:

> This could include identifying core values or philosophy or developing an overarching goal that guides practice and decision-making. A common framework and vision provides participants with shared language and a focused set of goals around which to engage people and interests, both inside and outside the community.

We argue that a theory of change must also acknowledge the numerous systems that operate within a community. The nonprofit organizations, foundations, local government entities, resident groups, schools, and other institutions, all have their own theories of change for their targeted underserved community. Each targets a different group or goal, and each has its own culture and approach for achieving these goals. To be effective, a CCI requires agreement among the various theories of change held by each system operating within a community. Otherwise, a CCI will develop programs and activities that keep residents and nonprofits busy, but fail to address the structural inequities that systems maintain and reproduce. Speaking from experience, Walsh (1997, p. ix) highlights this point in her review of Annie E. Casey's New Futures Initiative:

New Futures projects got busy putting case managers in schools, setting up health clinics, promoting education reform, and developing school-to-work initiatives. But by getting involved with new services, however innovative, they left the public systems they were designed to change mostly intact. Less than two years into the process, leadership divisions led the city of Lawrence to withdraw from New Futures (it was replaced by Bridgeport, Connecticut). Pittsburgh's entire collaborative resigned in the third year. Tension with school leadership plagued Dayton and Savannah, while Little Rock struggled to bring its business community on board.

The outcomes of this effort clearly did not target the key elements and essential relationships of the system. Programmatic changes and new initiatives worked outside the boundaries or at the edges of these systems, failing to engage key leaders and stakeholders in a process of comprehensive community change. In fact, defining the boundaries may be the most critical element of designing a CCI, as agreement among stakeholders on this issue demands iterative negotiations to clearly define the problem, determine the boundaries of the various systems impacted, and determine who should be involved based on the system boundaries (Checkland, 1981; Midgley, 2000). CCIs have implemented numerous innovative programs but these are often isolated interventions that fail to account for their role in the overall system, and, as a result, sustainable change is difficult to realize and maintain.

Systems theory thus offers a promising approach as it allows for the examination of systems as component parts that interact within a particular context and through those relationships can function as an entity or organism. Ferris and Williams (2009) argue that each system operates according to its own logic that influences the behavior and practices of actors within and outside the system. Neighborhoods targeted for CCIs are in essence systems, each with their own logic, and containing key actors engaging with each other within a particular environment influenced by their demographic, political, historical, and economic context.

Systems theory offers a new direction for examining CCIs that responds to the complexity of comprehensive change but, more importantly, it helps identify the key drivers or "levers" of change for underserved communities (Foster-Fishman and Behrens, 2007). By recognizing the contextual conditions that frame each community's interactions with outside funders, systems theory focuses attention on community as system but, more importantly, on other systems impinging on it, including foundations, local government, nonprofits, religious organizations, and local stakeholders. All are interacting in an effort to effect holistic change in the targeted underserved community. The interconnections between systems can provide clues as to the key levers needed for transformative change in an underserved community (Hirsch, Levine, and Miller, 2007).

Foundations operate as a system with their own logic for taking action, each guided by their own set of values that shape their relationships with underserved neighborhoods, key actors, institutions, and other funders. Differences in these system elements may result in a very different community development initiative than those proposed by foundations similar in size, history, or assets. We found evidence of these differences as we developed a typology of foundations engaged in comprehensive community change. We present two main approaches to neighborhood change by foundations engaged in CCIs, and within each there are subsystems that demand additional analysis. The first approach is foundations as supporters of CCIs. In these cases, the foundations typically provide a significant financial investment, they engage with the systems of stakeholders, but they eschew involvement in actual implementation. The second approach places foundations as managing partners in CCIs. These foundations also invest sizeable amounts of resources but they embed themselves in the community and pursue direct engagement, relationship building, and programmatic implementation with the systems of stakeholders.

Chapter 5 delineates the ways in which systems theory enables us to better understand and contextualize these varying dynamics. A comprehensive list of foundations engaged in CCIs and our effort at classifying these dynamic efforts is included in the Appendix.

# 5

# SYSTEMS CHANGE THEORY

## Advancing complex community change

Systems theory responds to a gap in the literature on community change that fails to account for the role of political, cultural, economic, and demographic context, creating a unique field of interaction in each community targeted (Milofsky, 2008). The perspective that each entity takes influences their interactions with internal and external systems. Without common agreement within the neighborhood as a system, or between the neighborhood and those systems impacting it, the targeted neighborhood as a field of interaction becomes a competitive and "turbulent environment" as each element seeks to impose its norms, values, and processes to move that community towards the desired end (Checkland, 1981; Flaspohler et al., 2003; Lasker, Weiss, and Miller, 2001). Using a systems approach to comprehensive community change calls for identifying the systems in place in the targeted community, identifying the external systems that impact the targeted community, recognizing the impact of numerous contextual conditions, and then finding the lever that will trigger significant change across system components (Foster-Fishman and Behrens, 2007).

The linear model of causation (x predicts y) used to identify ideal "models" for change in underserved neighborhoods fails to account for the complexity of system dynamics that are embedded in these neighborhoods (Foster-Fishman and Behrens, 2007). As Warren (1967) initially argued in his classic text on interorganizational fields, neighborhoods are composed of a multiplicity of organizations, groups, and institutions, what he terms "task-oriented systems," that make decisions about the community, claim resources, and provide legitimacy to social problems (Milofsky, 2008). In addition, the interaction between these parts within and between these task-oriented systems, gives birth to entrenched patterns of interaction and relationships (Senge, 1990). These patterns occur within a particular cultural, political, economic, and social context that shapes and influences each system operating within the field.

Systems theory thus provides an analytical approach that fits the context of comprehensive community change, which involves "change efforts that strive to shift the underlying infrastructure within a community" to achieve specific goals that may include policy change, community capacity building, and/or strengthening social capital (Foster-Fishman and Behrens, 2007, p. 192). While systems theory can be a useful tool for understanding the internal dynamics of a targeted community, we seek to highlight its potential for also examining the various external systems that strive to create positive change in low-income communities (see Figure 5.1). Thus our systems theory approach acknowledges the interconnections of entrenched patterns of interactions within a community to those of external systems (Emshoff et al., 2007). Responsibility for holistic or comprehensive systems change would thus not be placed completely in the laps of residents and nonprofits in underserved communities, but it would be shared with formal and informal systems (e.g., government, education, judicial system, health systems, etc.) that played a role in the policies that created poverty (Wilson, 1990). Thus systems change calls for transformation by altering the status quo, which is "maintained and constrained by the systems we live within" (Foster-Fishman and Behrens, 2007, p. 195; Seidman, 1988).

## What is a system?

A system is composed of parts that are interdependent and as a result of their interactions function as a whole in a process that leads to self-renewal (Ackoff, 1994; Kelly et al., 2000; Maani and Cavana, 2000). As we emphasized earlier, these interactions produce patterns of actions and responses that become entrenched in the system and are challenging to change (Senge, 1990). The properties of each system—meaning the values, beliefs, and norms—are important for understanding system behavior (Foster-Fishman et al., 2007). In the case of CCIs, the values and beliefs of each foundation as a system impact each foundation's theory of change, or their vision and assumptions about the process needed to achieve the desirable goals. The theory of change for some embedded foundations may include focusing on increasing community capacity and leadership; for other foundations, the theory of change focuses on the physical transformation of a neighborhood to catalyze social change.

Each system engaged in comprehensive community change efforts is driven by its own theory of change, including local government, the education system, health delivery systems, neighborhood organizations, nonprofits, the criminal justice system and foundations. As these various systems collaborate to effect comprehensive community change, agreement must first be reached on the definition of "the problem," a process that can be contentious as each system evaluates the community's conditions through its own theory of change.

Systems theory grew out of the natural and social sciences, as it began to shift towards an integrated approach to understanding phenomena in the 1920s.

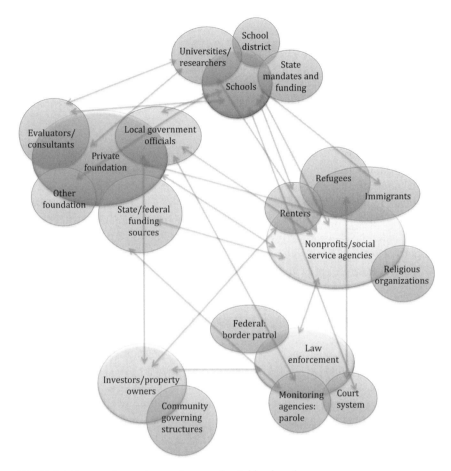

**FIGURE 5.1** Systems impacting underserved neighborhoods

Ludwig von Bertalanffy, an Austrian biologist, introduced the concept of general systems theory, arguing that observable phenomena cannot be understood by examining their component parts in isolation. To obtain a full perspective of an organism, social phenomena, or process, knowledge of the interrelations between elements was needed to make sense of "the complex dynamics of human bio-psycho-socio-cultural change" (Laszlo and Krippner, 1998, p. 4). More important for our understanding of CCIs is an understanding of systems as dynamic patterns, rather than static entities (Macy, 1991). Systems will seek to maintain their structure and function against internal or external forces. We see examples of this resistance as low-income communities work to convince formal systems, such as the banking industry or the employment sector, to engage with them in creative ways that can positively impact the revitalization of poor neighborhoods (Foster-Fishman et al., 2007).

As an example of the various systems operating in a community, and their competing theories of change, we examine stakeholder views in City Heights, a community targeted for comprehensive community initiatives from Price Charities, CalEndow, numerous nonprofits, and governmental agencies (see Table 5.1). Each foundation and institution belongs to a system with its own components, values, and theories of change; and each holds competing views on problem definition, the function or role of the neighborhood as a system, the system boundaries, and desired systems change outcomes.

Private foundations and public charities targeting low-income neighborhoods are powerful philanthropic systems. Their focus may be on increasing the capacity of nonprofit organizations, improving service delivery networks, or altering "policies, routines, relationships, resources, power structures, and values" (Foster-Fishman, 2002, p. 197). But for stakeholders within the community who may not share the same view of "the problem," these efforts fail to address inequities that originated beyond the neighborhood's boundaries. Unifying the neighborhood around a common problem is only half the equation for comprehensive community change; uniting external systems that impact the neighborhood around a common goal is the other half of the equation. And as evaluations of CCIs suggest, both are challenging efforts that to date have had limited success (Brown and Fiester, 2007).

As Foster-Fishman, Van Egeren, and Yang (2005) explain in their research on evaluating systems change in CCIs, systems contain a hierarchy of choices that determine capacity for that system. By identifying and focusing on strategic choices, those levers that can create a domino effect towards positive outcomes, "the system could be changed completely or we are just engaged in 'busy work' without effecting the system slightly" (Foster-Fishman et al., 2005, p. 26). Our task is developing the tools for identifying these system choices that can help leverage broader systemic and transformational change.

## Theory of change vs. systems change

Systems theory allows for a shift in the analytical gaze from a linear progression of community change to one that acknowledges the multiple systems, the shifting nature of relationships, and the complex dynamics and interactions that occur within underserved communities. But as evident from our analysis of approximately 60 foundations engaged in place-based initiatives, boundaries are often set by systems external to the target community, such as foundations, government officials, or other key stakeholders invested in community change. Joan Walsh, who worked closely with the Annie E. Casey Foundation for over a decade on the foundation's New Futures CCI, explains the challenges faced by foundations and other systems committed to community change but who continue to replicate programming:

**TABLE 5.1** Stakeholder views of neighborhood as a system in City Heights

| Stakeholders | The function of the system | Definitions of the problem | Relevant system boundaries | Desired outcomes |
|---|---|---|---|---|
| Neighborhood property owners | Maintain boundaries and provide safety, identity, seek relationships with similar others to improve neighborhood | Must keep community from declining and work to increase property values; increase "economic diversity" | Geographic boundaries; class boundaries; homeownership as boundary | Gentrification |
| Neighborhood renters | Provide affordable housing, safety, proximity to public transit, good schools | Rising rents; poor condition of rental units and unresponsive landlords; crime; lack of jobs with livable wages | Affordable housing areas; proximity to public transportation, schools and daily rounds (family, market, services) | Affordable rentals in good condition, in safe area for children, within daily round area |
| Schools | Preparing a diverse student body for future | Low-income, highly mobile, academically under-prepared new immigrants speaking more than 30 languages challenge schools | School zone boundaries | High daily attendance rates; meeting goals of high-stake testing; improve graduation rates; differ by school |
| Health providers | Creating conditions that lead to improved health outcomes | Low-income, diverse populations with no insurance; working poor; high number of children in densely populated area with negative health outcomes | Income requirements for services; school-based boundaries | Model that can be replicated elsewhere; providing services within budgetary constraints |

*Continued*

**TABLE 5.1** Stakeholder views of neighborhood as a system in City Heights, *continued*

| Stakeholders | The function of the system | Definitions of the problem | Relevant system boundaries | Desired outcomes |
|---|---|---|---|---|
| Foundations | Creating visible and measurable change that can be replicated in other communities | Poverty and disinvestment the result of inefficient public sector; underserved areas need external experts to resolve entrenched social, cultural, and economic problems | Fluid | Model that can be replicated elsewhere; policy changes at state and federal level |
| Local government | Improving tax base of community in crisis; lowering crime rate and improving image | Declaration of Emergency issued in 1990 due to crime, neighborhood decline; infrastructure needs attention yet lack of public funding limits action | Geographic boundaries as determined by Redevelopment Area boundaries | Limited gentrification, continued public–private development, decrease in crime rate; growth in home ownership rates |

On the one hand, Casey sent the message, "This is about systems change." But then on the other hand, they gave us a guidebook for our proposals that seemed to be saying "You must have case management," which is clearly direct service. "You should have a youth employability system," which usually meant new services. "And you've got to reach these benchmarks: You must decrease dropouts by X percent, and teen pregnancies by Y percent, and something else by this percent over these five years. And here's this enormous amount of money." So they give you the money, and they say "impact those numbers." And you set up clinics, you set up education, you set up case management, you do certain services that will impact numbers. But this wasn't really systems change. Systems change is a much more time-consuming process.

(Walsh, 1997, p. 4)

The Federal Reserve Bank hints at the need for a systems change approach in its summary of a conference on place-based initiatives (Cytron, 2010). The report cites the need for funders to base their decisions for collaboration with underserved neighborhoods on a variety of data that allow foundations to "make an effort to gain an understanding of the institutional assets and systems in a community; critically, this should be done before injecting significant capital into a community" (Cytron, 2010, p. 4). The report acknowledges the difficulties that CCIs continue to face to "move the needle" in a direction that ameliorates entrenched urban problems.

As we outlined in our historical survey, community interventions targeting low-income areas cycle through various approaches as funding agencies, policymakers, and stakeholders seek the newest or more relevant methods for impacting community systems. At the start of the Johnson administration's War on Poverty programs, the focus was on the "maximum feasible participation" of the poor in determining how to use federal funds funneled to municipalities, but the Community Action Programs were quickly dismantled as city mayors chafed at the challenges posed by local residents to entrenched systems. Community change efforts then shifted their gaze to social capital as a strategy for building social networks between low-income neighborhoods and resources outside their communities (Coleman, 1988; Granovetter, 1973; Jacobs, 1961). This view held that the answer to urban disinvestment was better connections for the poor to networks that could offer jobs, better housing, and role models for urban residents to mimic.

Community activists and scholars then sought to respond to the focus on the perceived deficiencies of low-income communities and shifted research towards asset mapping as a way to highlight a community's human, social, economic, and cultural resources (Kretzman and McKnight, 1993). Private foundations welcomed this approach and funded community development initiatives in the 1980s, seeking to partner with public entities in developing replicable multi-site models. Capacity building emerged in local change initiatives in the 1990s as the key catalyst for systems change as nonprofits and other local institutions were charged with developing more effective practices. Residents were targeted for training that would enhance their capacities to participate actively in community change (HUD, 1993). In the twenty-first century, CCIs are the newest iteration of community change efforts, and may be the more promising, particularly as public–private partners seek to move beyond programmatic change to "strategic initiatives designed to create system changes that will lead to intended long-term, sustainable impact" (Kellogg Foundation, 2007, p. 1).

Systems change allows for consideration of some of the gaps in earlier community change efforts. It allows for context to be placed at the forefront of the initiative, as each system is nested and connected to the other systems within and outside the neighborhood; it calls for a recognition and reallocation of power, acknowledging the political and economic systems that often have a stronghold on poor neighborhoods; it supports the caring relationships that exist within low-income communities and seeks ways to build relationships within and outside existing systems; and, finally, systems theory allows for boundary creation that provides a geographic, social, and cultural framework for focusing on neighborhood change, a particularly important issue for CCIs (Walsh, 1997).

## How does systems change work?

Systems theorists argue that this methodology offers an opportunity to examine the elements of systems as they interact through stakeholders seeking to change the social sphere. Stakeholders' roles, positions, core values, and experiences act as filters that result in various interpretations of the problem, its causes, and the solutions that can effectively impact the systems (Flaspohler et al., 2003). Systems theory thus highlights the subjective nature of systems analysis, and seeks to include insight into the different stakeholder interpretations of the problem situation (Checkland and Scholes, 1990).

To illustrate the challenges of engaging the numerous internal systems that operate in underserved communities, as well as the external funding systems that seek to impact change in these communities, we draw on two cases studies of comprehensive community initiatives. The first, LAUF, presents valuable lessons on strategies for acknowledging the subjective nature of this work while still engaging a variety of stakeholders in strategic funding initiatives aimed at responding to the 1992 L.A. riots. The second case, the Foundation for Community Empowerment (FCE) in Dallas, Texas, presents evidence of the challenges of understanding and working with existing entrenched community systems. Community history, political rivalries, and a lack of trust created a context that was difficult for the FCE to overcome as it tried to move its revitalization plans forward.

## Case study: LAUF

After the civil unrest in Los Angeles in 1992, the Southern California Association for Philanthropy (SCAP), a regional association of private grant makers, sought to increase the efficacy of philanthropy in addressing social needs and problems throughout Los Angeles County. Previous efforts to respond to the unrest, most notably Rebuild LA, were unsuccessful. Local and national foundations were initially skeptical about their ability to meaningfully support neighborhood change in an area ravaged by poverty, crime, and institutional negligence. However, after several years of discussion and conversations with neighborhood stakeholders, some foundations began to acknowledge the potential impact that was possible by strategically combining resources. This led to the creation of LAUF in 1996 to serve as a collaborative model of philanthropy. The vision was shaped by a desire to eliminate piecemeal grant-making in favor of a model that would lead to systemic change (Letts and McCaffrey, 2003).[1]

Preliminary research conducted in 1993 by SCAP identified a funding climate that was largely neglectful of L.A.'s most challenged neighborhoods and a service model that lacked collaboration and local stakeholder participation. The findings revealed that only 35 percent of the 20 funders interviewed targeted funds to specific neighborhoods in L.A. Additionally, one-third of community-based organizations in the survey indicated that they rarely participated in intra-community collaboration and 40 percent of the agencies surveyed had very little if any resident participation on short- and long-term planning.

Analysis of the research findings led SCAP to recommend the creation of a fund to support CCIs in specifically designated neighborhoods throughout the county. This was an innovative model for Southern California. One of the early participants in the efforts noted that in comparison to Northern California, Southern California had a weak history of philanthropic collaboration. With 33 private and corporate foundation members, LAUF assembled a five-year action plan (1995–2000) organized around a three-phase strategy designed to support four main goals. The first phase in the action plan involved capacity building at two levels: between the funders and among the neighborhood stakeholders. This approach is congruent with systems theory as it does not assume that the neighborhood as a system is the only target for change; philanthropies are also systems with values, boundaries, processes, and relationships that warrant examination. This assessment was followed by a comprehensive planning phase for each neighborhood through a collaborative process with the foundations, to prepare a long-term strategic plan. The third phase allocated two years to begin implementation of the plan.

During the first phase, a team of consultants and LAUF board members considered 29 neighborhoods as possible target areas. A rubric was designed to evaluate the suitability of the neighborhoods as well as their future potential and degree of risk. The evaluation led to the selection of one neighborhood in the San Fernando Valley, one neighborhood in northeast L.A., and a third neighborhood in south central L.A. All three of the neighborhoods shared similar challenges affiliated with neighborhood blight such as physical decay, crime, low levels of educational attainment, high levels of unemployment, and strained race relationships.

LAUF's four main goals were shaped by a desire to develop a model of comprehensive community investment and change that departed from traditional models of philanthropy. Its broader objective, as summarized in a Harvard University Kennedy School of Government case study, was

> to find community initiative and follow it, rather than design and implement its own program. This kind of consultative model of philanthropy, with its many feedback loops, and resident-driven advocacy, was a big departure from traditional grant making and was both revolutionary and liberating for early members.
> (Letts and McCaffrey, 2003, p. 5)

LAUF essentially turned the typical funding model around and instead of grantees shaping their neighborhood renewal approaches to match foundation priorities, foundations were now responding to neighborhood-identified needs (Hamilton, 2002). Towards this end, LAUF's four main goals included 1) educating the funders about the neighborhoods at a deep and substantive level and encouraging collaborative grant-making; 2) enhancing the capacity of individuals and organizations; 3) creating stable neighborhoods through comprehensive, holistic strategies; and 4) sharing lessons learned with participants and policymakers.

A critical component of LAUF's strategic model of philanthropy was the development of a unique bi-modal funding strategy designed to address two critical and simultaneous goals of capacity building and improving quality of life. This approach acknowledges the diversity of stakeholders within the philanthropic systems while also pooling resources in areas where foundations agree. This type of flexibility is a hallmark of systems theory. First, each funder contributed to a pooled fund of $5.5 million over five years designed to support capacity building at the organizational and individual level. Allocation of these funds was at the discretion of LAUF's executive director and they were used for organizing, comprehensive planning, convening agencies, management assistance, developing local leadership, and evaluating outcomes (Letts and McCaffrey, 2003). The executive director was given a considerable amount of flexibility to engage and support neighborhood participants in a way that moved the effort forward in direct response to stakeholder needs (Sharp, 2002). Second, LAUF members also provided categorical grants. This more traditional form of grant-making allowed the funders to provide support to those areas in alignment with their mission and areas of specialization. The 33 funders agreed to a five-year commitment and each foundation determined their individual contribution. They were asked to contribute a grant comparatively similar in size to other significant grants that they had awarded in the past (Letts and McCaffrey, 2003).

At the completion of its first five years, LAUF evaluated its accomplishments and the lessons learned offer invaluable insights on the limitations and potential of innovative philanthropic approaches to chronic urban problems. Evaluation of the outcomes was framed by a host of important evaluation criteria as identified by Letts and McCaffrey (2003):

*Clients*: Varying viewpoints emerged regarding the intended beneficiaries of the effort. While some participants only identified the foundations, other members identified three key clients: foundation participants, nonprofit service providers, and residents in the target neighborhoods.

*Short-term vs. long-term expectations*: Large-scale efforts such as neighborhood rehabilitation take a long time and may not be seen for many years, perhaps even decades. One foundation representative noted that the initial five-year time limit was artificial.

*Multiple contributing factors*: An initial criteria used by LAUF in selecting its three target neighborhoods was that there had to be ongoing community initiatives to build upon. This, though, presented measurement problems because it made it challenging, perhaps even unrealistic, to isolate and identify LAUF's unique contributions.

*Assessment objectives, process vs. outcomes*: At the onset of the effort, LAUF was committed to assessing both process and outcomes by focusing on improved capacity and improved quality of life. Actually doing this proved to be very challenging. Most of the data focused on process, and LAUF's executive director noted that during the first five years LAUF expected to see improved organizational and neighborhood capacity and that specific indications of community improvements would take longer and follow from this investment.

*Evolving evaluation model*: Since evaluation was an ongoing process and the larger model was based on a continual feedback loop, it was challenging for LAUF to establish an evaluation model at the beginning of the process. Different evaluation consultants were brought in to measure specific aspects of the effort and subsequently different models were implemented and critiqued from a range of standpoints.

In looking specifically at funder outcomes, the results of LAUF's first five years were encouraging. Many of the participating foundations reported that they changed their grant-making practices as a result of their involvement with LAUF, and they were unanimous in their assessment that the effort was successful. The experience also led to better communication between funders and local community agencies and a shift in the way that funders looked at and interacted with local communities (Letts and McCaffrey, 2003). Thus the systems approach taken by LAUF impacted philanthropies as systems in ways that traditional "top-down" philanthropic efforts could not, and it improved relationships between the community systems and funding systems.

Community agencies identified numerous benefits with LAUF's efforts. The final benefits were clear as over $15 million was cumulatively invested in the three targeted neighborhoods. Importantly, many local agencies developed relationships with foundations that were previously unknown to them and were able to gain access to information and communicate with them. At the resident level, benefits were also achieved but were more difficult to measure. Certain trends were observed, though, in the areas of increased capacity, more social capital, and improved cohesion and solidarity among residents.

Proponents of funder collaboratives including LAUF's executive director, Elwood Hopkins (2005), argue that funder collaboratives have the potential to unite philanthropic efforts, promote true partnerships, and ultimately produce tangible social returns. They are seen as having the potential to increase the capacity of foundations to impact social and policy change and incubate new ways of working (Sharp, 2002). The potential benefits of funder collaboratives include diversified funding streams, enhanced political clout, greater philanthropic efficiency, long-term sustainability, risk pooling, and knowledge sharing (Hamilton, 2002; Hopkins, 2005; Sharp, 2002).

## Case study: the FCE

Although similar in scope and vision to other foundations such as Price Charities and the Jacobs Family Foundation, the FCE, created in 1995, faced a much tougher battle as it sought to change Dallas' Frazier Courts neighborhood. J. McDonald "Don" Williams, chairman emeritus of Trammell Crow, a development company with assets of $55 billion (CNRE, 2011), worked to convince residents of a historically African American neighborhood that the foundation's intent was benign. But a contested history around the use of eminent domain and remnants of Jim Crow proved to be formidable obstacles for the FCE to overcome.

The vision of the FCE called for an asset-based, comprehensive community change effort through technical assistance, coalition building, and grant-making to support capacity building among community partners. In 2003, the FCE received a $578,892, three-year Compassion Capital Grant from the U.S. Department of Health and Human Services, Administration for Children and Families.[2] The grant's goal was to support faith-based and community-based organizations in South Dallas to increase their ability to compete for public and private resources through capacity building. To further strengthen CDCs in low-income Dallas neighborhoods, the FCE and the city of Dallas partnered with 15 donors that collectively raised $2.5 million to create the CDC Core Operating Support and Capacity Building Fund.

Don Williams worked to build trust with residents, meeting with South Dallas school principals, hiring a community engagement director, and working with the city to obtain a $20 million HOPE VI grant in 2003 to rehabilitate Frazier Courts, one of Dallas' largest public housing complexes. The 50-acre public housing development was built in the 1920s and 1930s, and by 2000 most of the 109 units were in deplorable condition and crime kept many residents indoors. After obtaining the HOPE IV grant, the Dallas Housing Authority hired Boston urban planner Antonio DiMambro to create a comprehensive land use plan for the 11,000 acres surrounding the Frazier Courts area. The plan was completed in 2004 and includes a Dallas Area Rapid Transit (DART) light rail line along the neighborhood's western boundary. In 2006, the foundation created Frazier Revitalization Inc., an independent 501(c)(3) nonprofit, to lead the physical and social rebirth of this largely low-income, African American neighborhood of approximately 33,000 residents.

Like many communities across the United States, Dallas' Frazier Courts neighborhood felt the impact of White flight to the suburbs, particularly after World War II when the federal government provided a variety of incentives for returning GIs to move to new homes using the new freeway infrastructure connecting the city's center with outlying areas. As Whites left south Dallas, poor rural Blacks seeking jobs in the booming Dallas economy moved into the Frazier Courts neighborhood near Fair Park. Racial tensions arose at the steady stream of rural African American newcomers, and Dallas' fledging Ku Klux Klan (KKK) chapter's enrollment boomed as the group capitalized on people's fears. On October 24, 1923, the State Fair of Texas held Ku Klux Klan Day and 5,000 new members were initiated, making the Texas chapter of the KKK the largest in the country (Mondell et al., 2007; Wooley, 2010). Streets around Fair Park were renamed to reflect the changing demographics and thus Congo Street remains today (Schutze, 2007).

South Dallas' Fair Park neighborhood continued its decline into the 1960s, further exacerbated when the city bulldozed a large number of homes for additional parking for Fair Park and the Cotton Bowl in an unsuccessful bid to lure the Cowboys football team back. The neighborhood has not forgotten the treatment of African American families displaced through the use of eminent domain for this project.

After working in the neighborhood for more than a decade, Frazier Revitalization Inc. sought a change in the use of eminent domain in Texas to allow them to acquire large parcels for the redevelopment project around Frazier Courts. Despite the shuttered stores, run-down strip malls, and crack houses prevalent in some parts of the neighborhood, residents angrily turned foundation officials away. At a heated neighborhood meeting in the Juanita Craft Recreation Center in Spring 2007, state senators and county commissioners representing this district worked to convince the crowd of the merits of this legislative tool. They argued that eminent domain would clear up the "tangled land titles, liens, back taxes and convoluted heirships" in the Frazier Revitalization area (Schutze, 2007, para. 19). But more than 300 residents jeered various speakers and cheered as State Senator Royce West, D-Dallas, told the crowd he would not sponsor the bill (Meyer, 2007, p. 2A).

The public rejection of FCE's initiative led to a reassessment of its projects. By 2008, the FCE had invested more than $3 million in Dallas city schools in an effort to achieve systems change through the Dallas Achieves Initiative in partnership with Texas Instruments. It also created the J. McDonald Williams Institute through grants totaling more than $550,000 to collect data on Dallas' distressed neighborhoods, including the development of an Indicators Project webpage to disseminate data. Accomplishments also included the development of a network of community gardens in South Dallas, and it kicked off an effort to engage churches across the city in community revitalization through a "Justice Revival" event. It also held a series of conferences at which community-based researchers shared data with neighborhood advocates on quality of life issues between the wealthier north and the underserved South Dallas neighborhoods.

The CEO of Frazier Revitalization Inc. resigned shortly after the controversial community meeting, and the research arm of the FCE was moved to the University of Texas at Dallas in 2008 and renamed the Institute for Urban Policy Research. In 2010, J. McDonald "Don" Williams resigned as chair of the FCE board, arguing that: "It was never our intention to create a permanent institution driven by the universal institutional imperative to persist and grow … the FCE's role was to illuminate, to enhance, to support, but not to own the problem or solution" (Williams, 2010).

Frazier Revitalization Inc. continues to exist, working to revitalize the community through smaller projects such as a wellness center, financial counseling for prospective homeowners, and through programs to encourage minority entrepreneurship. It is also working with a for-profit developer on a $30 million transit-oriented project in South Dallas/Fair Park that will include 25,000 square feet of commercial space. It continues to work with the Dallas Housing Authority as it completes the development of 300 new townhome-style multi-family units and 40 single-family homes in Frazier Courts.

The challenges faced by the Frazier Courts community development effort highlight the dissonance between two systems operating in the same contested field: the African American neighborhood and the FCE. As an experienced commercial real estate developer, Don Williams' definition of the problem was the aggregation of land needed to achieve large-scale redevelopment of this area, and eminent domain was the answer. But the Frazier Courts neighborhood as a system with entrenched values and beliefs could not set aside its historical experiences with eminent domain. *Dallas Examiner* reporter Jim Schutze (2007, para 16) describes the contextual conditions that derailed FCE's efforts:

> Somebody forgot to read the history. In southern Dallas, eminent domain is a phrase only slightly less odious than the old man himself, Jim Crow … White people have always had a divided theory of property rights in this country. If it's White property, the right of ownership is almost absolute. But if it's Black property, the rights of ownership are something less. Hence Dallas, like most American cities, has seen waves of property seizure—sometimes called slum clearance, sometimes called flood control, whatever—in which eminent domain has been used to seize Black-owned property. Black Dallas knows that. Black Dallas hates eminent domain. FRI [Frazier Redevelopment Inc.] didn't have that figured out.

The FCE failed to understand stakeholder interpretations of the problems in South Dallas. The dynamics of the neighborhood as a system precluded consideration of FCE's plans. Although the FCE had actively networked and worked with residents for a decade, eminent domain was not the lever the neighborhood saw as a catalyst for systemic change and instead it reinforced strongly held fears. Without common agreement between the neighborhood and funding systems, Frazier Courts became a contested field of interaction as each system sought to impose its view of the future of this community (Checkland, 1981; Flaspohler et al., 2003; Lasker et al., 2001). Ultimately, elected officials aligned themselves with residents reaffirming the importance of maintaining the particular cultural, political, economic, and social context that shapes and influences this neighborhood.

An important contribution of systems theory to understanding CCIs is its focus on philanthropic systems that must also make adjustments to their practices to partner effectively with community, nonprofit, and governmental systems (Ferris and Williams, 2009). Recognizing underserved communities as complex systems also allows for an examination of the formal and, more importantly, informal rules that guide action in these neighborhoods. Ultimately, systems theory offers an opportunity to develop truly collaborative community development efforts that acknowledge the dynamics, values, history, and culture of neighborhoods, as well as those of actors seeking to intervene, and presents a broader menu of policy options that respond to the complex conditions that led to the decline of underserved communities.

**PART II**

# Lessons from the field

# 6

# PRICE CHARITIES AND THE JACOBS CENTER FOR NEIGHBORHOOD INNOVATION

## An introduction to the case studies

As discussed in Part I of the book, CCIs exhibit a high level of heterogeneity. While there does not appear to be any specific determinants that lead to regional variations or trends, one city finds itself in the unique position of housing two innovative, and seemingly similar, cases. Price Charities and the Jacobs Family Foundation are two embedded family foundations working in contiguous neighborhoods in San Diego, California, motivated by the same goal of comprehensive community change. Both foundations began their efforts at approximately the same point in time in the 1990s and developed models that, on the surface, have many parallels. Both foundations are committed to deep levels of financial investment and hands-on policy and program development in clearly delineated underserved neighborhoods. This chapter introduces these two communities and situates the discussion in the broader history of growth and development in San Diego. We consider the factors in San Diego's history that may help us answer why it is that two parallel, innovative CCI models were seeded in San Diego and serve as exemplars in both the foundation and community development worlds.

San Diego's urban history has received little scholarly attention. Its neighbor to the north has overshadowed it for years and while a rich body of literature explores past and present planning efforts in Los Angeles, most notably with the Los Angeles School (see for example Abu-Lughod, 1999; Dear, 2002; Dear and Dahmann, 2008; Erie, 2004; Keil, 1998; Scott and Soja, 1996; Wolch, Pastor, and Dreier, 2004), San Diego has yet to benefit from this level of inquiry. While San Diego is best known for its close ties to the defense industry as well as its thriving biotechnology sector and a climate desirable to tourists and retirees, this oversimplifies a complex history that shares many of the traits from other Sunbelt cities, yet deviates from them as well.

## Planning and growth in San Diego

San Diego's history from the mid-1800s through the early twentieth century was characterized by frequent cycles of boom and bust and competition with Los Angeles to secure the infrastructure necessary to stimulate robust population growth and economic development. A lack of strong municipal leadership and public will was disadvantageous to San Diego and contributed to its inability to compete with Los Angeles to secure the major infrastructure improvements, such as railroad service and harbor access, necessary to ensure long-term growth. Whereas Los Angeles voters, for example, approved bond subsidies to fund the expansion of the Southern Pacific railroad, San Diegans were unwilling to do so and offered public land grants instead (Erie, Kogan, and MacKenzie, 2011). San Diego, it appears, was always a step or two behind L.A.

San Diego had its share of dynamic boosters in the nineteenth and early twentieth centuries. Alonzo Horton, John D. Spreckels, A. G. Spalding, and E. W. Scripps were among the most influential and used their vast resources to secure sizeable amounts of land and city infrastructure to steer growth in directions that would enhance their personal holdings (Erie et al., 2011; Hancock, 1996). They succeeded in large part due to a lack of municipal leadership and civic will to counterbalance their narrowly defined growth agenda. Between the 1800s and World War II, San Diego had relatively little growth with the exception of the projects spearheaded by wealthy business interests (Erie et al., 2011; Ford, 2005).

In the early 1900s, Progressivism was popular in San Diego and municipal reform took root to a certain extent (Bridges, 1997). However, the efforts encountered challenges. George Marston, a department store owner and City Beautiful proponent, was largely responsible for hiring the well-respected urban planner and landscape architect, John Nolen, to prepare a comprehensive city plan for San Diego in 1908. In his desire to see the plan implemented, Marston ran for mayor twice, in 1913 and 1917, but he lost to proponents of more aggressive growth dominated by industry and military expansion. The 1917 race, labeled the "Smokestacks versus Geraniums" contest, saw Marston portrayed as the anti-growth candidate and set up a long-lasting struggle in San Diego pitting aggressive pro-development factions against those in favor of more deliberate, planned growth (Hancock, 1996; Ports, 1975).

Public planning was finally adopted in San Diego in 1924 as Marston's "geraniums" held the mayor's office continuously between 1921 and 1931. Nolen and Marston lobbied once again for a comprehensive city plan but this time the support was deeper and Nolen, having learned from his past experiences, exercised more savvy in securing broad public support for his plan (Hancock, 1996).

By the end of the 1930s, the military was San Diego's biggest employer with the navy taking a particularly aggressive approach. This resulted in San Diego getting the growth it wanted but at the price of giving away sizeable amounts of land. By the end of World War II, the federal government controlled about 40 percent of the region's land and this impacted the city's tax base since this land was not subject to local taxation (Erie et al., 2011; Ford, 2005; Lotchin, 1992; Shragge, 1994). Not only did the federal government wield significant control over land, it held considerable influence over urban growth through its construction and expansion of local infrastructure. During World War II the rate of growth was so rapid that orderly planning fell by the wayside and the city's limited infrastructure was severely strained, thus increasing the city's reliance on the federal government. As defense workers streamed into San Diego, the already inadequate housing infrastructure was overburdened. Out of necessity, and against the wishes of local officials who disapproved of federally subsidized affordable housing, the federal government launched a building initiative to quickly provide low-cost housing for war workers. This was done without consideration of long-term planning objectives and the legacy of massive housing tracts contributed to new suburban growth detached from adequate infrastructure (Killory, 1993). In the years immediately following World War II, San Diego continued to take shape as a new type of city, a Sunbelt city (Phillips, 1969). With city hall largely controlled by a small cadre of business leaders, low taxes were favored at the same time that growth was promoted with a focus on the downtown core (Bernard and Rice, 1983).

Modern San Diego formed in the post-World War II era as close connections to the defense industry stimulated growth. Planning once again surfaced as a critical issue under the mayoral leadership of Pete Wilson in the 1970s. Wilson proposed a growth management plan that divided the city into tiers. The model, codified in the 1979 San Diego General Plan, was structured for growth to pay for itself. In order to encourage infill development in the inner core neighborhoods and simultaneously preserve open space in the outer tiers, developers were exempted from impact fees with the expectation that the city's budget could accommodate the costs for the infrastructure improvements in these older neighborhoods. The growth management plan created a division between residents in the newer areas who benefitted from adequate public services and those in the older urban core who required infrastructure improvements. The residents in the outer tiers, who were paying for their own public services via Mello-Roos taxes (development fees passed along by developers to homeowners) and homeowners association dues, did not want to see their taxes increase to pay for improvements in the older neighborhoods (Erie et al., 2011). Wilson's plan was in certain respects a re-circling back to George Marston's planning ideology that proposed cautious, deliberate growth. In 1974, with a grant from the Marston family, Donald Appleyard and Kevin Lynch, both urban planners and urban designers, prepared a report for the city of San Diego (Ports, 1975). Entitled *Temporary Paradise? A Look at the Special Landscape of the San Diego Region*, the report called for thoughtful planning and preservation of San Diego's natural resources (Appleyard and Lynch, 1974).

By the late 1980s, elected officials were also feeling the impact of Proposition 13. The initiative, approved by two-thirds of California voters in 1978, set property tax value at the 1976 assessed value level. Property tax increases on any given property were limited to no more than 2 percent per year as long as the property was not sold. Once sold, the property was reassessed at 1 percent of the sale price, and the 2 percent yearly cap became applicable to future years (californiataxdata. com, 1986). A reduction in tax revenues and lack of developer fees led city of San Diego officials and planners to revisit long-term planning goals and, in 2002, the city presented a smart growth plan known as "City of Villages." The plan directed growth towards existing neighborhoods with the goal of creating urban villages characterized by increased housing density, access to multiple modes of transportation, and vibrant mixed-used places. Opposition to the plan came from politically powerful community groups opposed to increased housing density and potential strains on existing infrastructure. The mayor, Dick Murphy, bowed to this opposition and planners were directed to remove from the plan all references to increased density. The city council adopted five pilot villages in 2004. Two of these selected pilot villages, City Heights and the Village at Market Creek in southeastern San Diego, were already in the process of revitalization utilizing innovative models of funding and planning in conjunction with embedded family foundations. As with many other communities in San Diego, stakeholders in City Heights and southeastern San Diego had become frustrated by the lack of public resources to assist their revitalization efforts. Price Charities in City Heights and the Jacobs Family Foundation in southeastern San Diego stepped in to fill the void of public sector leadership as major catalysts for community change. As we discuss later in this chapter, in many respects these two private foundations became de facto public planning entities.

At the same time that the City of Villages plan was undergoing completion and adoption, San Diego experienced significant growth as high tech and biotech, real estate, tourism, and foreign trade bolstered the local economy. The city encouraged this growth by pursuing a model of small government, low taxes, and a business-friendly environment directed by a small cadre of powerful businessmen (Erie et al., 2011). Unlike other Sunbelt cities that saw central city power erode as the metropolitan area enlarged and minority and neighborhood groups assumed increased power (Bernard and Rice, 1983), a narrow arm of the private sector still to this day largely dictates San Diego's development policy. San Diego development efforts are criticized as focusing on downtown "legacy projects" at the expense of neighborhood and regional improvements as well as larger social justice considerations (Davis, Miller, and Mayhew, 2003; Erie et al., 2011). These legacy projects were largely funded by the public sector and the military industrial complex and done so in a region known for its disdain of taxes, raising important questions about how growth has truly been funded in San Diego. With their recently published critique of San Diego's fiscal policies, Erie et al. (2011) observe that San Diego, as a region, has grown accustomed to someone else paying for necessary public services and infrastructure while maintaining a strong aversion to paying taxes.

With an aversion to taxes, San Diegans have had to look elsewhere to pay for civic improvements. Unlike other Sunbelt cities with a strong corporate philanthropic sector, San Diego is a branch plant town that has few corporate headquarters. The result is a city lacking in strong corporate civic leadership and local ties that has created a void in support for larger civic concerns. The private sector has been able to steer development in directions that support its narrow interests and public–private partnerships have become the primary vehicle for public redevelopment with the major emphasis directed to the downtown core. Older urban neighborhoods have been low priorities unless they show potential for future gentrification (Erie et al., 2011). Many of San Diego's older neighborhoods have strong community planning groups, but they are limited in what they can do by their lack of funding. In two neighborhoods, City Heights and southeastern San Diego, these gaps are being addressed by Price Charities and JCNI, two locally based private family foundations that have emerged as dominant forces in the neighborhoods' comprehensive community initiatives. We now turn to these two neighborhoods and look at the their unique histories and the factors that led to the emergence of the CCIs. This is followed by an analysis of the application of these two examples to the broader field of comprehensive community change.

## The neighborhoods

The city of San Diego encompasses the southwest corner of the United States, bordered on the south by Mexico and on the west by the Pacific Ocean. Its total population is 1.3 million, largely White, but with a growing segment of Hispanic residents (25.4 percent) and Asian residents (13.9 percent) (U.S. Census Bureau, 2010). The temperate weather, physical beauty, tourist attractions, military bases, and a thriving biotech industry have contributed to one of the highest housing costs in the nation. In April of 2012 DataQuick reported the median price of a home in San Diego at $320,500, almost $70,000 higher than the median price of a home in the state of California (DataQuick, 2012). San Diego's median income of $62,480, while at parity with the state's overall median income of $60,883, is not high enough to ensure adequate opportunities for affordable homeownership (U.S. Census Bureau, 2010). The rental market is equally challenging and in March of 2012 San Diego County reported the third highest rents in the country, after San Francisco and Los Angeles, at $2,083 a month (Bauder, 2012).

City Heights, located a few miles northeast of downtown San Diego, has one of the highest population densities in the county, whereas southeastern San Diego, situated a few miles southeast of downtown San Diego, still contains open space areas. Although the population total of both target areas is similar, as Figure 6.1 indicates, the land mass of southeastern San Diego is much larger than City Heights', but to date JCNI has targeted its efforts on a smaller segment in the larger catchment area.

# Boundaries of
# City Heights & Diamond Neighborhoods

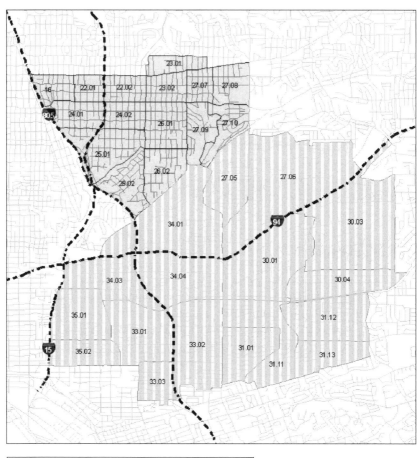

## Legend

 Diamond Neighborhoods Tracts

City Heights Tracts

▪ ▪ ▪ ▪ ▪ ▪ Highway

N

**FIGURE 6.1** Boundaries of City Heights and Diamond Neighborhoods

A clear divide exists between the northern and southern sections of San Diego. Both of the neighborhoods targeted by these two foundations are south of Interstate 8, often referred to as the racial and economic dividing line for this region. City Heights is composed of 16 neighborhoods with approximately 81,205 residents; the majority reside within a three-square mile area (U.S. Census Bureau, 2010).[1] One of the most racially and ethnically diverse neighborhoods in San Diego, over 30 different languages are spoken in the community. Southeastern San Diego is quite large, encompassing 19.1 square miles, but the primary focus of redevelopment has been ten distinct and underserved neighborhoods referred to by the Jacobs Family Foundation as the Diamond District, based on its diamond shape. With a population of 93,879 people, the Diamond Neighborhoods are a group of multi-ethnic and multiracial communities comprised of African Americans and Hispanics along with a growing population of Somalis, Laotians, Filipinos, and Samoans.[2] As illustrated in Table 6.1, the communities share a similar socioeconomic profile and have experienced comparable demographic trends over time, yet there are some clear differences, too.

**TABLE 6.1** Socioeconomic characteristics of City Heights, Diamond Neighborhoods, and the City of San Diego, 2010

|  | City Heights | Diamond Neighborhoods | City of San Diego |
|---|---|---|---|
| *Population* |  |  |  |
| Total population | 81,205 | 93,879 | 1,307,402 |
| Median age | 28.4 years | 29.6 years | 33.6 years |
| Median household income | $32,286 | $39,917 | $62,480 |
| Percent foreign born | 42% | 33.9% | 25.9% |
| Percent unemployed | 9.9% | 10.1% | 7.3% |
| Percentage without a high school diploma | 38.3% | 36.1% | 13.5% |
| Percent households in poverty | 26.5% | 20.4% | 9.5% |
| *Housing* |  |  |  |
| Median housing value[a] | $185,000 | $236,000 | $345,000 |
| Median monthly rent | $868 | $945 | $1,186 |
| Percent owner-occupied housing units | 24.9% | 51.5% | 49.5% |

[a] Housing values are for 2012 and based on DataQuick values due to inconsistencies with census data for 2010.

Source: U.S. Census Bureau, 2010 census, American Community Survey, 2010

Between 1990 and 2010, the Diamond Neighborhoods' rate of growth was more gradual and stable than that of City Heights. From 1990 to 2000, City Heights' population increased by 17 percent to 86,107 while the Diamond Neighborhoods' population increased by 4 percent to 92,128. However, in 2010, City Heights' population declined by 6 percent while the Diamond Neighborhoods' population grew by 2 percent. City Heights is slightly younger than the Diamond Neighborhoods. In 2010, City Heights' median age was 28.4 years while the Diamond Neighborhoods' was 29.6. Further, the age distribution for both communities from 1990 to 2010 shows that the Diamond Neighborhoods have had a greater percentage of residents 55 years and older. In 2010, 18.3 percent of the population in the Diamond Neighborhoods was over the age of 55 compared to 13.6 percent in City Heights and 20.8 percent in the city of San Diego. As discussed in more detail later in this chapter, City Heights, known as San Diego's "Ellis Island," has a high proportion of new immigrant and refugee families that tend to have young children, which thus explains the age distribution. In contrast, the Diamond Neighborhoods house one of San Diego's largest middle-class Black communities. Southeastern San Diego was one of the few areas in San Diego after World War II that did not enforce restrictive covenants, therefore making it one of the few areas for Black households to purchase a home. Many of these households have remained in the community and aged in place. The Diamond Neighborhoods' average family size has also been slightly larger than City Heights' over time. From 1990 to 2010, the Diamond District's average family size has increased from 3.7 people to 4.0 people, while City Heights' average family size has grown from 3.5 people in 1990 to 3.8 people in 2010.

Both City Heights and the Diamond Neighborhoods are among the poorest communities in San Diego. City Heights' median household income has been consistently lower than the Diamond Neighborhoods' from 1990 to 2010. In 2010, the Diamond Neighborhoods' median household income was $39,917 while City Heights' was $32,286 compared to $62,480 for the city of San Diego. Poverty and unemployment levels have been consistently high in these two neighborhoods as well. City Heights' poverty rate decreased from 28.1 percent in 1990 to 26.5 percent in 2010, while the Diamond Neighborhoods' poverty rate was 20.4 percent in both 1990 and 2010. In contrast, between 1990 and 2010 the city of San Diego's poverty rate fluctuated between 9.7 percent and 9.5 percent, increasing to 10.6 percent in 2000. Unemployment rates in City Heights and the Diamond Neighborhoods have remained consistently higher than the city. In 1990, for example, the unemployment rate in the city of San Diego was 6.2 percent compared to 12 percent in City Heights and 10.4 percent in the Diamond Neighborhoods. By 2010 the unemployment rates in City Heights (9.9 percent) and the Diamond Neighborhoods (10.1 percent) had declined slightly, but they were still higher than the city's unemployment rate of 7.3 percent.

Elevating educational equity is also a challenge in these two communities. City Heights' percentage of residents without a high school diploma has fluctuated dramatically since 1990, while the Diamond Neighborhoods' percentage has only shifted marginally. From 1990 to 2000, City Heights' percentage of residents without a high school diploma increased from 36.5 percent in 1990 to 50.5 percent in 2000. The Diamond Neighborhoods' percentage of residents without a high school diploma increased from 33.9 percent in 1990 to 36.5 percent in 2000. In comparison, the city of San Diego experienced a significant decrease in the percentage of residents without a high school diploma, dropping from 17.7 percent in 1990 to 13.5 percent in 2010. But positive change may be occurring in City Heights, as the percentage of residents without a high school diploma declined from 50.5 percent in 2000 to 38.3 percent in 2010. It is unclear whether this is a result of improved educational opportunities, or newcomers potentially gentrifying the neighborhoods.

Like many communities across the United States, both City Heights and the Diamond Neighborhoods experienced a high percentage growth in their Hispanic population from 1990 to 2010. In 2010, Hispanics made up over half of City Heights (56.1 percent) and the Diamond Neighborhoods' total population (52.2 percent) compared to 28.8 percent city-wide, and they represented the largest immigrant group in the communities. In addition, 16.7 percent of City Heights' population was Asian in 2010 compared to 14.1 percent in the Diamond Neighborhoods and 16 percent in the city of San Diego. The Asian population represented the second largest immigrant group in both communities. Both City Heights and the Diamond Neighborhoods also experienced declines in their White and Black population from 1990 to 2010. While both communities' Black population decreased over time, in 2010 the Black population made up a larger percentage of the Diamond Neighborhoods' population (20.7 percent) than in City Heights (12.9 percent) or the city of San Diego (6.3 percent).

A challenge to active participation in the governance structures that guide the changes in their neighborhoods is evident in the growth of households where English is not the first language. In City Heights, this population has grown from 45.4 percent in 1990 to 71.4 percent in 2010. In the Diamond Neighborhoods, it has increased from 39.4 percent in 1990 to 59.5 percent in 2010. These rates are significantly higher than the city of San Diego which, in 2010, counted 38.8 percent of households where English was not the first language. Residents of both communities also speak numerous languages and schools are challenged to respond to the more than 30 languages spoken by children and their parents, particularly in City Heights. Lastly, with the growth of the Hispanic population in City Heights and the Diamond Neighborhoods, 51 percent of City Heights' residents spoke Spanish in 2010 compared to 46.2 percent in the Diamond Neighborhoods and 22.2 percent in the city of San Diego.

Not only are the socioeconomic characteristics of City Heights and the Diamond Neighborhoods significantly different than those of the city of San Diego, but this is also the case when we look at physical infrastructure, particularly housing. From 1990 to 2012, the median housing value in the Diamond Neighborhoods was higher than that found in City Heights. Most recently, in 2010, City Heights had a median housing value of $185,000 compared to $236,000 for the Diamond Neighborhoods and $345,000 for the city of San Diego.[3] Similarly, from 1990 to

2010 the Diamond Neighborhoods' median rent values have remained higher than City Heights by approximately $75. In 2010, the median rent in the Diamond Neighborhoods was $945 compared to $868 in City Heights and $1,186 in the city of San Diego. Nevertheless, this statistic in relation to the communities' median housing value suggests that City Heights has become a more attractive community for home buyers over time. As discussed in Chapter 8, some neighborhood stakeholders have expressed concern that the redevelopment activities spearheaded by Price Charities may be contributing to gentrification.

The two neighborhoods have experienced stable, but different, housing tenure patterns over time. Between 1990 and 2010 the Diamond Neighborhoods have maintained parity between owners and renters with 50.1 percent homeowners in 2010, a trend similar to city-wide patterns with 49.5 percent homeowners in 2010. City Heights has also experienced a consistent pattern, but one that has renters consistently outnumbering homeowners approximately 75 percent to 25 percent between 1990 and 2010. As the first, and often temporary, stop for new low-income immigrants and refugees, the large inventory of apartments serves an important need but contributes to instability in the neighborhood. In contrast, many of the households in the Diamond Neighborhoods are long-term residents. For example, in 2010, of the 51.5 percent of owner-occupied housing units in the Diamond Neighborhoods, 21.7 percent were comprised of households that moved into their housing units in 1989 or earlier. In contrast, of the 24.9 percent of owner-occupied housing units in City Heights in 2010, 6.7 percent of these households moved into their housing units in 1989 or earlier.

Emblematic of the demographic changes occurring in communities across the U.S., both of these case studies exemplify the challenges faced by public and private partners as they seek to engage residents in planning, developing, and evaluating comprehensive community initiatives. The high mobility rate of low-income households, particularly renters, as is the case in City Heights, is problematic. The language differences, lack of knowledge of U.S. participatory practices by immigrants, and poverty can be formidable obstacles for residents; the lack of capacity or failure to understand these contextual obstacles by organizations seeking to effect comprehensive change can also test the best intentions and lead to resentment and discord.

As examples of neighborhoods targeted for community development initiatives, City Heights and the Diamond Neighborhoods not only share some similar demographic trends, but they also have related challenges regarding their physical infrastructure. Both communities have experienced decades of public- and private-sector neglect. The response to this disinvestment by residents of these two communities presents valuable lessons as they ushered in a new era with the arrival of CCIs spearheaded by private family foundations.

## A new era: the arrival of CCIs in City Heights and the Diamond Neighborhoods

In response to the variety of problems that plagued its declining urban neighborhoods in the later part of the twentieth century, the city of San Diego created redevelopment mechanisms to stimulate revitalization. In 1981 the city established the Southeastern Economic Development Corporation (SEDC), a nonprofit public benefit corporation responsible for overseeing revitalization in a 7.2-square mile area in southeastern San Diego, encompassing the Diamond Neighborhoods. In 1994 it created a 1,984-acre redevelopment project area, the city's largest, encompassing City Heights. The City Heights project area generates approximately $10 million in tax increments per year and has spent approximately $129 million to date on housing and other infrastructure (City of San Diego Redevelopment Agency, 2009b). SEDC also generates robust annual tax increments and, as an example, in 2009 it generated approximately $6.9 million (City of San Diego Redevelopment Agency, 2009a).

Price Charities and the Jacobs Family Foundation began their redevelopment work in these communities at approximately the same point in time, independent of one another but motivated by the same desire to target resources in older urban neighborhoods in need of significant redevelopment. The Price Family Charitable Fund was created in 1983. Sol Price was seeking a community in which to focus his philanthropic efforts and, in 1994, he chose City Heights after meeting with residents and city officials. In 2000, San Diego Revitalization Corporation was established as an operating arm to fund capital programs in City Heights and was later renamed Price Charities.

The Jacobs Family Foundation was founded in 1988 and, in 1995, it created its operating arm, JCNI, in order to address the needs of the Diamond Neighborhoods in southeastern San Diego.[4] The Jacobs Family Foundation targeted this neighborhood for its work after its own internal evaluation of its goals and objectives was found to be in consonance with the challenges present in the Diamond Neighborhoods.

Although the two foundations, Price Charities and JCNI, do have much in common, their theories of change and resultant approaches to community development differ markedly (see Table 6.2). Price Charities' approach is described as a collaborative, pragmatic process that engages a variety of nonprofit, foundation, and public partners both within and outside the community to leverage the foundation's resources to maximize impact. Price's approach is one focused on the foundation serving as a catalyst for physical change based on a deep trust in the market, but it is also characterized by a willingness to work and fund a variety of neighborhood groups, nonprofits, and other stakeholders resulting in a thick web of organizations that are loosely linked through the Mid-City Community Advocacy Network (Mid-City CAN), an existing nonprofit organization. Price has provided funding for this collaborative to continue to serve as a forum for community decision-making.

**TABLE 6.2** Comparison of Price Charities' and the Jacobs Center for Neighborhood Innovation's approaches to community engagement

| Community context | Price Charities | Jacobs Center for Neighborhood Innovation |
|---|---|---|
| Political | Support from city officials and staff | Skepticism from city officials |
| | Fragmented and diverse resident population | Resistance from African American leadership |
| | Strong property owner group | Scandal-plagued redevelopment agency |
| Cultural | Culture of collaboration and partnerships with nonprofits | Strong resident participation but few nonprofits |
| | Foundation supports a variety of nonprofits' programs | Competition between nonprofits and Jacobs for grants |
| Impact | Extensive physical change | Infrastructure changes occurring at a slower pace |
| | Fast-paced program development that does not always elicit resident input | Extensive community participation slows down process |
| | Community governance is fragmented | Community governance is challenged by lack of consensus and trust |
| Foundation mission | | |
| | Physical change of community as outcome is most important | Process of building resident participatory capacity is most important |
| | Leveraging of public funds with private sector is important | Deliberations and extensive consultation with residents is the norm |
| | Resident capacity for engagement will occur naturally as physical change transforms community | Capacity building is a long and difficult process |

The Jacobs Family Foundation has a clearly articulated theory of change premised on what it believes is a new model of community development. Jacobs' goal is to increase community capacity to the extent that resident capacity building in intellectual and social capital ultimately leads to community ownership of all local assets. This theory is characterized as holistic and comprehensive. While building the capacity to own, manage, and sustain its future development is a priority for Jacobs, it also supports physical redevelopment. Through the creation of its operating arm, JCNI, staff members work closely with residents through numerous working teams in order to facilitate resident-driven change. Local nonprofit and public sector entities partner with Jacobs but, until very recently, these external partnerships were secondary to the internal, or "inside," infrastructure that serves as the core of Jacobs' work. Both foundations can be described as entrepreneurial in their response to each community's needs.

Price Charities and the Jacobs Family Foundation have each made a significant impact on their respective partner communities. These two family foundations have members of the founders' family actively engaged in their philanthropic work; they are similar in the amount of assets they hold, and both are 501(c)(3) nonprofit corporations. Each has played an active role in developing "urban villages" in their targeted communities, although the scope and size of each differ. The City Heights Urban Village is the beneficiary of public and private investment totaling approximately $137 million in an eight-block area that encompasses a public school, public library, affordable housing, a community college continuation center, medical clinic, sports facilities including a swimming pool, and a shopping center with a major supermarket as its anchor tenant. The Village at Market Creek is a 60-acre site located in the Diamond Neighborhoods of southeastern San Diego. Developed by JCNI, it is anchored by a retail center, Market Creek Plaza, containing both national chains and local businesses. The plaza also houses an amphitheater for community events and the 78,000-square foot Joe and Vi Jacobs Community Center completed in 2008. While there are a number of similarities between the two partnerships, their theories of change and resulting outcomes differ in many respects. The detailed comparative analysis of these two on-going efforts as presented in Chapters 7, 8, and 9 considers the reasons for this difference and offers larger insights on the structure, function, strengths, and weaknesses of CCIs.

# 7

# THE JACOBS CENTER FOR NEIGHBORHOOD INNOVATION

The Jacobs Family Foundation was established in 1988. Joseph Jacobs, the family patriarch, accrued his wealth from the success of his engineering consulting firm, the Jacobs Engineering Group, which he established in 1947 in Pasadena, California, and which eventually went on to become a Fortune 500 company. After Jacobs Engineering went public, the family discussed ways to distribute its wealth and subsequently decided to establish a foundation. Jacobs relinquished control of the decision-making authority and turned the foundation over to his daughters. However, his personal beliefs and views on philanthropy have integrally shaped the direction of the foundation. A self-described compassionate conservative (Jacobs, 1996), Jacobs sought to uphold the primary principles of responsibility, respect, and empowerment at the grassroots level through his foundation's work. Joseph Jacobs was an engineer who understood the value of calculated and well-developed plans, reflected in the "Four Rs" that serve as the framework for the Jacobs Family Foundation's work: risk, respect, responsibility, and relationships. With one of Jacobs' daughters as the foundation's first executive director, the Jacobs Family Foundation had all the hallmarks of a traditional family foundation. The initial focus was conventional grant-making, and many of the first grants were awarded to international microlending organizations such as the Foundation for International Community Assistance and ACCION International.

Over the course of the next ten years, the foundation awarded grants to numerous organizations both domestically and abroad. Exposure to the complex demands of capacity building and long-term investment required by nonprofits to realize significant and lasting changes in the communities they serve led the board of directors, comprised exclusively of family members during its early years, to re-evaluate the foundation's mission. According to one of the current board members, writing checks was not fulfilling to family members, and they increasingly believed that they needed to fund organizations that were in alignment with their principles. The events of the 1992 Los Angeles uprisings also led the foundation to a reassessment of how best to support local community development (Sojourner et al., 2004). With the desire to facilitate resident-driven community revitalization at the grassroots level, the Jacobs Family Foundation restructured its approach and embarked on a new direction that moved away from programmatic funding in favor of organizational support for entities that embodied the mission of the Jacobs Family Foundation.

With its retooled mission, the Jacobs Family Foundation embraced the overlapping principles of what is now known in the literature as embedded philanthropy, placed-based funding, social justice philanthropy, and CCIs. In order to take a more active role in the community, in 1995 Jacobs established an operating foundation, JCNI.[1] Jacobs was interested in finding a community in which it could serve as a partner in holistic community development. Even though the corporate headquarters of Jacobs Engineering is located in Pasadena, California, the family considered communities beyond the greater Los Angeles metropolitan region. Through a discovery process that included some preliminarily partnerships that ultimately were not in alignment with the foundation's goals and objectives, and taking into consideration where some of the family members lived, in 1997 the foundation identified its target area. It selected a group of contiguous neighborhoods in southeastern San Diego which it referred to as the Diamond Neighborhoods due to its geographic configuration. Efforts were initially made by the foundation to work through existing nonprofits, a problematic move as many of these organizations did not have the capacity or community ties necessary to effect substantive changes in the target neighborhoods. The Jacobs Family Foundation realized that in order to broker and negotiate the partnerships required to support the type of community development it envisioned, JCNI would need to help build the physical and social capital that would enable the neighborhood to grow itself. A primary objective, and something that is repeated often in the foundation's publications, is that people must "own their own change" (Jacobs Center for Neighborhood Innovation, 2004, p. 1).

In 1998 JCNI moved its office into the Diamond Neighborhoods in order to serve as an active partner in its revitalization. It initially purchased office space on a site situated approximately one mile away from the center of many of the community's social service agencies, churches, schools, community clinics, and other resources. In May of 2008, JCNI relocated to a newly constructed, $23.5 million, 78,000-square foot community center adjacent to a trolley stop and in closer proximity to the community's core services and resources. The Joe and Vi Jacobs Community Center was built to serve as the headquarters for the Jacobs Family Foundation and JCNI and contains staff offices as well as provides community meeting and social space. The new center is located adjacent to Market Creek Plaza, a retail center developed by JCNI in the heart of 60 underutilized acres that the foundation is developing into an epicenter for social, commercial, cultural, and educational activities, known as the Village at Market Creek.

JCNI's efforts are targeted in the 60 acres that will ultimately encompass the Village at Market Creek. JCNI refers to itself as the coordinating partner in this endeavor. At its completion, the Village at Market Creek will include afford-able housing, retail, office, and light industrial space, childcare centers, conference facilities, open space and parks, and cultural venues. The physical development will embody the core principles that fulfill JCNI's mission.

## Governing principles, leadership model, and operational structure

The creation of an equitable partnership between the foundation and the com-munity served as the cornerstone of JCNI's governing principles and operational structure and served as the basis for its systems change theory. Comprehensive, col-laborative development as conceptualized by the foundation requires a long-term investment in the neighborhood (Brown and Fiester, 2007), and JCNI realized that the first step in the process was to become an accepted member of the community. Unlike some place-based philanthropies that have long-standing connections to the neighborhoods they serve, JCNI came into the neighborhood as an outsider. Acutely aware of the challenges this presented, JCNI was deliberate and strategic in the first phase of its work in the neighborhood. As one board member noted, JCNI "gently introduced" itself to the neighborhood. After securing office space in its first location, JCNI made this space available for free to community organi-zations in need of meeting facilities. Under the leadership of its founding CEO and president, Jennifer Vanica, it engaged in a considerable amount of outreach that entailed listening to the community and asking them what they wanted. One of the first staff members hired by the foundation in 1997, Roque Barros, was a veteran community organizer tasked with spearheading the organization's resident engagement efforts. Barros began talking with residents and encouraging them to host informal living room meetings to both introduce Jacobs to the community as well as initiate resident-based dialogue about existing challenges and visions for the future. An early participant recalled that she met Barros at a community meeting where he was soliciting volunteer hosts for living room meetings and door-knock-ing campaigns. She volunteered and in 2000 became one of the first members of JCNI's Community Coordinator Program, designed to have residents go door-to-door, meet their neighbors, and conduct surveys. This volunteer organizer lived on a block in the community with four different apartment buildings segregated by race or ethnicity; Samoan, Hispanic, and Black households lived in separate apartment buildings. As a way to create community, the residents decided to hold a block party. After two months of planning by the residents, the party was held and the beginnings of new relationships were established between the different cultural communities. These types of activities and experiences embody Jacobs' early efforts.

At the same time that the living room meetings and door-knocking campaigns were underway in the early 2000s, critical relationships were established with individuals and organizations that had deep histories in the neighborhood. An early partner and someone who encouraged their presence was Doris Anderson, executive director of the Elementary Institute of Science (EIS). Founded in 1964, the EIS is a nonprofit science enrichment center that offers science education to low-income children in southeastern San Diego and other parts of San Diego County. JCNI became a supporter of EIS's work and helped it launch a capital campaign to raise funds for a new facility by offering a $1 million challenge grant. In October of 2000, the EIS broke ground on a new $6 million, 14,700-square foot facility located across the street from the future site of Market Creek Plaza and the headquarters of JCNI.

This early work at building community partnerships was done in somewhat of an *ad hoc* manner as JCNI realized that it had to be a flexible problem solver if it was to make inroads in the neighborhood. There were significant challenges along the way and developing community acceptance was not always an easy process. The local city council member who held his position from 1991–2002 provided limited support for the organization. Under his tenure, several beneficial community development projects were pursued in southeastern San Diego, including the construction of a public library and multicultural community center, but issues of community ownership and territoriality were clearly present. The primary power brokers in southeastern San Diego were in the Black community, and these community leaders exercised caution when newcomers arrived. The local redevelopment agency, SEDC, also kept JCNI at arm's length for many years and viewed it as a competitor.[2] A change in SEDC's leadership in 2008 led to a more collaborative relationship and SEDC's office is now located in the Joe and Vi Jacobs Center. In addition to the lack of acceptance from local elected officials and other organizations, JCNI also confronted a considerable amount of skepticism from community members who were wary, and to some extent continue to be wary, of the organization's motives.

According to then CEO Jennifer Vanica, from its inception, JCNI saw building trust and relationships as integral to its community development efforts, particularly as an "outsider" to the Diamond Neighborhoods. Vanica noted that the pervasive community distrust of outsiders was critical to JCNI's decision to move into the community and establish its headquarters there as a way to engage in direct contact with the residents. Vanica described the move as "catalytic." Nonetheless, this move failed to alleviate community skepticism. The foundation is still not completely embraced by the community. The neighborhood has grown accustomed to broken promises from foundations and other public and private entities, and, according to Vanica, many in the community expected Jacobs to study them and leave, just as so many other outsiders had done in the past.

In order to build a sustainable model for community development, JCNI approached its community partnership building on several concurrent fronts. With comprehensive community change and shared decision-making as its primary objective, JCNI developed a complex organizational and communal infrastructure that is unusual in its scope and depth. It is also fluid and while the core objectives have remained the same, the methods and internal organizational strategies have evolved over time. Working teams are the core component of JCNI's organizational model. The teams are comprised of staff members, community members, and community partners. JCNI refers to this structure as their "integrated network of stakeholders" (Jacobs Center for Neighborhood Innovation, 2007, p. 47). Resident involvement serves as the cornerstone of these teams and supports Jacobs' belief that engaged residents can find the "pathway to change" by working together (Jacobs Center for Neighborhood Innovation, 2009, p. 5). The teams are designed to address every facet of the neighborhood's social, economic, physical, and cultural needs. As such, teams have been created for affordable housing development, property management, asset management, social fabric, evaluation and policy implications, and strategic direction. These teams are organized into the five larger umbrella categories of social infrastructure, civic engagement, economic opportunity, physical development, and innovation/shared learning (Jacobs Center for Neighborhood Innovation, 2009).

In order to create cohesion and effective communication between the teams and respond to the pressing concerns brought on by the recession, in 2008 JCNI launched the project Voices of Community at All Levels (VOCAL) with the goal of creating broader coalitions. This outreach effort was supported by the formation, in the same year, of the Village Teams Council. JCNI has over 40 working teams and the council was designed for working team representatives to meet on a quarterly basis and coordinate their work. These quarterly Village Center meetings are planned and organized by residents. In 2009 these meetings attracted 1,800 participants, up from 750 in 2008 (Jacobs Center for Neighborhood Innovation, 2009).

JCNI has been able to support this undertaking as a result of consistent funding from the Jacobs Family Foundation. Unlike many other community-based organizations that are often understaffed due to limited resources, JCNI has more than 100 staff members, including a four-member management team, and it has the financial resources to ensure that all aspects of the organization function properly. Combined, JCNI and the Jacobs Family Foundation had approximately $168 million in assets in 2010.[3] The typical nonprofit, neighborhood-based organization is short on both time and resources, but JCNI has both available. JCNI plans to sunset and transfer all of its remaining assets to the neighborhood by approximately 2030.

JCNI's access to resources is also instrumental in expediting other objectives. JCNI has hired consultants to provide vital services and guidance. Gus Newport, the former Berkeley mayor and local community development activist, served as a JCNI consultant when the Jacobs Foundation created its strategic plan. Known among other things for his work as the executive director of the DSNI in Boston, which was one of JCNI's early inspirations, Newport was able to impart his experiences on the foundation. This type of strategic and invaluable consulting was realized because of the foundation's access to financial capital as well as its deep social networks; resources not available to the typical community-based nonprofit.

The foundation also views its role as an innovator in community-based philanthropy and has promoted a culture of shared learning both within the immediate community as well as with interested parties from around the world. However, JCNI's leadership team and board members have made it clear that its approach cannot and should not be directly replicated. Rather, their objectives are to identify new ideas to incorporate into JCNI's own efforts as well as to stimulate innovation in the larger field of local community development and CCIs. In order to do this within the community, JCNI aspires to promote an environment where diverse voices and opinions are heard and respected. It also encourages learning exchanges with other foundations, civic leaders, and community-based organizations. Since 1997, it has hosted visitors from 27 states and 15 countries (Jacobs Center for Neighborhood Innovation, 2010). As part of its learning process, JCNI expends a considerable amount of effort documenting its process through multiple multimedia strategies including video documentation of meetings and community events, policy briefs, and annual reports from the executive director. This reflects a desire to promote transparency and is a deviation from many other small family foundations that rarely produce the depth of reports and policy briefs found at JCNI. This sets Jacobs apart from many of its peers. Transparency is a critical element of the foundation's work and figures prominently in how it has developed its own systems change theory.

## JCNI's definition of community development and change theory

JCNI describes its work as a new model of community development and it has a well-theorized model to support this belief. JCNI's dedication to resident ownership of community change drives its theory of community development and its focus on capacity building in intellectual and social capital.

JCNI focuses on processes of resident engagement and stakeholder relationship building, and this drives its community development work. One of the foundation's board members defines JCNI's approach to community development as holistic and comprehensive, explaining that this is in contrast to the programmatic and categorial focus of traditional community development initiatives. Former JCNI president and CEO Jennifer Vanica defined the foundation's approach to community development as working across the four quadrants of social, political, economic, and physical development. Physical improvement is certainly a priority for JCNI, but the process that generates this change is given priority. However, from its early involvement in the neighborhood Jacobs realized that it had to produce physical improvements, even if they were only at the small scale through, for example, the demolition of dilapidated structures, to demonstrate to the residents that it was committed to community improvement.

Many residents of the Diamond Neighborhoods share similar conceptualizations of community development, viewing it as a large holistic process that unites physical and social improvement. Through the process of conducting in-depth interviews with a range of neighborhood stakeholders, we gained insights into their viewpoints on community development. One Diamond Neighborhoods resident, who also works for a neighborhood-based nonprofit, defines community development as "all aspects that make the community a good place to live, work, and do business." Another resident who is actively involved with JCNI and other planning efforts in the neighborhood defines community development in a similarly broad manner noting that it is "physical things, there's spiritual things, there's, you know, all of those things that can be developed which for me is finding all that everybody has to offer and allow it to flower and to grow."

Many of JCNI's staff members began their involvement with Jacobs as volunteer resident participants, only to be hired as staff when their value to the organization was identified. Interviews with two residents on the staff at JCNI illustrate the extent to which JCNI as an institution has a very clearly articulated definition of community development that is strongly upheld by staff. When asked to define community development, one resident staff member said that "Jacobs taught me that everyone should define it for themselves," and she then proceeded to articulate a definition that emphasized residents participating in the process and shaping the vision for the future. This individual had a passion for her work and expressed gratitude for how her involvement with the Jacobs Family Foundation had generated numerous positive outcomes in her life. She noted that "Jacobs is my life. Everything I do is part of Jacobs. It changed my life and way of thinking." Another resident staff member, a charismatic woman whose husband and father-in-law are prominent members of one of the local cultural communities, described JCNI's community development work as being "about building people's capacity and being able to carry on the work of the future."

One of the public partners defined community development in a much more traditional manner. As a member of the city's planning staff who works with community planning groups in JCNI's catchment area, this individual explained that community development is focused on physical and economic reinvestment. However, he also noted that JCNI has an impressive commitment to the community that is atypical and unusual.

Stakeholders from the local nonprofit sector differed from JCNI the most in their definitions of community development. Although they shared the foundation's conceptualization of community development as requiring resident ownership and partnership, they were among the most vocal critics of JCNI's work in the neighborhood. The president and CEO of a nonprofit organization that does a lot of work in southeastern San Diego explained, "community development is not a physical thing. Long-lasting sustaining communities are ones where residents have a stake in them." However, this individual was critical of Jacobs, questioning the integrity of its participatory process and its true motives. Similarly, the executive director of another nonprofit organization that works in southeastern San Diego defined community development as "a way by which local resources and land can benefit local people; and how do you make sure that jobs, housing, health care, and access to a healthy community is rooted in that community?" This individual was equally skeptical and critical of Jacobs' motives. These two interviews bring to light the challenges of building trust between outsiders, including benevolent foundations, and skeptical residents and existing community organizations that may feel used by these outsiders. We have informally heard this issue raised repeatedly over the years throughout the course of our research: How can it be that organizations with a vision of community development shared by Jacobs can nonetheless call into question Jacobs' community development work? This raises important questions about the role of foundations in community development and whether or not collaboration with the community can occur when there is resistance. It highlights the challenges of building trust, something that JCNI continually addresses. While many residents are supportive of Jacobs' work and believe strongly in its mission, over the years many residents, some of whom participate on various JCNI committees, continue to express skepticism and distrust. While one of JCNI's perceived strengths is its emphasis on process, oftentimes these processes are lengthy and test the patience of stakeholders who are eager to see their ideas translated into action.

Building from its definition of community development, JCNI articulates its systems change theory as the intersection of what it identifies as the four main existing models of community development: the philanthropic model, the organizing model, the nonprofit model, and the for-profit development model. In theory, JCNI's approach to community development takes attributes of the four models, mitigates their limitations, and crafts a new hybrid approach (Hapke, 2004). From philanthropy, the model acknowledges the value of philanthropic resources, but it encourages an approach that is more willing to take risks and engage in long-term neighborhood partnerships, not short-term piecemeal approaches. Foundations have long been criticized for their risk-averse approach to philanthropy (Brown and Fiester, 2007). Foundations are typically driven by maximization of their investment, which is often a short-term infusion of resources, and is focused on quick, measurable results. However, longer-term funding commitments that take a more systematic approach are believed to lead to more democratic and meaningful collaboration and results, as well as to a more holistic approach to community improvement (Silver, 2006; Viederman, 2005). JCNI's board and senior staff support this long-term approach.

From the organizing model, JCNI acknowledges the critical value of neighborhood organizing, but it aspires to create a model that promotes power sharing, asset control, and decision-making authority for the residents themselves. This is a significant paradigm shift from the typical philanthropic model. As the former president of the Jessie Smith Noyes Foundation, Stephen Viederman observed, activists and community organizers are rarely involved in discussions with foundations. Instead, foundations view community-based movements as less efficient than national organizations that promote a more top-down approach to advocacy (Viederman, 2005). Most foundations are unable to catalyze significant change because they typically do not support activist organizations that are grounded in the targeted community. As such, deep levels of citizen engagement are largely ignored by a majority of foundations (Faber and McCarthy, 2005). JCNI's approach to comprehensive community change strives to treat the target communities as participants, not clients, an approach that overlaps with the main underpinnings of social justice philanthropy (Shutkin as cited in Faber and McCarthy, 2005). As discussed in Chapter 3, this is a type of philanthropy that works to change institutions and defines issues based on community priorities. It emphasizes grassroots organizing and democratic civic participation in community work (Faber and McCarthy, 2005). This is a model that focuses on the root cause of problems and calls for structural and systematic change with an emphasis on inclusive, collective action and leadership development at the grassroots level (Foundation Center as cited in Gould, 2011). However, this type of work is expensive to fund, challenging to coalesce in a diverse community, and requires a long-term commitment. Jacobs' approach embodies these core principles, accepts the time commitment, and recognizes that it is crucial for its success.

From the nonprofit development model, JCNI acknowledges the essential role played by nonprofit CDCs in neighborhood revitalization, but it faults this model for its lack of access to capital and expresses concern that the interests of neighborhood residents are not always a priority. The history of CDCs is well-documented[4] and their evolution from neighborhood-based community organizing entities to successful developers of affordable housing calls attention to their efforts to stimulate community economic development. The CDC model, while notable for its contributions to affordable housing production, has some significant challenges. Federal devolution of housing policy resulted in a greater reliance on CDCs as housing producers and community revitalizers leading to increased professionalism, more competition, and a shift away from advocacy (Bockmeyer, 2003). Although some contend that CDCs have diverse portfolios (Melendez and Servon, 2007), others argue that the CDC model faces competition for affordable land and constraints resulting from fluctuating housing markets (Bratt, 2009). CDCs also must address the challenges of assembling projects financed by multiple sources as well as maintaining core operating support (Glickman and Servon, 1998; Vidal, 1997; Walker, 1993). Capacity building is particularly challenging for CDCs and the emphasis is often placed on real estate development capacity to the detriment of building capacity for community organizing and other soft skills (Lowe, 2008; Stoecker, 1997). As a result, many CDCs need, but struggle to secure, adequate capacity-building support (Nye and Glickman, 2000) and numerous CDCs have subsequently failed, downsized, or merged, thereby leaving many low-income neighborhoods without an organization to advocate for, and serve, their community development needs (Rohe and Bratt, 2003). JCNI shares many of the attributes found in CDCs including a clearly defined neighborhood-based geographic focus, a mission emphasizing physical, economic, and social renewal, and resident engagement. Several years ago JCNI's then chief operating officer asked stakeholders whether or not Jacobs was more like a CDC than a foundation. While the parallels are clear, JCNI differs in many respects, including its access to capital. In addition to the resources of the foundation, JCNI has been able to leverage its connections in the foundation world and secure funding from many large foundations including the Ford Foundation, the Annie E. Casey Foundation, the James Irvine Foundation, the Rockefeller Foundation, and CalEndow. The infusion of external funding helped Jacobs acquire blighted or unused land for JCNI's development projects. In this respect, Jacobs operates like a CDC for the Diamond Neighborhoods, "land-banking" unused physical assets for future development.[5]

The fourth component of JCNI's systems change theory addresses the role of the private sector in community revitalization. JCNI acknowledges the ability of the private sector to access capital and use its knowledge to develop and run projects, but it simultaneously faults this approach for lacking the commitment to listen to, and work with, neighborhood residents in a way that realizes projects that reflect neighborhood needs and nurture local capital. In 2001, concerns about overzealous development potentially contributing to gentrification led Jacobs to develop a seven-point plan to counterbalance this dynamic. The plan included the following elements: 1) resident control of land planning; 2) structures for capturing the appreciating value of land within the neighborhood; 3) a system for capturing a significant percentage of all new job creation; 4) comprehensive support systems for local entrepreneurs; 5) support for affordable housing and home buyers; 6) broad-based training in financial planning and disciplined investing; and 7) networks of social, cultural, educational, and economic partners. As discussed later in this chapter, Jacobs has achieved varying degrees of success with the different elements of this plan.

An overarching component of JCNI's systems change theory is its explicit goal to sunset within a distinct time frame. Jacobs' trustees intend to close the Foundation and JCNI in or around 2030. As one of a small subset of foundations with a planned sunset date, Jacobs shares the view that foundations should be used as vehicle for change (Ostrower, 2011). In contrast to perpetual foundations, Jacobs' trustees and staff believe that sunsetting provides the opportunity to experiment and engage in greater risk and ultimately yield a more significant impact on the community. Its framework for sunsetting is guided by the board's desire, influenced in large part by Joe Jacobs' vision, to ensure that the time and effort invested in the Village will be sustainable. To this end, by the time both foundations sunset, the goal is for the community to own the assets and to ensure that the social capital and local leadership has been developed to maintain and further Jacobs' investment (Ostrower, 2011). Illustrating the challenge of developing and ascertaining the achievement of adequate community capacity, Jacobs' sunset date continues to change and is not delineated in the sunset clause of the foundation's bylaws. However, the bylaws do call for the foundation to sunset along with the end of Joe Jacobs' daughters' generation and this date is currently set around 2030.

With a well-articulated systems change theory, JCNI has spent the past 15 years translating its theory into action. It has not necessarily been a linear process as board members and senior staff respond to unforeseen changes such as the recession of the late 2000s, delays with city bureaucracy and entitlement approvals, and, perhaps most importantly, the feedback it receives from community stakeholders. JCNI is well known for its emphasis on process, but it has been making inroads on the physical articulation of its larger systems change theory.

## Evolution of the Village at Market Creek

By the time it sunsets in 2030, JCNI hopes to realize the completion of a comprehensive village redevelopment plan with its Village at Market Creek. Virtually every component of comprehensive and holistic community development is incorporated into JCNI's strategic long-range plan for this 60-acre former brown field (Urban Land Institute, 2007) in a strategically central location in southeastern San Diego. It is the physical embodiment of Jacobs' theory of community development. A trolley line runs through the neighborhood, thereby enabling JCNI to include transit-oriented design and smart growth principles as a significant component of the redevelopment. Market Creek Plaza, a ten-acre cornerstone commercial center, broke ground in 1999 and the first phase was completed in 2004. It brought the first chain grocery store into the neighborhood in 30 years. The plaza itself provides much needed services and products to the neighborhood, but it has also stimulated job training and employment. Not only were 69 percent of the construction contracts awarded to local minority-owned businesses, but also 91 percent of the initial hires at the grocery store were neighborhood residents (Robinson, 2005). The planning and design process also embodied Jacobs' approach to embedded philanthropy. JCNI organized cross-cultural teams to both plan and implement the project, and approximately 2,000 adults and 1,000 neighborhood youth participated in various aspects of the planning process (Robinson, 2005).

In alignment with JCNI's goal of facilitating community engagement and ownership, in 2006 it offered ownership shares in Market Creek Plaza through an initial public offering (IPO) to people who lived, worked, or volunteered in the neighborhood. This unique community development investment approach offered residents of the Diamond Neighborhoods the opportunity to purchase $10 shares in the plaza. It was a novel but risky venture that initially faced opposition from the California Department of Corporations. After submitting over 30 drafts of the IPO and pursuing the plan for six years, JCNI finally received approval of its application (Stuhldreher, 2007). The IPO exceeded expectations and by October 2006, when it closed, it had secured 415 investments amounting to $500,000 (Jacobs Center for Neighborhood Innovation, 2009). In 2018, resident owners in partnership with the Neighborhood Unity Foundation, a resident-led community foundation established by the Jacobs Family Foundation, will have the option to buy out JCNI, which is currently the majority shareholder. The Neighborhood Unity Foundation was designed to gradually take over many of the roles and functions of the Jacobs Foundation (Ostrower, 2011).

Market Creek Plaza is a central node in the Diamond Neighborhoods, but it has encountered some challenges. Food 4 Less, the anchor grocery store, enjoys robust sales and is one of the top-performing stores in the chain owned by Kroger, and the onsite Starbucks (partially owned by Magic Johnson Enterprises) and Coldstone Creamery have also generated a steady stream of traffic and sales. However, the small businesses in the plaza run by local entrepreneurs have not benefitted from the same level of success. A multicultural gift shop designed to provide retail opportunities for micro-entrepreneurs closed its doors after several years of operation despite receiving business planning assistance. Locally owned restaurants situated in the mall have also struggled to stay open and their experiences draw attention to the challenges of small business development in low-income, historically underserved communities. JCNI did not have adequate internal capacity to mentor and support these local business people.

As the Jacobs Family Foundation continues to realize its vision for the Village, plans are underway to bring in a national drug store. This would be the first one in the neighborhood. Jacobs has also been in discussions with Walmart to locate a store on an eight-acre site that it owns, located across the street from Market Creek Plaza. Numerous well-attended community forums have been held to discuss the Wal-Mart plan, and residents' comments about the plan speak to the structural challenges in the community. Some residents are advocating for living wage jobs and believe that Wal-Mart is not a good fit for the community. Other residents are eager for any new employment opportunities and speak of the need to find jobs for young adults as a deterrent to gang activities, as well as the need to provide additional income to senior citizens on fixed incomes. JCNI's staff has openly acknowledged its own lack of consensus on the plans, highlighting the downside of resident-driven community development.

In addition to its retail component, Market Creek Plaza was also designed to provide community facilities. The Joe and Vi Jacobs Community Center has an area of 78,000 square feet and houses JCNI's staff along with meeting rooms, a community room, and a social hall, all for the use of the neighborhood. Market Creek Plaza also houses an amphitheater used for community events. Through its many partnerships in the neighborhood, JCNI supports education and cultural development. The organization is also in the early stages of designing a mixed-use development that is planned to house both light industrial and office space.

The provision of affordable homeownership opportunities is a main component of JCNI's plan for the Village, but it is one of the most elusive objectives to realize. JCNI ultimately plans to build 1,000 affordable housing units but to date it has been unsuccessful in its attempt to build any units, and a combination of factors has contributed to its inability to make progress. In 2005, in the midst of the rising housing market, JCNI launched an effort to build its first affordable housing development. Trolley Residential, located adjacent to the trolley stop in Market Creek Plaza, was envisioned to contain 42 affordable, owner-occupied housing units. In alignment with JCNI's philosophy of developing community wealth and building local equity in the community, promoting homeownership made sense. A housing team comprised of residents, JCNI staff, local stakeholders, and affordable housing experts was assembled to craft the plan for Trolley

Residential. As the team worked on the project, it developed a list of criteria for eligible buyers including that they either lived or worked in the community and had a commitment to community service. JCNI's plans were greeted with tremendous enthusiasm from the community. An early meeting to announce plans for the development drew over 200 people, and JCNI quickly assembled a list of interested buyers. The foundation's goal was to develop units affordable to those within the neighborhood's median income of $35,000.

In alignment with JCNI's theory of community development, the community, and especially prospective buyers, helped design the housing development. JCNI subsequently embarked on a unique participatory design process led by the project architect, Carlos Rodriguez. Over the course of several months in 2007, Rodriguez and his staff facilitated a series of charrette/workshops that had the participants work on, and learn about, different components of the design process from site planning, to financing, to the design of individual units. One memorable workshop occurred approximately halfway through the process. In a previous meeting, discussion had turned to optimal square footage for the different units, and it was soon apparent that it was difficult for many of the participants to envision how plans on paper translated into three dimensions. Several weeks later Rodriquez and his staff took over the central community room in JCNI's offices, hung room dividers, and for one evening "built" life size models of the units, complete with furniture. It was a unique example of participatory design that was very much in alignment with JCNI's goals and objectives.

The design process was lengthy and JCNI staff struggled to assemble the funding and secure the city approval necessary to break ground. Part of the delay resulted from JCNI's lack of capacity in developing affordable housing. While key staff members were experienced real estate developers, the successful development of affordable housing requires a unique cadre of skills and experience that JCNI did not have at this point in time. As market conditions subsequently changed, the housing team decided that it made more sense to build rental units instead of owner occupied units and it pursued a partnership with a nationally recognized developer of affordable housing. As the country entered into a recession, JCNI continued to experience setbacks and, as of 2012, Trolley Residential has not yet been built. The experience with Trolley Residential was one of many challenges that Jacobs encountered as the economy weakened. However, it led JCNI to rethink its overarching model of partnerships and strategies for leveraging resources.

## Collaboration and financing

JCNI is clear that residents are the most critical stakeholders and relationships with them are given primacy. JCNI staff engages in continuous outreach designed to bring different constituents into the process. It has also developed working relationships with nonprofit organizations in the neighborhood. The Coalition of Neighborhood Councils (CNC), a spin-off from the Jacobs Foundation's early work, was one of the largest nonprofits in southeastern San Diego until it experienced organizational challenges in 2009. CNC was known for its community organizing and community development efforts and worked closely with, and received funding from, the Jacobs Foundation for many years. JCNI has had varying degrees of interaction with other nonprofits in the community, but not to the extent that one sees with other foundations such as Price Charities. This is the result of two primary factors. First, JCNI believes strongly in its own ability to catalyze change through its staff members and the community stakeholder infrastructure that it has developed. Second, the Diamond Neighborhoods do not have the same broad established infrastructure of nonprofit social service and community development organizations found in City Heights. Unlike City Heights, for example, which has an established CDC that has engaged in successful neighborhood organizing and improvement projects, the Diamond Neighborhoods do not have such an entity. Little has been written about this phenomenon, but it could be due, in part, to the history of the neighborhood as a stable lower-middle-income community of African American homeowners following World War II. With a high percentage of homeowners in the years following the war, perhaps there was less need for social service and nonprofit entities, especially given the presence of numerous African American churches that likely served as informal providers of assistance. However, as the neighborhood dynamic changed over the years with the influx of new immigrant groups such as Hispanics and Samoans, social service provision became increasingly important and the neighborhood is now playing catch-up, with JCNI in the lead and even developing independent nonprofits to fill in these gaps. As discussed earlier, JCNI was created in response to the absence of a strong nonprofit core in southeastern San Diego.

Recently JCNI acknowledged that it would need to broaden its web of partners. The economic downturn has undoubtedly impacted the foundation's resources, and several other recent events contributed to an awareness that the foundation needs to expand its political clout and partnerships beyond its existing circle. Over the course of several months in 2009, JCNI experienced some significant setbacks. In partnership with a leading national developer of affordable housing, JCNI submitted an application for state funding to build over 200 units of affordable housing. The application was denied, in part, because the city of San Diego did not provide the support necessary to make Jacobs' application competitive. In its early years, Jacobs somewhat naively failed to develop relationships with high-level political powerbrokers at the city level. During this same time period, Jacobs also failed to receive federal stimulus dollars for infrastructure improvements to the neighborhood despite the support of the district congressman. Its lack of political capital, fed by distrust from past local elected officials, continues to negatively impact its community development efforts.

Even though the city of San Diego abolished its planning department in 2011 and merged its functions with the Development Services Department, the city is updating several of its community plans. In the 1960s the city established over 50 community-planning groups designed to provide a vehicle for citizens in each neighborhood to formally participate in the planning process, largely in an advisory role. The planning group that represents the Diamond Neighborhoods is embarking on an update of its community plan, and JCNI has adopted a proactive approach to participating in this recently initiated process. At a kick-off meeting in October of 2009, Jacobs hosted over 60 staff members, neighborhood residents, and other partners and stakeholders who expressed the shared desire to take a prominent role in this planning process. In many respects, JCNI has become the de facto planning agency for southeastern San Diego and its willingness to respond to these types of efforts will be increasingly valuable in light of changes made to San Diego's public planning process. The city government is reeling from budget shortfalls and community plan updates are expensive and take a long time to complete. Southeastern San Diego may be at an advantage due to Jacobs' efforts, and its ability to bring experts into this process.

Setbacks often provide avenues of opportunity, and this may be the case for Jacobs as it opens itself to engaging in larger public processes than it has in the past. This change in attitude is articulated in one of JCNI's social and economic impact reports. The report's conclusion states:

> Working comprehensively at the intersection of social, economic, physical, and civic strategies also requires a national community of leaders, working side-by-side with residents. As partners in community change, it requires us to stay open to new voices, be willing to try new solutions, and be prepared to assume new roles.

> The key lesson of 2008 was about learning to partner like never before. To reinvigorate disinvested neighborhoods, we must create new platforms for investment and work across the public and private sectors. Success depends on our ability to bring to the table diverse types of capital at the right time to best support community teams. Now, as we launch the next phase, we are inviting many other partners to join us.
>
> (Jacobs Center for Neighborhood Innovation, 2009, p. 40)

Receptive to new partners and partnerships, the Jacobs Family Foundation may now actually be in a position to assuage some of the concerns of those organizations and neighborhood residents who question its motives. This move towards a more public and diverse approach to community development may bring new partners and resources into the fold, ultimately strengthening the efforts of JCNI and others to bring about holistic comprehensive change in the Diamond Neighborhoods.

## Lessons learned from the Jacobs Center for Neighborhood Innovation

While each foundation has its own unique structure and approach, the Jacobs Family Foundation and its operating arm, JCNI, present all of the significant defining features found in the CCI approach as identified by Sojourner et al. (2004) and Brown and Fiester (2007). With its long-term commitment to the Diamond Neighborhoods, in concert with its efforts to develop an inclusive, participatory approach to holistic community development, it is attempting to build relationships and social capital as much as it is rebuilding the physical infrastructure of the neighborhood. For the Jacobs Family Foundation, process and outcome are inexorably intertwined and equally important. In its self-described efforts to "re-engineer" philanthropy, Jacobs strives for an approach that "promotes[s] an authentic resident voice in a process of shared decision-making." In doing so, it believes it is promoting "the resident ownership of change" (Jacobs Center for Neighborhood Innovation, 2004, p. 1). Furthermore, its access to a deep pool of financial resources has enabled it to bring in the staff and consultants necessary to effectively work towards its vision.

To date, JCNI has built a solid base to help it achieve its long-term objectives. It has been effective at building grassroots community partnerships with some segments of the population and developing a participatory process that seeks resident input. While this is promising and the processes are certainly in place, some stakeholders, even those who participate in JCNI working teams and purchased shares in Market Creek Plaza, still question the foundation's motives. Trust is difficult to build and sustain. Others point to JCNI's inability to engage certain segments of the community as successfully as others. JCNI has made significant inroads with the Black community, but many of its meetings lack a visible Hispanic or Asian presence despite their growing numbers in the neighborhood. JCNI has also faltered at times in implementing its plans. The larger process is well developed, but Jacobs has been criticized for taking too long to act as it checks with residents and other stakeholders for input on proposals. While transparency is an expressed cornerstone of Jacobs' work, the internal staff hierarchy of JCNI has been described by some stakeholders as difficult to discern, particularly as the foundation continues to hire internal and external experts, and as JCNI transitions into a new phase with the selection of a new CEO in 2012.

The approach developed by JCNI is both organic and deliberate. While the processes in place are designed to adapt to community conditions and resident input, JCNI's board and staff members proceed with a considerable amount of introspection. Each step in the community development process has been thoroughly and thoughtfully documented by JCNI as well as outside consultants. Foundations such as JCNI acting as managing partners in CCIs do not necessarily aspire to replication (Brown and Fiester, 2007; Jacobs Center for Neighborhood Innovation, 2004), but it is apparent that JCNI wants others to be able to learn from its experiences. This introspective approach to community development is also unique, since JCNI's resources afford it the opportunity to take the time to step back and consider both process and outcomes. This availability of time and resources is scarce among nonprofit community development organizations. This deliberate approach has yielded a range of transparency, as JCNI has been willing to publicize and share many of its experiences to date.

In August of 2011 the two top executives at JCNI, CEO and President Jennifer Vanica and her husband, Chief Operating Officer Ron Cummings, left the organization. It was a sudden departure that was unanticipated by many. Both the Jacobs Family Foundation and JCNI were at a crossroads and the board members and senior staff were engaged in a substantive internal analysis. With the 2030 sunset date looming, much of the vision for the Village still unfinished, and the first generation of family foundation members nearing the age of retirement, a second generation of Jacobs' family members was becoming increasingly involved. In addition to its internal evaluation, the Jacobs Family Foundation was aware of external influences. Jacobs had been subject to criticism due to the lack of community members holding senior staff positions. If Jacobs was to realize its vision of transferring ownership of local assets to the community in 2030, it was not unreasonable to expect it to develop a cadre of local leaders capable of managing and further growing these resources past the sunset date.

The foundation continues to make progress in other areas. In February of 2012, JCNI successfully negotiated the purchase of a small townhouse development in close proximity to the Village. The original developer experienced financial problems and the timing was fortuitous because Jacobs had a $1.35 million Catalyst Project Grant from a new State of California pilot program, and it had a short window left in which it could use the funds. Jacobs' purchase of these units has enabled it to add housing to its portfolio of community resources.

JCNI's accomplishments to date have been identified as a successful model of transformative, comprehensive community change. This is evident by the number and variety of interested parties that visit it every year to observe its work in action. Compared to other family foundations, JCNI clearly shares and articulates its systems change theory. It has, to a certain extent, catalyzed change in southeastern San Diego, but the most important lessons from Jacobs' efforts are to be found in the challenges that it faces through the process of translating the theory into action. As it continues to move forward towards realizing its mission, it will need to maintain focus on building community trust, engaging multiple communities, and securing the resources necessary to complete the Village as planned and promised to the neighborhood.

# 8

# PRICE CHARITIES

Some of City Heights' residents argue that the start of their community's decline can be traced back to the approval by California voters of Proposition 13 in 1978, which set property taxes at the 1976 assessed value of the property. The referendum challenged many cities such as San Diego to maintain the infrastructure of older neighborhoods such as City Heights. In the interim, growth continued as developers addressed a need for affordable housing by tearing down small homes in these older areas and replacing them with low-quality apartment buildings. As density increased, overcrowded schools became the norm. Children played in alleys or streets as parks were scarce; sewer and water systems were taxed; parking became a major problem due to high population density; and shoddy construction and poor maintenance resulted in blighted areas.

City Heights' decline was exacerbated by delays in the completion of a 2.2-mile section of Interstate 15, which routed 40,000 cars per day through residential streets. For approximately 25 years, residents knew that the freeway was coming. The California State Transportation Department (Caltrans) bought homes on the path of the new highway and boarded them up. These vacant homes became a haven for drug dealers, prostitutes, and gang members, and several were the targets of arsonists. By January of 2000, when this stretch of freeway was finally completed, more than 500 dwelling units were torn down, and the surrounding community bore the scars of 25 years of neglect. The physical condition of City Heights' neighborhoods provided an ideal site for Price Charities' comprehensive approach to revitalization.

## Governing principles, leadership model, and operational structure

In 1990, as Sol Price and his son Robert were researching strategies for focusing their philanthropic resources in one location, the San Diego City Council made a

"Declaration of Emergency" in City Heights due to an "increasing crime rate and lowered standard of living."[1] City Heights' high levels of poverty, low levels of educational attainment, and diverse population comprised of many immigrants and refugees all combined to present challenges to community stability.

The closing of the last major supermarket in City Heights in January of 1994 spurred Price to examine this community. The city was also looking at using the closed supermarket site as a new police station but had no money to develop it. Price approached the city with a partnership proposition. Price agreed to loan the city the approximately $3 million needed to build the new police station, if Price's for-profit partner, CityLink, Inc., was allowed to develop a master plan for the area that incorporated the new police station and eight contiguous, densely populated city blocks. In June of 1994, the city council approved the development of a master plan for City Heights' new "Urban Village" that included a new public library, shopping center, park and sports field, recreation center with tennis courts and a swimming pool, a new community college district facility, and, through negotiations with San Diego Unified School District (SDUSD), a new elementary school as an anchor for the nine-block core area. San Diego city staff contend that Price successfully compelled three very independent institutions to collaborate: the city, the school district, and the community college district, by using his financial assets and business acumen.

Price's theory of change also sought to leverage private donations through a mix of public and private funding to speed up the physical change in City Heights. For example, the first priority identified by residents and the city for City Heights' renewal was a need for a stronger police presence. Rather than give the city the funds needed to realize the police substation project, Price lent the city the funding necessary, allowing construction to occur 3–5 years ahead of schedule, with the caveat that the station be designed to be "community friendly." This strategy allowed Price to recoup his $3 million loan to reinvest in future projects in this community, and it gave him the needed leverage to design an attractive 39,000-square foot station with bullet-proof windows that looks onto the park and library, contains public meeting rooms, and a youth gym attached to the west side of the station that encourages local youth to engage in sports in a safe environment. The foundation's strategy of loaning funds to catalyze programs continues to serve as a type of revolving line of credit to fund new housing, parking structures, and community facilities.

Sol Price and his son Robert founded Price Club membership warehouses in San Diego, California. A decade after opening the first Price Club in 1976, the stores were generating $2.6 billion in sales and earnings of $75 million a year.[2] Later they merged the chain with Costco Wholesale Inc., but they retained a number of other business interests including commercial real estate enterprises and discount warehouses overseas. This business acumen and entrepreneurial spirit influences their approach to philanthropy and community change.

Price Charities' theory of change is grounded in the development of an approach to neighborhood revitalization that is holistic in scope. Using the graphic of a wheel, Price's vision of a healthy community consists of a number of spokes in balance with each other that include housing, health services, childcare, a library, schools (kindergarten to twelfth grade), recreation, community organizations, safety and security, shopping, eldercare, non-government services, and local ownership of assets. At the center of the wheel are residents, nonprofits, government, businesses, labor, and religious organizations. This core group would work with the foundation to effect comprehensive change in City Heights.

## Price Charities' definition of community development and the foundation's theory of change

After a lengthy process of relocating hundreds of low-income residents from the approximately 400 housing units slated for demolition, bulldozers began to tear down blighted apartment buildings, corner stores, and older homes to make way for the Urban Village (Martinez-Cosio, 2003). As trucks cleared the debris, Price began working with San Diego State University's (SDSU) College of Education and the SDUSD to develop an educational collaborative. Price advanced funding to the school district to build Rosa Parks Elementary in 1997, and hired its principal a year ahead of schedule to allow her to get her team in place and begin networking with the community. The school was built for 900 students and opened its doors with approximately 1,200 children. Through the City Heights Education Collaborative, Price funds innovative practices by SDSU researchers that aim to impact learning at Rosa Parks Elementary, Monroe Clark Middle School, and Hoover High School, which enroll predominantly very-low income, English-language learners. Each school has active parent volunteer groups, social workers, full-time nurses, and school psychologists. Price also funds the "School in the Park" program whereby 3rd, 4th and 5th graders spend 25 percent of their school time in San Diego's Balboa Park, home to dozens of museums that become classrooms away from school. Teachers in the partnership schools were offered opportunities to earn master's degrees funded by the foundation and engage in innovative practices such as looping which allows students to stay with the same teacher for 3–4 years. While other schools in the district struggle to survive one of California's worst budget deficits, the Price Charities' partner schools enjoy more freedom and a staggering amount of resources. But has this investment translated into academic achievement? The results are mixed; the elementary school's Academic Performance Index, the state's tool for measuring academic achievement and progress in public schools, was 3 out of 10 (California Department of Education, 2010), and the high school continues to be one of the lowest performing in the city. School administrators contend that the high transiency and impact of poverty on families is challenging but the investment in resources is making an impact (Alpert, 2008).

## *Program dimensions*

The physical development of the community is at the core of Price Charities' renewal effort, and now includes the police station, an elementary school, a junior high school, a park with tennis courts and other sports amenities, a library, a performance space, community and city offices, a pre-school program (Head Start), a satellite community college campus, office space for nonprofit agencies, parking structures, a shopping center, and senior market-rate and low-income housing (see Table 8.1 for a complete description of some of Price Charities' projects in City Heights).

Quantifying the amount and variety of program activities sponsored by Price Charities in City Heights is a daunting task. Since its $18 million donation to SDSU in 1998, the foundation continues to partner with numerous organizations and funds a variety of programs. Most recently, the Price Family funded the Sol Price School of Public Policy at the University of Southern California through a $50 million endowment that encourages young researchers to use the San Diego and Los Angeles urban areas as living laboratories (Magee, 2011).

The fast pace of the foundation's physical change initiatives, as well as the creation of new program initiatives, are described by former and current staff members as both positive and negative:

> As long as we are running, I think internally we feel like we are succeeding. I don't see us being very self-reflective or just having the spaces to talk much about whether we are running in the right direction and really "why" we are running. So I think sometimes it's good, because we get a lot of stuff done … it requires a certain willingness to take risks, a certain entrepreneurism, and yeah, I guess not too much of a concern of failure, and partly I think that helps that we are not that self-reflective, so we really don't have much of a chance to dwell on failures because … we are already focusing on the next five things. So we are definitely forward looking and I think relatively pragmatic too.

This pragmatic approach is at the core of the foundation's theory of change that aims to provide low-income families with basic resources such as affordable housing and higher-quality education for their children. This approach ultimately focuses on residents' "own initiative and resourcefulness and responsibility" in making best use of the opportunities provided. Price Charities thus provides direct services through social workers that operate out of the three schools that form the Educational Collaborative in partnership with SDSU's College of Education. It also funds a food stamps coordinator, two school-based health centers staffed with full-time nurses, and a variety of programs aimed at improving the academic achievement of the approximately 4,500 students enrolled in three partnership public schools.

**TABLE 8.1** A sample of Price Charities' programs in City Heights

| Community development activity | Partners | Description |
| --- | --- | --- |
| City council approves urban village master plan and business/finance plan (October 1995) | Price Charities, City of San Diego, City Redevelopment Agency | Price Charities donated $5 million towards master plan development. |
| Mid-City Division police substation and community recreation facility (May 1996) | Price Charities, City of San Diego | Includes gymnasium for area youth. The police substation is "community friendly," offering windows to the park and a community meeting room. Price Charities' $3 million loan allowed for construction 3–5 years ahead of schedule. |
| Rosa Parks Elementary School (1997) | Price Charities, SD Unified School District, San Diego Educational Association | Price Charities funded the school principal's salary for a year before the school opened and played a role in the design of the school and joint-use playground/park space. |
| City Heights Weingart Public Library. (November 1998) | Price Charities, Weingart Foundation, City of San Diego | $5.25 million, 15,000-square foot facility, the busiest library in the system with more than 2,000 patrons per day; free computer access; community meeting room. |
| San Diego Community Policing Program (1998) | Price Charities, San Diego Police | Social workers and community organizers worked with police to build alliances between residents and business owners. The San Diego Police Department was one of the first to implement community policing city-wide, starting in 1973 and continuing for almost 20 years. |

*Continued*

**TABLE 8.1** A sample of Price Charities' programs in City Heights, *continued*

| Community development activity | Partners | Description |
|---|---|---|
| School-based health care | Price Charities, La Maestra Community Health Clinic, the San Diego Unified School District, San Diego Family Care | Funding from Price Charities allowed two licensed medical professionals to operate a clinic at Central Elementary; the three schools in the SDSU Educational Pilot program have full-time nurses and social workers. Hoover High School also houses a clinic managed by La Maestra. |
| Masters in Education | Price Charities, SDSU College of Education, SD Educational Association | More than 100 teachers have been awarded an SDSU Master's in Education degree funded in partnership with Price Charities, with classes held at schools in City Heights. |
| "Home in the Heights" | Assists first-time, low- and moderate-income home buyers to purchase homes in the project area. $1.75 million dollars set aside from tax increments. Price Charities provides $30,000 per homebuyer, SD Housing Commission provides $40,000 per homebuyer. The City Heights Redevelopment Project Area contributes $15,000 per homebuyer | The program targeted residents displaced by four new public schools built in the community from 2002–2006. Also available to first-time home buyers who are employees of nonprofits or public institutions, or renters in City Heights. |
| Senior Housing Complex at City Heights Square (completed in 2007) | Price Charities, City of San Diego Redevelopment Agency, Senior Community Centers of SD | 150-unit affordable senior housing complex, owned and operated by Senior Community Centers of SD. On-site social support and meal delivery are offered to low- and very-low-income seniors. The total development cost was $21.1 million, with the redevelopment agency contributing $9.1 million. |

| Community development activity | Partners | Description |
| --- | --- | --- |
| New Roots Community Garden (2009) | Price Charities, public donors and the City of San Diego | A city-owned lot was transformed into 80 plots farmed by immigrants and refugees. It is a project of the International Rescue Committee which helps relocate refugees fleeing violence. In 2011, the Price Family Charitable Trust funded an urban compost worker plus two outreach workers to educate residents on composting. |
| La Maestra Community Clinic (completed 2010) | Price Charities, La Maestra, Bank of America Foundation ($100,000 grant), Kaiser Permanente ($1 million grant), Anthem Blue Cross, the U.S. Department of Health and Human Services, the Parker Foundation, the Robert Wood Foundation, the San Diego Gas and Electric Sustainable Communities program, and the Tides Foundation | A state-of-the-art, $24 million three-story, 36,440-square foot "green" health center opened in the heart of City Heights. The building received a Gold LEED certification. |
| City Heights Square Apartment Homes and Retail (completed 2011) | Price Charities' development arm, San Diego Revitalization Corporation; ConAm, City of San Diego Redevelopment Agency, and a grant from the Affordable Housing Program (AHP) | Five-story housing project, includes apartments for 150 very-low-income seniors (62 years and older). On-site clinical services, health education, and counseling, mental illness and substance abuse intervention on site. Also includes 92 market-rate apartments above a 10,000-square foot Walgreens plus 11,000 additional square feet of commercial uses. The units have one, two, and three bedrooms with washers and dryers, secured underground parking, and other amenities. |

*Continued*

**TABLE 8.1** A sample of Price Charities' programs in City Heights, *continued*

| Community development activity | Partners | Description |
|---|---|---|
| Job creation (2010–11) | Price Family Charitable Fund | The fund began supporting the employment of local residents by community nonprofits through grants for salaries. Two jobs were created to clean up and restore local canyons; three positions were funded at La Maestra Family Clinic; a coordinator for Head Start was hired, in addition to bilingual student advocates, parent coordinators and assistants for the fledging Dad's Club. More than two dozen jobs have been directly created by the fund. |
| USC Sol Price School of Public Policy (2011) | Price family | A $50 million endowment helped create the Price School that now offers five professional master's degree programs, three executive master's degree programs, doctoral programs, and an undergraduate degree program. USC students utilize City Heights and neighborhoods in Los Angeles as urban laboratories to develop innovation, entrepreneurship, experimentation, and collaboration around urban problems. |

Price Charities implicitly defines community development as catalyzed by physical change and, as a result, the foundation continues to actively acquire property made available due to the deepening recession in California, serving as a "land bank" for the community, a role that the city does not have the resources to pursue. Most recently, the foundation purchased a five-acre site that formerly housed an auto dealership and is working to redevelop it into a YMCA.

## Collaboration and financing

Philanthropist Sol Price and former San Diego city councilman William Jones tapped into the organized community groups in City Heights as they sought to begin their partnership. These are a predominantly White, active core group of residents who own property in this area. An affinity existed between the values, beliefs, and goals of City Heights' core group and Sol Price's interests. This property-owner group had developed a strong social network with city staff members, particularly the city's manager, through their efforts to gain attention for their neglected community. The residents cultivated relationships with nonprofit corporations, elected officials, key decision-makers, and others of influence; and they used political tactics. After three teens were killed in a gang-related fight at the local high school in 1993, the City Heights Business Improvement Association erected billboards that declared "Welcome to City Heights, San Diego's Crime Capital. Won't Anybody Help?" to gain city officials' attention. Although the homeowners in the area were the most vocal and actively engaged in Price's partnership, they represented only 25 percent of City Heights' population, as 75 percent of residents in ten census tracts that largely comprise City Heights were renters (U.S. Census Bureau, 2010).

Sol Price and former San Diego city councilman William Jones worked in partnership with the group of residents to create a model public–private partnership with the city. William Jones stated that the decision to invest in City Heights was strategic, as they saw the possibility of the blighted conditions in City Heights spreading to adjoining neighborhoods. But partnering with a community with the demographic, cultural, and economic diversity typical of many large urban areas presented unique challenges to Price Charities. Residents in City Heights speak more than 30 languages. Translation is necessary at major meetings. But this diversity manifests itself in many other ways that affect participation: cultural differences regarding the role of participants in a public forum; immigrants' and refugees' experiences with government in their home countries; citizenship status; and recruitment, retention, and engagement efforts that are appropriate for ethnically and racially diverse communities. A nonprofit staff member that interacts actively with refugee groups explains:

> The multiple languages is incredibly challenging. It's not necessarily about just providing translation. It's about people being able to talk to each other within the group, given the translation needs. And having enough time to have meaningful conversation, and the amount of time that takes through translators.

Price Charities works to address this diversity by collaborating closely with non-profits grounded in the community, particularly those that actively engage with immigrants and refugees. It supports efforts by a large social service agency to develop a leadership program for Spanish-speaking residents in City Heights called Latinos y Latinas en Acción. Initially funded by a $50,000 grant from the Waitt Foundation in 2002, Price Charities supported the program in subsequent years in an effort to increase participation by the growing Latino community in City Heights' governing structures. The project continues to recruit and train Spanish-speaking leaders and its alumni are active in a number of community advocacy teams that focus on housing, immigrant's rights, and health issues.

Sol Price's son, Robert, has also started to connect with the vast immigrant business community in City Heights in recent years. Some businesses were hard-hit by the redevelopment process due to relocation, the impact of construction, and the subsequent economic downturn. Residents say that Robert Price visited several establishments in an effort to hear directly about their concerns. A Vietnamese activist and small business consultant provides a perspective on the challenges the foundation faces in connecting to this sector:

> From this population [Vietnamese and Southeast Asian businessmen], they're sort of culturally isolated. They say look, I am doing business with my community. My clients are the same people that come from the same country and speak the same language, same culture. Why do you want me to be involved? It could be because they have experienced, their upbringing experience has been in that manner and not wanting it to be involved in any type of effort that has government … the idea of government participation, some of them want to stay away from that.

Opportunities do exist through the foundation's work in education to increase immigrant participation in redevelopment. Price Charities has a strong parent involvement program in each of the three schools in its partnership through the creation of parent rooms designed to improve communication between schools and parents, work in partnership with parents on academic achievement, and develop parent leadership. Each of the partnership schools has an active parent-room coordinator who engages daily with parents from each of the community's resident groups. Parent leaders representing the Vietnamese, Hispanic, African, and other immigrant communities provide a valuable link to newcomers to the U.S. and inform them about the many courses, workshops, and other opportunities for parents to become advocates for their children. The foundation is investing in these parents and exploring opportunities for congruence between the community organizing efforts by these three schools and the engagement of residents in the future development of their community.

Price Charities' pragmatism also translates into collaboration. The foundation actively engages with a thick web of neighborhood and social organizations. The foundation provided small grants for the formation of neighborhood associations, developed a Town Council, provides grants to a variety of nonprofits groups including one for a community garden targeting refugees, and helps support the Mid-City Community Action Network (CAN) collaborative, a 23-year-old umbrella organization with members representing over 150 public and private organizations such as schools, faith communities, businesses, and nonprofits. Since 2009, Price Charities began a monthly listing of the grants it approved, providing a short description of the work to be accomplished by the nonprofit organization funded but not the amount granted. The list encompasses a broad menu of the foundation's work to improve City Heights and its interest in supporting social justice issues including programs in Israel, such as an early childhood education for Arab children, a pedagogical class for Arab high schoolers interested in pre-school education, and educational exhibits at the Jerusalem Zoo. The Price Family also funds the Aaron Price Fellows program that began in 1991 to honor the grandson of Sol Price who died from cancer at age 15. Approximately 40 high school students from the San Diego area are chosen every year to learn about policy through visits to local government entities, nonprofits engaged in public policy, and trips to Sacramento and Washington, D.C.[3] Price Charities' collaborative ethic has served City Heights well, as the foundation continues to attract other foundations, private donors, and, most importantly, the public sector to continue to address the many challenges facing this older, urban community.

## Public sector role

In communities such as City Heights and the Diamond Neighborhoods, "citizens as owners of the public enterprise" is a challenging concept for city officials to implement, particularly as the economic recession leads to deep budget cuts. Local government's role in community development has devolved into a silent partner, focusing on responding to local political and fiscal crises. One outcome of local government's changing function is innovation as foundations assume quasi-public roles, filling in the gap of resource allocation and programming traditionally assumed by public planning agencies.

Critics of Price Charities' role as a catalyst for change argue that the foundation's brisk pace to realize physical change precludes careful assessment of outcomes. Some argue that the foundation moves so quickly that it often reacts "impulsively" to funding opportunities, rather than planning purposefully. Although Price Charities developed a "vision plan" in collaboration with City Heights' residents and city staff, the foundation's funding strategy is not always clear to residents and nonprofit staff. This perception may be a function of Price Charities' broad vision for the community and its entrepreneurial and pragmatic approach to community development that does privilege fast-paced change as a lever for systems change. A nonprofit administrator cautiously commented on their perception of the foundation's entrepreneurial approach, which, she argues, does not address the systemic conditions that negatively impact this community:

and [Price Charities have] got all these resources. And they, because they have so many resources, don't fit in. They kind of plow their way in. And we're suddenly having to figure out how to work around the [new initiative] or task force, or whatever. Whatever new thing they want. And then nothing changes.

In the case of Price Charities' work in City Heights, the city's role is one of enthusiastic supporter. The charity's efforts at leveraging its own contributions into more than $140 million in projects would be difficult, if not impossible, for the city to develop on its own. From the perspective of city staff charged with administering the redevelopment district, Price Charities' financial resources, experience, and its cadre of professionals allows the foundation to fulfill a role that has all but disappeared in the current economic climate—that of urban developer of large mixed-use projects. A city staff member explains Price's role in building a 92-unit housing project with 26,000 square feet of retail in the heart of City Heights:

They fronted a lot of money and then they also just took it through the whole city's redevelopment process to get all the permits and everything that was needed for that … They just have a lot of people who are very experienced with this stuff. They have an experienced legal team, they have experienced consultants, they have done these projects before, so that, I mean, that's invaluable, especially when you are dealing with a large organization like the city and the redevelopment agency as well.

But nonprofit staff expressed concern over the lack of transparency regarding the use of redevelopment funds, community input on projects, shared evaluation of projects and programs, and the lack of information shared by the foundation with the public. Although Price and Jacobs fill the void left by the inaction and lack of resources from the public sector, questions about accountability and transparency continue to plague their efforts. Foundations do not typically function as quasi-public entities, but in this case innovation may result in traditional partners assuming nontraditional roles that must be explained and justified to all stakeholders. Although respondents to our interviews clearly appreciated the magnitude of the resources that private foundations bring to their communities, they also raised concerns over governments' and nonprofits' diminished capacity to evaluate and assess the impact of the private-enterprise model of community development.

Encompassing these concerns is the very tangible fear that successful revitalization of these underserved neighborhoods will lead to gentrification. Interestingly, those who spoke directly about gentrification in the San Diego case studies, particularly property owners and investors active in City Heights' civic sphere, did not perceive this process as completely detrimental. But for foundation and nonprofit leaders, there is significant discomfort surrounding a foundation facilitating gentrification through its community development projects.

## Lessons learned from Price Charities

Community change initiatives typically have long-term agendas that go beyond the sponsoring foundation's projected timeline. This makes it especially important to build resident ownership, knowledge, and skills; develop the community's infrastructure; and embed the change effort in the larger geographic and political context, because those are the capacities that will move the work forward and maximize the sponsor's investment (Brown and Fiester, 2007).

The work of Price Charities demonstrates the potential for catalyzing and implementing large-scale, comprehensive community change in disenfranchised urban neighborhoods. Foundation-driven community development can fill important gaps left by decades of public sector retrenchment and neglect. Yet these efforts are not monolithic, and their many nuances must be further analyzed to better understand the increasing complexity of differing approaches to community development. As outsiders to underserved communities, trust is a key variable that can facilitate or, in its absence, impede change efforts. But, as outsiders, foundations are also very important in linking resources, such as social, economic, cultural, and political capital to those of underserved communities.

Price Charities moved quickly to present physical evidence to the neighborhood that it was committed to the CCI. It forged important relationships with local elected officials, even hiring the former San Diego City Manager to head Price Charities' redevelopment projects. Its educational collaborative gave teachers unparalleled control, allowing them to choose their school principal, hire qualified teachers without concern for seniority, choose their own textbooks, and design their curriculum, including using block scheduling. The social capital built through the parent rooms in each of the schools is fueling leadership efforts in other venues, and the dense network of nonprofits and community groups that Price has supported over the last two decades is helping attract outside funding to this underserved community.

Yet, one of the more important lessons from Price Charities' City Heights Initiative is that achieving holistic change in an underserved community is very challenging. It is not only about the amount of funding allocated, but it is also about the other components of the system: education, health, crime, jobs, and housing. As Price Charities attempts to impact each of these system elements as outlined in its theory of change, it is evident that its partnerships with other nonprofits, foundations, city officials, and residents are becoming more valuable as each group becomes stronger and impacts its own sphere of influence and the systems within which it operates. The growing participation of CalEndow in this community may provide the statistical analysis and evaluation skill-set that Price lacks and may provide the evidence needed to show best practices in their approach.

This raises an underlying issue among those stakeholders who are critical of Jacobs' and Price's work: some stakeholders adhere to an older model of community development whereby roles and activities are clearly assigned to certain types of organizations. Since foundations typically have not engaged in direct, hands-on community development, the fact that the Jacobs Family Foundation established an operating arm, JCNI, to do community development, is potentially threatening.

The Price Family created, merged, and dissolved a number of nonprofit and for-profit entities to engage in their work in City Heights. Grasping the extent of their holdings and operations is a formidable task, which we attempted to decipher by examining U.S. Securities and Exchange Commission Filings, IRS 990 Forms required of all nonprofits, newspaper articles, and other archival sources. City Heights' transformation is occurring through a maze of limited liability corporations (LLCs) that manage property (City Heights Realty LLC with assets in 2010 of $5,950,369[4]) and the Urban Village Residential LLC (assets in 2010 of $18,067,269) that owns and manages the 115 townhomes that Price Charities rents in the heart of the community. Price Charities' development arm, San Diego Reinvestment Inc., and other limited corporations purchased property in the community and managed large-scale construction projects. San Diego Reinvestment Inc. was recently folded back into the broader Price Charities umbrella. But there are numerous components to the Price Family's holdings, from the transfer of stock that funds the initiative and serves as payments for senior staff, to the creation of for-profit entities that serve the nonprofit work, that challenge efforts at transparency and accountability.

Thus accessing information that can assist in maintaining foundations accountable is an onerous process (Covington, 1994; Fleischman, 2007; Lowe, 2004). In theory, both the Jacobs Family Foundation and Price Charities only need to answer to their boards, which are largely composed of family members and friends, and this poses understandable concerns among community stakeholders, particularly when the board does not reflect the ethnic, racial, or economic diversity of the neighborhoods targeted (Jagpal, 2009). Other foundations have addressed transparency concerns by creating governing boards or collaboratives composed of residents, foundation staff, and others that can plan, oversee, and evaluate the place-based philanthropic project (such as the Riley Foundation working with the Dudley Street Neighborhood Initiative in Boston). Some foundations take on the role of "connector" by bringing residents, funding sources, and city officials together, serving as "neutral conveners" to help change occur and maintaining transparency by allowing the agenda to be driven by others in the community (such as the Birmingham Foundation in Pittsburgh's South Side; the Rosamond Gifford Charitable Corporation in Syracuse's Southside; and the Humboldt Area Foundation in California).

Price Charities tried to achieve a middle ground by developing an educational collaborative board that included principals and Price Charities' board members and staff. It only met briefly to oversee the restructuring of the three City Heights' public schools. But the foundation resists efforts to develop a governance group that can oversee the physical redevelopment of City Heights. This is not unusual, according to researchers at the Chapin Center for Children at the University of Chicago. Foundations that have invested substantial resources in a community want some control over the outcomes. The Hass Foundation in San Francisco has similarly expressed reticence in forming a community leadership group to oversee the revitalization of two low-income areas in lower Oakland, California, arguing that it "wants to maintain control of its own decision-making and fears having its range of action unduly constrained by a designated community leadership group" (Sojourner et al., 2004, p. 45). For Price Charities, working with the community takes precious time and as a staff member explains, the foundation's theory of change demands fast action that may preclude full participation and transparency:

> I work for people who want to see things happen quickly. Who are used to seeing things happen quickly and try to make things happen quickly, is part of what we struggle with … The one thing that we have … that non-profits don't have is capital. So we "blow and go" … we'll be done with probably three developments before a non-profit can finish one because we don't have to wait for the money to come through, we can acquire [properties] and that's scary too. Because I think for the community, it's like, my God, we are working at like warp speed.

As an underserved community in a desirable location, City Heights is the target of a number of interventions and initiatives by nonprofits and foundations. The California Endowment, a private health foundation, leads the newest effort as it named City Heights one of 14 disenfranchised California neighborhoods that will be part of a $1 billion initiative focused on improving a community's health through place-based interventions. Mid-City CAN, resident leaders, and neighborhood nonprofits were tapped by the endowment to engage in a discussion about "Building Healthy Communities." Nonprofits and residents were initially pressed to respond as yet another entity demanded scarce resources, to launch this initiative under a very short timeline. By 2007, 105 house meetings were held in 13 languages, involving approximately 1,500 residents. The outcomes of these meetings form an agenda for change that focuses on youth leaders, particularly around issues of violence, access to recreation, and job opportunities. Resident momentum teams are now working in the community addressing access to health care, the built environment, food justice, peace promotion, resident participation, and school attendance. Many of these elements are also the focus of Price Charities' resources and although Price has met with CalEndow officials to support their efforts, staff contend that a true partnership has yet to materialize between the two foundations.

As Price Charities nears the twentieth anniversary of its partnership with City Heights, the foundation faces a number of challenges. While the physical change is extraordinary, serious urban problems continue to plague this area. Affordable housing is still a challenge for many families in this community and fear of gentrification is still alive in sections of this diverse community. The Rev. Jim Gilbert from the City Heights' Fairmount Baptist Church tried to encourage the late Sol Price to consider strategies to create affordable housing, but, as he shares, was unsuccessful:

I have tried to get Mr. Price to look into community land trusts and limited equity housing cooperatives, as well as just providing more help to non-profit, affordable housing developers. But frankly, he is not enthusiastic about helping very-low income people. He is eager to help those of modest incomes to purchase a home … but the majority of residents, who make less than $26,000, cannot benefit from such programs and are in danger of being priced out.

Between 1990 and 2002, more than 1,100 dwelling units were torn down in City Heights, leading to the relocation of approximately 3,000 low-income individuals. Almost 700 additional dwelling units were torn down from 2002–2007 as a result of the construction of three new elementary schools, the Metro Career Center, and a new Regional Transportation Center, affecting close to 2,500 residents. By 2011, the city of San Diego's rental vacancy rate hovered at 3.8 percent (Leung, 2011). Price Charities built the 116-unit townhomes in 2003, out of which 34 are low-income. The Metro Career Center, opened in 2004, offers 120 affordable housing units; City Heights Square opened in October of 2011 and offers 92 market-rate units. Clearly, more affordable housing will be needed if the community is to maintain the ethnic, racial, and economic mix that makes it so unique.

As City Heights' façade continued to change, it no longer became the community people moved to because they could not afford to live elsewhere. Evidence seems to indicate that rents began to climb in City Heights. Respondents to a door-to-door survey on community satisfaction (N=83) stated, on average, rents had increased by 39 percent in the past three years (2000–2003), 49 percent of respondents knew someone who had moved in with family because they could not afford a home of their own, and 32 percent knew someone who had moved out of City Heights due to affordability. But these residents were also generally pleased with the changes occurring in their community and 63 percent of the renters interviewed indicated that they would seek to buy a home in City Heights if such an opportunity arose largely due to the quality of local schools (Gibney, 2004[5]).

Maintaining the character of this neighborhood was one of the key goals espoused by the foundation as the community began to change. In an interview, a former Price Charities staff member explained:

The mission for everything we do, simply stated is to make City Heights a community that retains its current residents and attracts new ones. So the idea being that we could do a lot of work in City Heights and make it so that the people that live here now are completely priced out of the neighborhood. If that happens we failed in our mission and I think that's an important thing to keep in mind here every day.

Price Charities clearly played an important role as a catalyst for change for a community that needed serious help. As the physical transformation of City Heights began to take place, the foundation sought out additional partnerships with other entities such as the City Heights CDC to increase the number of affordable housing units in the area. The foundation's willingness to engage with other systems to achieve broader change is a hallmark of its theory of change and its vision of a desirable process for transformation of underserved communities. A more detailed analysis and lessons learned from both the Jacobs Family Foundation and Price Charities' efforts are presented in Chapter 9.

# 9

# APPLYING SYSTEMS THEORY TO PRICE CHARITIES AND THE JACOBS CENTER FOR NEIGHBORHOOD INNOVATION

## Lessons learned

After more than 15 years of dedicated embedded philanthropy, Price Charities and the Jacobs Family Foundation have helped deliver change in two under-served communities in San Diego in ways that have considerably impacted the local fabric. Their work is not yet done, but with significant progress already completed, a comparison of these two efforts offers lessons on the complexity of comprehensive community change and the value of applying systems theory to both analyze and implement these multilayered efforts. Their experiences are representative of other foundations' involvement with CCIs and serve as instructive examples. As explained in Chapter 5, systems theory provides the framework for better understanding the intricate web of systems and their relationships with one another at the neighborhood, regional, state, and federal level. Systems theory accounts for the diversity between and among internal participants, such as residents and local nonprofits, along with external ones, including foundations and public sector agencies, and analyzes the processes through which they interact. It enables us to use a holistic lens to better understand the ways different stakeholders interpret community challenges and, more importantly, places context at the forefront of the analysis.

Acknowledging the significance of context enables participants to reallocate resources in order to identify the levers for triggering proactive, sustainable change in a collaborative environment. Systems theory supports the contention that it is more effective to look at systems, rather than models, since models can be rigid and often ignore local context. Furthermore, systems theory shifts the focus from a linear trajectory of outcomes to a recognition of the importance of identifying the multiple systems in existence and the ways in which they intersect, or have the potential to intersect, as well as the importance of process to these types of community change endeavors.

The discussion in this chapter is framed by the foundations' roles in these intricate systems. Foundations are systems that operate in diverse neighborhood contexts. Given their financial resources, foundations have the potential to significantly impact local community development efforts to best meet their own internal mission, especially when they do not share the same view of the critical challenges that exist in a particular community. At moments in history, this has certainly been the case. However, systems change theory posits that a foundation's role in community change is to unite external systems around a shared definition of community problems that is also in alignment with internal definitions. We contend that when foundations are willing to partner in a truly collaborative method with other local stakeholders and help develop more equitable participatory processes, they maximize the levers that have the potential to catalyze meaningful change and improvement. Throughout this book we have highlighted examples of numerous CCIs. In this chapter we provide a more focused analysis of two case studies, Price Charities and the Jacobs Family Foundation, in order to demonstrate the value of using systems change theory to frame and analyze comprehensive community change efforts.

## Community development in the context of systems theory

Comparing the efforts of Price Charities and the Jacobs Family Foundation demonstrates that in order to analyze the relationship between systems at the neighborhood level, it is essential that stakeholders begin with a clear definition of community development as this impacts the ways in which foundations conceptualize the broader context, their role in it, and subsequently their method and approach to community change. If foundations' community development definitions diverge from those of other stakeholders in the larger network of neighborhood systems, then change will be difficult to realize. Potentially opposing paths will be implemented leading to dissent and perhaps even systems failure. Additionally, in looking at Price Charities and the Jacobs Family Foundation as exemplars, we see that while many foundations involved in community change efforts often share the same fundamental definition of community development, it is one that may differ from that of community stakeholders, local representatives, and business interests—all representing different systems that interact at the neighborhood level.

Our analysis shows that foundations create hierarchies within the larger system whereby greater or lesser emphasis is placed on certain internal or external subsystems. This impacts outcomes considerably and demonstrates the intricacies of realizing change. The different orderings of the systems and its impacts are reflected in the efforts of Price Charities and the Jacobs Family Foundation. We begin with a look at Price Charities.

Price Charities' definition of community development is rooted in its founder's entrepreneurial roots. Price Charities operates through a collaborative, pragmatic process that engages a variety of nonprofit, foundation, and public partners both within and outside the community to leverage the foundation's resources to maximize impact. Price's systems change theory is structured around the foundation serving as a catalyst for physical change based on confidence in the workings of the free market. With its primary emphasis on physical change, Price Charities has emphasized its relationship with the systems that can best help it achieve this goal. This includes public sector partners and other private foundations such as the Weingart Foundation that have helped Price Charities leverage the funds necessary to realize large-scale physical renewal.

Local property owners also figure prominently in Price's overall strategy because the foundation recognizes that its goals for physical development complement homeowners' desires to see their property values rise. To this end, the foundation supported the creation of a Town Council including rent subsides for space and an executive director that worked to improve the image of this embattled community. In addition, the foundation implemented a neighborhood grants program to create neighborhood associations and, at its peak, approximately 11 neighborhood associations were active in City Heights. All were composed primarily of property owners and most held monthly meetings. Unfortunately, without the foundation's subsidies, the City Heights Town Council was unsuccessful in raising sufficient funds to keep its offices open, but several of the neighborhood associations are still in existence. With a strong desire to maximize as much return on investment as possible, Price Charities adheres to a pragmatic definition of community development that places physical development at the center of its larger systems change theory. Its staff and board members do not publicly articulate the foundation's definition of community development; rather, it was discerned from interviews conducted and identifiable outcomes. On rare occasions, Price Charities has publicly stated its view. An example is the following quote from Robert Price who assumed leadership of the foundation after his father's death in 2009:

> One of the things that we really did right when we started was that we didn't start with programs but with something very tangible—the Urban Village … It's very important to immediately get something tangible that's produced—it establishes real credibility.
>
> (as cited in Abraham, 2007, para. 20)

According to staff members at the foundation, Price Charities annually invests approximately $5–6 million of its own money that it then uses to leverage redevelopment funding or funding from other private foundations. Former and current Price Charities' staff members describe the way in which the foundation expedites its efforts as having both positive and negative outcomes. On the one hand, staff members admit to operating with very little self-reflection, yet at the same time they understand that this pragmatism has enabled them to achieve tangible results in a relatively short amount of time.

Price Charities' pragmatic approach to community development also means that the foundation seeks to provide local residents with basic resources such as affordable housing and higher-quality education for their children. Interestingly, as one staff member explained in an interview, the foundation emphasizes resident initiative and responsibility as the key to maximizing local opportunities. Price's entrepreneurial roots are evident as the foundation improves schools, housing, and the community's physical space as basic tools that residents are expected to use through their own initiative to obtain better-paying jobs, buy a home, and improve their family's outcomes. This presents a contradiction as the foundation has invested relatively few resources in capacity building, particularly in the areas of community organizing and individual empowerment. While it partners with local nonprofits that have a strong track record with these efforts, the foundation itself has been largely hands-off in this area.

Price's privileging of formal, institutional systems has resulted in strong partnerships with the SDUSD, the city of San Diego, and a host of well-established local nonprofits such as the Mid-City CAN. As a result, one of the largest internal stakeholder systems, specifically the low-income renters that comprise approximately 75 percent of City Heights' population, are not placed as high in Price Charities' hierarchal system. Given the strong network of internal nonprofit systems in the community, we could argue that it would be redundant for the foundation to invest much of its time working directly with renters. However, it certainly reflects the foundation's conceptualization of community development as physical renewal. In interviews, residents offer contradictory views, with some criticizing Price Charities' focus on rental housing rather than affordable homeownership; while others call for more focus on social services, and yet others want more "economic diversity" which some interpret as gentrification. Here we see a potential discord in the larger system. When the multiple components of a larger neighborhood system do not share a common definition of community development, it creates fissures in the system.

According to a series of interviews conducted over several years, for many low-income residents of City Heights community development is defined in more personal terms. For those interviewed, it means addressing inequities that affect their day-to-day routines, such as a lack of sidewalks, poor street lighting, combating crime, and regular trash pick-up. As some local nonprofit staff and residents explain, for a large segment of this ethnically, racially, and economically diverse neighborhood, community development is not a relevant term. A nonprofit manager for a refugee group explained that her clients are most concerned with learning the English language and finding work, and the city bureaucratic processes, including public meetings to gain community input, are not pertinent to their day-to-day life. Nonprofit leaders addressed structural concerns, challenging the role of private foundations as policy actors in the public sphere. A nonprofit CEO said this about CalEndow, which is investing millions of dollars in City Heights to improve the health of families: "These endowments are doing something that the city public official should be doing but aren't held accountable." Accountability and transparency were themes in several of the interviews. Another nonprofit CEO also expressed strong disdain for foundations taking over work that, in his opinion, should be done by organizations already present in the neighborhood. He argued that "Foundations should find partners and create partnerships and invest in them over the long term—but not supersede them … you are not from there, it is not what you do."

Based on its definition of community development, Price's systems change theory is premised on its belief that physical renewal is the primary engine of community change and relationships should be built, and stakeholders assembled, based on this main objective. This has resulted in a hierarchical conceptualization of the larger neighborhood system where partners with financial resources, or access to them, are assigned greater value. With the absence of deep public sector pockets for low-income neighborhoods in San Diego, Price Charities' role as a catalyst for physical change intertwines strategically with those partners in the larger system that can help it realize its goals. Price Charities does not adhere to a consultative system to the same extent found in other CCIs. Stakeholder input is acknowledged, but the foundation has placed a greater emphasis on working with organizational partners (nonprofits, public sector agencies, and private sector investors). This approach to systems change has enabled Price Charities to make a significant impact on the physical fabric of City Heights in a relatively short period of time. It has successfully leveraged its systems partners to catalyze physical renewal that otherwise would not have occurred, or that would have taken significantly longer to realize without the support and resources of the foundation.

In contrast to Price Charities, the Jacobs Family Foundation and its operating arm, JCNI, has articulated a definition of community development that places greater emphasis on resident stakeholders and community ownership of all assets, physical and otherwise. JCNI's commitment to resident ownership of community change has led it to develop a systems change theory that places local residents at the top of its hierarchy. JCNI focuses on processes of resident engagement and stakeholder relationship building, and this drives its community development work. The Jacobs Family Foundation's approach to community development is defined by its board and staff as holistic and comprehensive, leading it to conceptualize community change as individual empowerment at the same level in the hierarchy as neighborhood physical improvement, if not higher. Physical improvement is certainly important for JCNI, yet, unlike Price's approach, the participatory process that generates this change is given greater emphasis. Similar to Price, JCNI recognizes that in order to realize comprehensive change, multiple systems must be engaged. But in an effort to promote community ownership, JCNI works to create local organizations, hire local leaders as JCNI staff, and thus work to build a nonprofit network that can partner with the foundation to effect community change. The result is a less dense nonprofit network as the one in existence in City Heights, an issue that JCNI is working to change.

JCNI's systems change approach differs from Price Charities in terms of how external systems are incorporated into the model. Whereas Price Charities has been successful at engaging public sector partners, Jacobs has been slow to do this. In the early years of its work, its emphasis on empowering resident stakeholders led it to eschew forming partnerships with public sector agencies and nonprofit agencies outside of the community. Many of these organizations and their staff members did not have the opportunity to build relationships with JCNI and subsequently the foundation was viewed as being very inward focused. The executive director of a nonprofit organization that supports community development efforts across San Diego noted that there was a certain degree of suspicion about the foundation's work because it was slow to introduce itself to stakeholders outside of the community. Rumors circulated that it was land banking large swaths of property in order to gentrify the neighborhood. Because it was slow to partner with the city's planning department, it found itself at a disadvantage when it came time to apply for certain funding sources that required city endorsements or when it sought planning approvals for new projects. Whereas Price Charities leveraged its connections to City Hall very effectively, including hiring the former San Diego City Manager to oversee its redevelopment projects, the Jacobs Family Foundation was somewhat slow when it came to connecting its internal systems with those external systems that could facilitate its efforts. Concerns about ceding control to outside entities and disempowering resident stakeholders impacted its ability to engage those external systems that had potentially beneficial resources. The financial crisis of 2008 along with other internal factors led the foundation to seek outside institutional partners to assist in funding the type of change JCNI envisioned.

The one external system that has consistently figured prominently in JCNI's work is philanthropic systems outside of the community. JCNI has realized success in this area and has been able to leverage funds from many prominent national private foundations including the Ford Foundation, the James Irvine Foundation, the Rockefeller Foundation, and the Annie E. Casey Foundation. These entities serve somewhat as a shadow system in JCNI's larger systems change approach. While the support of large national foundations is not hidden by JCNI, they do not receive the same high level of public acknowledgement found with many of Jacobs' other stakeholder systems. JCNI values transparency, yet this is one area where we see lower levels of it.

A comparison between JCNI and Price Charities suggests that the two foundations are working with somewhat dissimilar systems both by choice as well as by necessity. Price Charities has been able to rely heavily on the deep network of nonprofit organizations in the community and leverage their resources to provide a full menu of social service programming. This has enabled it to focus on its primary goal of physical renewal. If the community did not have this strong internal system of social service provision, Price Charities would have found itself operating in a different system that may not have provided the latitude to emphasize physical redevelopment to the extent to which it has occurred. In contrast, JCNI is operating in a system that has strong informal social service networks, such as the resources offered by the many churches in the community, along with a few strong nonprofit organizations. But the larger southeastern San Diego area lacks the level of nonprofits one would expect to find in a neighborhood of this size. For example, the community does not house a single CDC nor does it have a large multipurpose social service nonprofit or a networking tool for nonprofits such as Mid-City CAN which operates in City Heights. As a result, the context in south-eastern San Diego is different from that of City Heights and this leads to different holes in the larger neighborhood system. Price Charities has been able to focus on physical renewal because social service issues can be effectively addressed by exist-ing nonprofit systems, whereas the Jacobs Family Foundation has placed greater emphasis on building the overall capacity of the community.

Integral to JCNI's definition of community development is an emphasis on strengthening individual stakeholder capital. The foundation contends that with-out this approach, its efforts will be unsustainable and systems failure will occur. Another point of contrast between the two foundations is that, unlike Price Charities, the Jacobs Family Foundation is intended to be a terminal founda-tion and has set 2030 as its sunset date. Unlike perpetual foundations that do not face the same urgency considering transference of assets, the board of the Jacobs Family Foundation and JCNI is acutely aware that, in order for the larger neigh-borhood system to operate after its departure, it needs to ensure that community capacity is in place and qualified to assume these responsibilities. Concerns about this capacity along with the slow pace at which it has realized its objectives has led the Jacobs Family Foundation board of directors to revise its sunset date sev-eral times.

## Systems interactions

Ferguson and Stoutland (1999) argue that an effective community development initiative is one in which stakeholders trust one another, develop the needed capacity to effect change, and work as allies across interest groups on projects that improve the lives of residents in underserved communities. We extend this reasoning and apply it to the larger context of systems theory. The multiple internal and external systems that interact at the neighborhood level should be synchronized based on a shared definition of the community's challenges and the optimum approaches for addressing them. Both Price Charities and the Jacobs Family Foundation play a major role in the revitalization of their two target communities. This work has resulted from systems that have been effectively integrated and coordinated to achieve a common goal. Analysis of their efforts demonstrates that the structuring of different systems, both internal and exter-nal, can vary substantially. In comparing the two larger systems in which Price Charities and the Jacobs Family Foundation operate, we see that Jacobs places more primacy on neighborhood, or internal, systems, whereas Price's strength is building relationships with individuals and systems external to the neighborhood. We see this when we look at the ways in which the two foundations have lever-aged resources to implement community change.

Both Price Charities and JCNI recruited Magic Johnson's urban investment company to open a Starbucks in their respective urban villages. Price Charities also partnered with the Weingart Foundation to fund a new public library; and it has collaborated with the city's redevelopment agency, public hospitals, the SDSU, and other entities to invest more than $140 million on a variety of projects. The Jacobs Family Foundation views neighborhood residents as the most critical partners in its work. And in fact, it has garnered national attention to its process of actively engaging hundreds of residents in the Diamond Neighborhoods' community development process, including the sale of shares in an IPO for the Market Creek Plaza shopping center.

For nonprofit partners in City Heights, Price Charities' role also encompasses the support of a vibrant systems infrastructure of neighborhood and social organizations. The foundation provided small grants for the formation of neighborhood associations, developed the City Height's Town Council, provides grants to a variety of nonprofit groups including one for a community garden targeting refugees, and helps support the Mid-City CAN collaborative, a 23-year-old umbrella organization with 120 members representing over 70 public and private organizations such as schools, faith communities, businesses, and nonprofits.

Jacobs has also developed valuable relationships with nonprofit organizations in the neighborhood. CNC, a spin-off from the Jacobs Foundation's early work, was for many years one of the largest nonprofits in southeastern San Diego. Until several years ago when it experienced internal problems, its work in community organizing and community development contributed to its relationship with Jacobs. JCNI has varying degrees of interaction with other nonprofits in the community, but not to the extent that one sees with Price. This is the result of two primary factors. First, JCNI believes strongly in its own ability to catalyze change through its staff members and the community stakeholder systems that it has developed. Second, the Diamond Neighborhoods do not have the same broad established infrastructure of nonprofit social service and community development organizations found in City Heights. In addition to relationships with internal systems of nonprofits and resident stakeholders, both foundations have engaged with the public sector and, to a certain extent, become de facto public agencies.

JCNI is clear that residents are the most critical stakeholders and relationships with them are given primacy. Jacobs engages in continuous outreach designed to bring different constituents into the process. Like City Heights, the Diamond Neighborhoods contain a diverse population, and Jacobs works with these different "culture" communities on many levels and via many formal channels. Internally, JCNI has its International Outreach Team that is comprised of residents representing seven different cultural communities found in the community including Samoans, Filipinos, and Laotians. Additionally, Jacobs has close to one dozen working teams, all of which have significant resident representation.

Price Charities' relationships with residents has at times been marked by frustration as the foundation's efforts to develop its plans efficiently are not always met with support. The sale of the townhomes presents an example of systems clash, as the expectations of the mostly immigrant renters were clearly contrary to those of the foundation. The 116 townhomes were eagerly anticipated by the community, particularly low-income renters who aspired to purchase a home in City Heights. But as the project developed, it became clear that Price wanted moderate-income residents to occupy the units as it began to quietly market the units to nonprofit employees as well as teachers, police officers, and professors from the university that operates the educational pilot. As this information trickled out to the community, the foundation's credibility was questioned. Price held a number of informational meetings at which they explained, with the help of translators, the intricacies of condo ownership and the unveiling of a program that allowed residents to engage in community service and receive "mortgage credit." Residents were befuddled and kept pressing the land ownership issue, presenting another example of systems clashing. For these immigrants, owning a home means owning land; for Price Charities, owning a home means owning a unit. The system's lack of congruency was evident as a Price Charities' executive responded to those in attendance in frustration:

> It is what it is. Don't mess around with the deal we are trying to create. You can't over-engineer this thing. If you don't like community service, this deal isn't for you. Then the ground rent isn't such an attractive piece of it. But it is a very fair deal; a very attractive deal for you. We don't know the market-ability of these units when you decide to sell. You are in the boat with us. It's a partnership. We are going to own this ground forever.

## Foundations, the public sector, and systems change

During the 1960s a clear division of roles separated private foundations and the public sector. Foundations served as funding sources for research and development, supporting new approaches to entrenched social problems. If a demonstration project proved successful, the federal government would likely fund it on a larger scale as it did with many of the War on Poverty programs (Letts, Ryan, and Grossman, 1997). As government continued to streamline its structure and processes, initially under the 1982 Grace Commission recommendations and later through Vice-President Al Gore's National Performance Review Task Force, "reinventing government" became the new mantra for government turning to private entities to provide public services in a more efficient fashion (Schachter, 1997). The federal retrenchment initiated under the Reagan Administration in the 1980s contributed to an increased burden placed on nonprofit organizations, or the "third sector" (Wolch, 1990), to fill in critical gaps in social service and community-related programming, and foundations' support became even more critical.

Although under some War on Poverty programs residents of decaying urban neighborhoods were seen as partners in community revitalization, power sharing was challenging at best. The reinventing government movement of the 1990s developed a new model for delivery of services whereby urban residents were customers and service delivery would be improved once customers' needs were identified (Osborne and Gaebler, 1992). For some public service sectors such as schools, parents and students were the customers and a plethora of programs and evaluation tools were used to discern appropriate service delivery so that customers' interests were addressed and performance improved. What these approaches missed, according to Frederickson is "that citizens are not customers of government; they represent its owners who elect leaders to represent their interests" (as cited in Schachter, 1997, p. 9).

Turning to the Jacobs Family Foundation's work in the Diamond Neighborhoods, the city's role is different. The local redevelopment agency, SEDC, is in the midst of an internal reorganization stemming from allegations that its long-time executive director was misappropriating funds for her own gain. Since her departure from the organization, JCNI has developed a more amicable relationship with SEDC. However, prior to her departure, SEDC viewed JCNI as a competitor, not a partner, and this prevented the two organizations from effectively leveraging their resources and partnering on projects. Furthermore, when the Jacobs Family Foundation entered the Diamond Neighborhoods the council member representing southeastern San Diego eyed the foundation with suspicion and was reluctant to support its work. These adversarial relationships had perhaps the unintended consequences of leading JCNI to believe that it would do better to disengage from some of the more established institutional actors in the neighborhood. This was problematic, though, because SEDC and the council member were prominent among the neighborhood's well-established, old guard, African American community.

JCNI met with less resistance from the city's planning department, especially after it made the effort to develop a relationship. According to one of the city's long-time planners who worked in the neighborhood for many years, the city planning department views Jacobs' work favorably. The local community planning group is generally supportive of the foundation's work, especially now that it has proven itself with the completion of Market Creek Plaza.

## Accountability, transparency, and systems change

As Price and Jacobs fill the void left by the inaction and lack of resources from the public sector, questions about accountability and transparency have surfaced. Foundations do not typically function as quasi-public entities, and this unfamiliar role raises legitimate questions. It also identifies a challenge to CCIs when innovation leads to traditional partners assuming nontraditional roles that must be explained and justified to all stakeholders. This upsets the traditional relationship between the neighborhood systems and requires further consideration. Although respondents to our interviews clearly appreciated the magnitude of the resources that private foundations bring to their communities, governments' and nonprofits' diminished capacity to evaluate and assess the impact of the private-enterprise model of community development raises questions about accountability and transparency, particularly in the use of redevelopment monies.

Unlike Price Charities' implicit conveyance of its approach, JCNI's theory is clearly communicated by the foundation staff and board members in many of its publicly disseminated reports and publications as well as when it meets with different stakeholder groups both in and outside of the community. Its former CEO was the public face of the foundation and traveled across the country sharing lessons learned and discussing its efforts. While Jacobs has been commended for making its approach clear to all interested parties, this has proven to be problematic at times because stakeholders have taken the foundation's words at face value and question it when it deviates from these statements or when it takes longer than originally planned to realize a stated objective.

One of the benefits of JCNI's relative transparency is that it has enabled it to outreach to a range of resident stakeholder groups from across the community, particularly the African American community which has a long history of residency and community engagement in the neighborhood. Through a series of interviews, many residents of the Diamond Neighborhoods shared similar conceptualizations of community development, viewing it as a large comprehensive undertaking that contributes to a strong quality of life and unites physical improvements with economic development and a vibrant social core. However, some of the nonprofit organizations that serve the community have challenged JCNI's definition of community development even though when asked to state their own definition it was essentially the same as that of JCNI. Further discussion with nonprofit staff members revealed concerns about the foundation's influence in the community. Unlike City Heights, which has a rich network of established nonprofit organizations, southeastern San Diego has a surprisingly small network of nonprofit social service agencies, given the size of the community. In fact, many of the nonprofits that provide services to residents of southeastern San Diego are located outside of the community's boundaries. This has led to greater visibility for the Jacobs Family Foundation in the Diamond Neighborhoods and has most likely contributed to its attempts to provide a comprehensive menu of programs and services to residents. The foundation therefore has assumed a more prominent position in the larger system that drives community change in the neighborhood.

JCNI's approach to community development is unlike that of typical public sector approaches, and this leads to stakeholder uncertainty about Jacobs' actual role in the community. JCNI's emphasis on process and the delays this yields in promised outcomes has led to suspicion. Ever wary of promises from outside investors that never materialized, or the seemingly endless stream of studies of neighborhood problems that never led to actual improvements, some of the Diamond Neighborhoods' nonprofit and resident stakeholders expect to see tangible, physical improvements, such as Market Creek Plaza. Others vent frustration over larger systematic breakdowns and question why foundations should be doing the work that they believe is the public sector's responsibility.

Many of the interviews with staff members of local nonprofits pointed to concerns about competition between the foundations and existing social service and community development providers. At least three individuals recounted stories of applying for grants from other private foundations, only to find out that Jacobs was applying for the same grant. One director of a small neighborhood nonprofit organization told the story of contacting Jacobs for a letter of support for a grant she was writing and was told that Jacobs had plans to submit an application for the same grant. Another individual interviewed asked "Is it appropriate for one institution to soak up all the financial resources in a given community and allocate it out?"

Encompassing these concerns is the very tangible fear that successful revitalization of these underserved neighborhoods will lead to gentrification. Several of the interviews for the Jacobs case study directly addressed the issue of gentrification, whereas others alluded to it. Interestingly, for those who spoke directly about gentrification, it was not necessarily perceived as completely detrimental with some people eager to see economic improvements in their community. However, as one person articulated it, and another inferred, there is significant discomfort surrounding a foundation facilitating gentrification through its community development projects. This raises an underlying theme among those stakeholders who are critical of the Jacobs Family Foundation's and Price Charities' work; some stakeholders adhere to a more traditional model of community development whereby roles and activities are clearly assigned to certain types of organizations. Since foundations typically have not engaged in direct, hands-on community development, the fact that Jacobs established an operating arm, JCNI, to do community development, is potentially threatening. Price's development arm, San Diego Reinvestment Inc., was recently folded back into the broader Price Charities umbrella.

Jacobs is acutely aware of the potential for gentrification and has crafted and implemented a framework to thwart potential gentrification by developing systems to "recycle" assets back into the community's hands. While this is a well-conceived plan, Jacobs must work hard to convey the message to its critics that its gentrification prevention plan is sincere. Price Charities has not been as clear in its stance on gentrification, and initially it espoused a goal of building "economic diversity" among residents of City Heights. Price Charities has constructed a number of affordable housing units in the community, particularly senior housing, but redevelopment projects as well as new school construction has resulted in the displacement of several thousand, largely low-income, residents from the area (Martinez-Cosio, 2003). Further aggravating the housing situation was the construction of four new elementary schools in City Heights to alleviate overcrowded classrooms. Voters approved Proposition MM in 1998, a $1.51 billion bond measure to modernize 161 existing schools and construct 21 new schools. Approximately 2,500 City Heights' residents were relocated between 2000 and 2005 as the school district acquired 163 parcels of land for four new schools in one of the city's most densely populated areas (San Diego Unified School District, n.d.[1]). Under state law, school districts are not required to build replacement low-income housing taken to construct educational facilities.[2]

Further complicating the matter is that public accountability of private founda-tions' work is a challenging task (Fleischman, 2007). Although private foundations have played an increasingly important role in supporting local community devel-opment since the 1980s, the degree to which they are held accountable for their impact on communities varies widely (Covington, 1994; Lowe, 2004). In theory, both the Jacobs Family Foundation and Price Charities only need to answer to their board members, and this poses understandable concerns among community stakeholders. Family foundations are in a unique position as a result of their organi-zational structure and mission. Unlike other foundations engaged in community development efforts, family foundations are by definitions often led by family members and are accountable to their boards of directors. A useful comparison is the community foundation model. Since the 1980s, community foundations have played an increasingly important role in supporting local community development (Lowe, 2004). These permanent community endowments receive support from local individuals and organizations and the funds are then earmarked for local use in areas ranging from education to affordable housing. Community foundations are markedly different from family foundations because as public charities they are held to higher degrees of community accountability and transparency (Covington, 1994).

A key question was raised as we examined the significant contributions private foundations continue to make to the urban landscape and to underserved commu-nities across the country: is process more important than expediency in achieving community change? Expediency is important in spurring change and growth in low-income communities, as Price Charities clearly illustrates; but process is also important in developing community capacity to sustain change, as JCNI eloquently contends. Does a middle ground exist? We argue that the middle ground is deter-mined by the context of each community, including its history, culture, values, beliefs, demographics, and all the other elements that make a community unique. Each community as a system must be understood before an effective intervention can be initiated. Otherwise, funders and their partners risk system clash with often disastrous results for underserved communities.

# 10
# CONCLUSION

Community development philanthropy in the United States has significantly evolved since its first introduction by European colonists over 350 years ago. With its roots in informal charitable efforts based on Judeo-Christian doctrines, it began a gradual trajectory towards greater formality leading to the creation of charitable institutions funded by both private and public sources. The complementarity between public aid and private philanthropy was established early on and continues to this day with community development efforts. Philanthropy has become increasingly more sophisticated as evidenced by the diverse typology of philanthropies in existence varying from community foundations to private family foundations. The emphasis in this book has been on foundations that support community development efforts. Evidence from the field highlights the variety of foundation-types, and range of approaches employed to fund these initiatives across the country in distressed neighborhoods. Within the past 30 years progress has been made in the philanthropic world to support emerging models that more rigorously incorporate systems theory and approach community development in a comprehensive, integrated manner linking human services, social capital, economic development, and physical redevelopment. These CCIs are realizing varying degrees of success and with a significant track record in place we can identify lessons learned and challenges for the next generation of CCIs. Progress has certainly been made, but philanthropic support for community development in the twenty-first century is still encountering some of the same challenges that existed over a century ago, along with some new ones brought on by the complexities engendered by persistent gaps in public support for low-income communities.

The approximately 60 CCIs reviewed for this book demonstrate the potential for catalyzing and implementing meaningful community development in disenfranchised urban neighborhoods. Foundation-supported community development can fill important gaps left by decades of public sector retrenchment and neglect.

Yet these efforts are far from monolithic, and their many nuances require careful analysis to better understand the increasing complexity of differing approaches to community development. It is clear that paramount to understanding CCIs, particularly for private foundation partners entering the fray, is to consider the contextual issues that ground this type of work. Systems theory provides a meaningful framework for developing CCIs so that context is front and center. With context at the forefront and all relevant internal and external systems in alignment with problem definition, the likelihood of achieving positive outcomes is enhanced. Systems theory acknowledges the complexity of community change and recognizes that when the numerous systems at play in local communities are acknowledged, coordinated, and granted equal value, resource maximization can occur. Systems theory not only operates as a framework for constructing holistic community development efforts, it also provides a lens for outsiders to understand and analyze the efforts.

In the past, it has been extremely challenging to measure the outcomes of CCIs for several reasons discussed in our case studies. Positive community change takes a long time to implement and many times the results are not apparent until well beyond the initial grant period. Most foundations, like other funders, operate on short time lines and are required by those with decision-making authority to demonstrate results quickly. This is contrary to the process through which community change occurs. Community change also includes many outcomes that are difficult to measure. How, for example, should social capital be quantified and how can evaluators measure relationships between community stakeholders? Systems theory enables us to assess the viability of relationships and partnerships between the internal and external systems in operation at the neighborhood level. It permits both participants and evaluators to look at the structures for community change. Systems theory is applicable in a variety of contexts and thus the theoretical framework is transferable and does not have to contend with the unique exigencies that make model transference between communities difficult, if not impossible.

Often the key questions raised in examining CCIs are focused on process versus outcomes. Systems theory enables us to address this dichotomy. The many case studies included in this book reveal that the answer is complicated and contentious, and, ultimately, it depends on whom you ask. In communities where CCIs are in place, many stakeholders would agree that their community benefited from the engagement of private foundations in community development efforts. But since context matters, the vision and philosophies of private foundations differ, as do the political, cultural, and demographic histories of each community. These differences in approach can be addressed by using systems theory to investigate how stakeholders define community development and how this in turned shaped the understanding of the relationship between the stakeholder systems impacting the neighborhood. This facilitates a movement away from the utilization of metrics that only quantify physical and economic change and enables an equal valuation of relationships and processes.

Systems theory requires patience and a paradigm shift. This is beginning to occur. The work of funder collaboratives such as LAUF is yielding significant outcomes. Employing consultative strategies that allow for meaningful dialogue and engagement between all stakeholders, foundations involved with these efforts are changing the ways they engage with communities and have moved away from top-down strategies where the funding source dictates programmatic decisions. Instead, all stakeholders are afforded equal value and foundations are realizing the benefits of partnering with the community rather than looking at it as a client with needs that should be served. We recognize, though, that funder collaboratives are a very small percentage of all philanthropic efforts with approximately 40 in existence. The jury is still out on how quickly and widespread these efforts will evolve. However, interviews with leaders in the funders collaborative field reveal cautious enthusiasm and a belief in their potential to significantly impact the role of philanthropy in local community development.

As foundations continue to rethink new approaches to meaningful investment in community development, several elements of their approaches will continue to require attention. At times in the past, foundations have used heavy-handed methods based on power imbalances stemming from access to resources. This has created distrust and ambivalence from stakeholders. For systems change theory to succeed, trust must exist between all stakeholder systems and true partnerships must be put in place. One way for foundations to do this is to operate with greater transparency. The laws governing private foundations do not require detailed reporting. For neighborhood system networks to effectively engage, foundations should clearly disclose their missions, goals, and funding priorities. Rather than creating an environment of second-guessing about a foundation's true intention, greater transparency will lead to higher levels of trust, which will maximize the successful interaction and coordination of system partners.

Increased transparency will also lead to higher levels of accountability, which is central to systems theory. Systems theory is based on the premise that the success of the larger system is dependent on the integration of all internal and external partners. This requires high levels of accountability from all community partners, particularly foundations. Dialogue and follow-through must take place as our case studies illustrate.

As more private foundations refocus their efforts towards a holistic place-based approach to philanthropy, they will assume an increasingly important role in local policy development and local funding. Many of the foundations involved with CCIs are essentially becoming de facto public agencies. In this era of public sector retrenchment, large funding gaps exist in low-income communities. Public planning agencies do not have the staff resources and/or financial resources to invest in low-income communities that do not have the political clout to demand otherwise. This provides a fertile opportunity for foundations eager to impact change. However, in relation to the point made above regarding transparency and accountability, we must question whether or not it is appropriate for foundations to assume this role. If all neighborhood system partners are in alignment, then greater foundation involvement may ultimately allow for increased flexibility in local community change efforts. Bureaucracies could be avoided and local stakeholders could benefit from more agility to effect change. However, if foundations have success in filling local funding gaps, will this lead to increased public sector retrenchment? This may not be a desired outcome. If neighborhood systems effectively incorporate city agencies, then these concerns could be mitigated because the public sector will be part of the interdependent network of stakeholders. The success of the foundation and neighborhood stakeholders would be intertwined with the integration of city government.

As CCIs continue to increase in number, and the trends identified in our research indicate that this will be the case, certain issues require further study. Our survey of CCIs across the country reveals a geographic imbalance in the location of these initiatives. The majority of CCIs are located on the East Coast and in older cities in the Midwest along with a few major urban areas on the West Coast that share a history of strong philanthropic support. Traditionally, foundations have invested in areas where they, or other foundations, have a track record. Other factors contribute to this pattern, and more research should be done to determine why and how private foundations, particularly ones with a national reach, select their target neighborhoods. Our research on the two CCIs in San Diego, Price Charities and the Jacobs Family Foundation, suggests that local family foundations have the potential to fill the gaps left by national foundations. In fact, the success of Price Charities and the Jacobs Family Foundation was effectively leveraged to secure resources from large, mainline foundations such as the Ford Foundation and the Annie E. Casey Foundation. As we discussed, the history and political climate in San Diego led to significant neglect of many of the city's low-income communities. However, local wealth was instrumental in seeding community change and attracting investment from local and national sources as well as public and private ones.

In recent years some CCIs have attempted to diversify their geographic targets. CalEndow's Building Healthy Communities Initiative, for example, is investing in 14 cities across the state of California, many of which have been overlooked by major foundations in the past. In addition to its investment in Los Angeles and Oakland, it is also working in cities in California's Central Valley such as Salinas and Merced along with Del Norte County and neighboring tribal lands in the northwest corner of the state adjacent to the Oregon border. Not only is the foundation investing in smaller, second-tier cities, it has included semi-rural ones. This is another area ripe for further analysis. Most CCIs focus on urban neighborhoods, with a few including rural ones, but regional systems have largely been overlooked. Neighborhoods and cities are interconnected in larger regional systems in areas such as food, housing, and job opportunities, among other systems. Given the increasing scarcity of resources (natural, financial, and other), the relationship between local and regional systems should be explored in more detail by foundations. Recently the Ford Foundation, under its "Promoting Metropolitan Land-Use Innovation" initiative, awarded $350,000 to Sustainable San Diego, a collaborative of groups dedicated to promoting equitable development, to explore strategies for integrated land use including housing, social equity, the environment, and economic development. This may prove to be a new area of interest for CCIs, or networks of CCIs, to pursue.

Of importance to the expansion of CCIs is a more coordinated method of documenting philanthropic investment. In order to monitor the impact of CCIs, the entities that quantify and track philanthropic investment should rethink the ways in which community development support is identified. One of the largest sources of data on philanthropic investment, the Foundation Center, does not include community development as a discrete category. This makes it impossible to monitor philanthropic support for community development over time. Oftentimes community development initiatives are identified as anti-poverty or quality-of-life programs, but they may also be included in public health or environmental policy categories. As we discussed throughout this book, for systems change to occur, all stakeholders must agree upon and share the same definition of community development. The Foundation Center should work with foundations, community development professionals, and others in the community development field to craft an umbrella definition for community development that will facilitate more systematized monitoring of philanthropic investment in low-income communities.

There is no magic bullet for communities suffering from physical, economic, and social distress. The challenges are complex, the stakeholders are diverse, and the solutions require coordination, cooperation, and adequate resources from multiple sources. Foundations are among the many investors in community development initiatives. The historical record of their efforts is uneven, yet at certain moments in time foundations have positioned themselves at the front lines of debate and policy innovation. Over the past several decades an increasing number of private foundations have engaged in CCIs. The appeal is based on the holistic, comprehensive, coordinated approach incorporated into these efforts. This enables foundations, and other investors, to minimize redundancies, effectively leverage their financial contributions, and eschew piecemeal efforts. The findings from this research point to the potentially transformative impact of the community development philanthropy that we see with many CCIs. Regardless of their approach, they generate physical, social, economic, and/or cultural change.

Foundations involved with CCIs often share the same role as first-stage responders. They are frequently among the first entities able to facilitate large-scale urban revitalization in a distressed neighborhood. This has both positive and negative repercussions. All neighborhoods have their own systems of stakeholders, many of which are dedicated to the neighborhood's well-being. These stakeholder systems precede the arrival of foundations and while existing stakeholders benefit from their social and historical connections, oftentimes they lack the political and financial capital necessary to realize comprehensive change. This is where CCIs offer opportunities of change. The ways in which these efforts proceed to capitalize on these opportunities varies considerably, as evidenced in the case studies presented here. Variation occurs based on the unique context of each neighborhood, the network of internal and external systems, and the ways in which the stakeholders define community development.

The history of philanthropic support for community development, especially through CCIs, demonstrates the merit of holistic community development. Over the past several decades, community development organizations, especially CDCs, have become savvy developers. They have excelled in the area of physical development, especially the construction of commercial and public-use facilities and affordable housing. Often lost in the process, though, was a focus on building the whole neighborhood and strengthening social, cultural, and economic foundations. Large intermediaries such as the LISC have recently realigned their programmatic efforts to focus on comprehensive community development.[1] This bridging effort is gaining traction, and financial resources are now being allocated for such efforts. These combined resources will further facilitate local neighborhood revitalization particularly when the efforts are framed as systems with multiple moving parts that are optimized when they move in sync with one another effectively catalyzing capacity for change.

# APPENDIX

## Typology of foundations engaged in community development

Comprehensive Community Initiatives (CCIs) bring together public, private, and nonprofit partners in strategic efforts to improve underserved low-income neighborhoods. At times referred to as public–private partnerships, these change efforts vary on a number of levels: organizational and operational logic; sources of funding and focus of expenditures; governing principles and/or values that guide their work; programmatic dimensions and scope of work; and type of leadership structure, and partnerships involved.

Efforts to respond to the complex interplay of structural, economic, and social conditions that led to the entrenched urban problems evident in U.S. cities and, increasingly, in older suburban areas, cross a number of disciplines. Thus CCI research is conducted by scholars and practitioners from planning, sociology, social work, education, nursing, and other areas that seek to reverse the conditions that marginalize a significant portion of the U.S. urban population. To move the discussion of this rich area of research in a direction that allows for a clearer understanding of best practices, we propose a typology of CCIs with a focus on the role of private and public foundations as key partners in holistic community change efforts.

The criteria for inclusion of CCIs in our typology include: must be a place-based effort, seek comprehensive change, use a mix of public and private funding sources, incorporate community-based decision-making, and be committed to community change. As we examined summary reports, IRS records, research reports conducted by a number of public and private institutions, evaluation reports, and literature on the topic, these elements were evident in many of the foundation-led community development efforts. Two broad classification categories emerged from our analysis:

> *Foundations as supporters of CCIs*—these are public, private, and community foundations that use on-the-ground partners such as nonprofits, public entities, and other foundations to target change within defined geographic areas.

The lead foundation may provide the bulk of funding, often long term (7–10 years) with the goal of achieving comprehensive change that can influence policy. Foundation staff and board rely on community partners for information on needs and programmatic responses, and the foundation may fund multi-site projects to facilitate cross-site learning. Community collaboratives in each site are prevalent as a vehicle for linking the resident base with funders, and may have oversight over management of projects.

*Foundations as managing partners*—these are largely embedded philanthropies, focused on place as a significant unit of analysis and as a target for comprehensive change. They are committed to significant direct interaction and relationship building with community members (residents, nonprofits, key stakeholders); engage in long-term funding commitment (5–10 years or even longer); may provide technical assistance, data, and information that can inform change efforts; work to build networks to resources outside the targeted neighborhood; flexible and "entrepreneurial" in funding approach; "hands-on." The level to which the foundations are embedded in the targeted community results in frequent interactions with residents and other stakeholders; they do not follow a prescribed model and vary in terms of funding strategies and approaches.

The broad menu of options for effecting comprehensive community change in underserved communities is as varied as the causes for disinvestment. This typology thus aims to start a conversation that begins to unravel the complexity of urban problems and the responses that have succeeded in activating key levers for comprehensive community change. The foundation initiatives are organized chronologically.

**Typology of foundations engaged in comprehensive community initiatives**

## I. Foundations as supporters of CCIs

| Name and governing principles | Funding | Program dimensions and outcomes | Accountability |
|---|---|---|---|
| *MacArthur Foundation—LISC New Communities Program (NCP); 1980–present* Foundation established in 1975.<br><br>Type: private foundation.<br><br>The New Communities Program (NCP) helped 16 Chicago neighborhoods develop partnerships to address challenges involving employment, education, housing, and safety.<br><br>*Governing principles:*<br><br>The NCP seeks to develop comprehensive, coordinated approaches to neighborhood investment through a partnership between a national foundation, its local chapters, and community groups (e.g. LISC San Diego, LISC Chicago).<br><br>The goal is to develop a relational approach by building collaborations as a "platform" for broad and sustained improvement, even as local conditions change. It is operationalized through its partnership with LISC Chicago.<br><br>Source: www.newcommunities.org | With assets of more than $6 billion, the foundation makes approximately $225 million in grants annually.<br><br>MacArthur's overall $150 million, ten-year investment in Chicago's neighborhoods, includes transforming public housing, enhancing community safety, and increasing the income and economic security of residents.<br><br>Since 2002, MacArthur has committed $21 million to the LISC for the program in Chicago; that early support has already leveraged more than $255 million in overall investment in the 16 targeted neighborhoods. Partners providing additional funding include Annie E. Casey Foundation, Bank One (Chase), Joyce Foundation, Living Cities, Mayor's Office of Workforce Development, Partnership for New Communities, Polk Brothers Foundation, State Farm Insurance Companies, and the Steans Family Foundation. | Examples of successes made possible by the NCP:<br><br>The Greater Southwest Development Corporation partnered with the Inner-City Muslim Action Network to build a new neighborhood health clinic.<br><br>The Logan Square Neighborhood Association helped 54 families keep their homes in the face of redevelopment plans. Quad Community Development Corporation is establishing a commercial district on the city's mid-south side that will include shops and residences.<br><br>Approximately five million square feet of retail/commercial business efforts received financing through its active relationships with CDCs. New Communities estimates that the partnership has invested $153.3 million in the 16 neighborhoods, for a total of $4.9 billion leveraged to benefit these communities. | The MacArthur Foundation believes as a foundation they are a private trust operated for the public good. Consequently, it makes public information about the operation of the foundation and knowledge derived through its activities. MacArthur regularly seeks external evaluations of its grant-making strategies. Summaries of those external reviews are posted at www.macfound.org in a section titled "What We Have Learned." |

| Name and governing principles | Funding | Program dimensions and outcomes | Accountability |
| --- | --- | --- | --- |
| *Annie E. Casey Foundation (AEC)—New Futures Initiative; 1987–1994* <br> Foundation established in 1948. <br> Type: private foundation. <br> The first long-term, multi-site initiative by the AEC focused on reforming public policy. Ten mid-sized cities were invited to compete for grants and five were selected. <br> *Governing principles:* <br> Existing service and support systems, despite growing expenditures, were inefficient in meeting the needs of children and families in low-income urban areas. <br> The AEC believes that these failures were partially due to deficiencies in the transactions between helping institutions/professionals and the children and families targeted for help. <br> Institutions helping the poor often work in silos and privilege punitive or expensive interventions at the expense of preventive work, are geographically and culturally remote from clients, and evaluation is typically based on quantity vs. quality of services. <br> Source: www.aecf.org | The foundation selected five cities—Dayton, OH; Lawrence, KS; Little Rock, AK; Pittsburgh, PA; and Savannah, GA—and gave them from $5–$12.5 million each over five years to improve the life chances of disadvantaged youth. <br> The five cities selected received five-year grants that ranged from $7.5 million to $12.5 million, depending on the size of the city. The cities were required to raise matching funds through a combination of new money and locally redeployed funds. <br> In 1993 no-cost extensions were offered to all of the cities, which extended the formal period of New Futures beyond June 30, 1993. In addition, the foundation reviewed the progress of each site and awarded an additional $1 million over two years to Savannah and Little Rock. <br> Originally designed as a five-year initiative, New Futures was extended to the end of 1994 when it officially ended. | New Futures interventions focused on youth and included after-school programs, teen health centers, developing teams of teachers and students within a school, and career education centers to target youth employability. <br> Key structural components included formation of school/nonprofit collaboratives that were later incorporated into nonprofit corporations; a case manager system anchored in schools; and service integration. <br> Despite extensive collaborative efforts, lowering of dropout and teen pregnancy rates, changing school practices, and employer hiring policies have proven considerably resistant in all the New Futures cities. <br> The Savannah and Little Rock sites did perform better and became lasting homegrown institutions for innovation and reform post 1994. | The foundation hired outside evaluators and reports are available online: *The path of most resistance: Reflections on lessons learned from new futures* (August 1995); *The Eye of the Storm: Ten years on the front lines of new futures* (undated). Available at: www.aecf.org/KnowledgeCenter.aspx |

| Name and governing principles | Funding | Program dimensions and outcomes | Accountability |
|---|---|---|---|
| *Ford Foundation—Neighborhood and Family Initiative (NFI); 1990–2000*<br><br>Foundation established in 1936.<br><br>Type: private foundation.<br><br>The NFI targeted four neighborhoods in four different cities for a ten-year commitment: Detroit, Memphis, Milwaukee, and Hartford. NFI is one of the first long-term funding programs for comprehensive change.<br><br>*Governing principles:*<br><br>Two principles underlie the initiative: comprehensive change (making use of interrelationships between social, economic, and physical opportunities); and organizational collaboration/citizen participation.<br><br>The NFI is based on the belief that building and strengthening resident leadership and creating synergies between housing, economic, and human capital can create comprehensive change.<br><br>The Ford Foundation's internal team created the governing principles and the general operational structure for the NFI initiative.<br><br>The cities chosen contained "assets on which to build" including resident leadership, active CDCs, or networks of nonprofits that could partner for comprehensive change.<br><br>Source: www.fordfoundation.org | Ford provided $3 million per site for operations and programs, in addition to support for technical assistance and evaluation. A $3 million investment fund was established for development projects for NFI sites (Turnham and Bonjorni, 2004).<br><br>Grant period for sites varied from 9 months to 3 years. | Each site had a partner community foundation that helped pick target neighborhoods, hire staff directors, and create community collaboratives as local governing structures. The community foundations also served as de facto fiscal agents for the foundation.<br><br>The sites developed small, discrete, time-limited projects:<br><br>*Hartford:* Food Shares Project distributed garden produce; summer program for children.<br><br>*Memphis:* The NFI collaborative created the Orange Mound Development Corporation (OMDC) to rehabilitate affordable housing.<br><br>*Milwaukee:* The collaborative joined with four organizations to purchase 33 acres of land vacated by American Motors and developed an industrial park.<br><br>*Outcomes and lessons:*<br><br>Sufficient funding is needed at start of initiative to effect the type of change envisioned.<br><br>High staff turnover impacted site collaboratives; some did not survive beyond the demonstration project.<br><br>Outsider/insider tensions between foundation and community impacted change efforts.<br><br>Neighborhood change results were at a very small scale and difficult to attribute to the initiative. | The Chapin Hall at the University of Chicago conducted an evaluation of the NFI and the report is posted online: www.chapinhall.org/research/report/evaluation-ford-foundations-neighborhood-and-family-initiative.<br><br>The sites were reluctant to conduct local evaluations without additional funding available for evaluation and there were conflicts with the national evaluator. |

| Name and governing principles | Funding | Program dimensions and outcomes | Accountability |
|---|---|---|---|
| *The Lilly Endowment—GIFT initiative; 1990–present* | In 2011, the Lilly Endowment approved $67,422,336 in community development grants. | The foundation supports community development initiatives through GIFT—Giving Indiana Funds for Tomorrow program—that funds community foundations in each of Indiana's 92 counties. | Endowment makes its annual reports available online from 1998 to 2011 at http://www.lillyendowment.org/annualreports.html#2011. |
| Foundation established in 1937. Type: private foundation. The endowment's community development division focuses on central-city and older neighborhood revitalization in Indianapolis and Indiana. | Lilly Endowment ranks #11 in the 100 largest U.S. grant-making foundations, ranked by market value of their assets. Lilly's assets were $5,184,625,647 (July 29, 2012; The Foundation Center). | By supporting the arts and cultural organizations, the intellectual capacity of a community increases resulting in a more prosperous economy. Employers will want to stay in communities that are thriving in these various levels. | It also maintains a news archive of Lilly Endowment press releases available at http://www.lillyendowment.org/newsarchive.php. |
| *Governing principles:* The endowment's philanthropic vision focuses on the development of a "virtuous circle." In a type of domino effect, a thriving business sector leads to a virtuous circle of community, one that is actively building social capital. | The endowment granted $67 million in community development grants to a variety of community-based organizations from assets totaling $6,225,629,363 in 2011 (Lilly Endowment Annual Report, 2011, available at www.lillyendowment.org/annualreports.html#2011). It also supports more than 60 United Ways throughout Indiana. | | |

Source: www.lillyendowment.org

| Name and governing principles | Funding | Program dimensions and outcomes | Accountability |
| --- | --- | --- | --- |
| *Living Cities—The National Community Development Initiative (NCDI); 1991–current*<br><br>Foundation established in 1991.<br><br>Type: foundation collaborative with own 501(c)(3) designation.<br><br>The NCDI is a collaborative of 22 foundations and financial institutions, HUD, and private corporations. The LISC and the Enterprise Foundation served as intermediaries. Pew, Rockefeller, Lilly, Knight, MacArthur, Hewlett, Surdna Foundations and Prudential Insurance were initial funders. The U.S. Department of Housing and Urban Development is now the largest single funder.<br><br>*Governing principles:*<br><br>Living Cities' focus is on CDC capacity-building; real estate development by CDCs, and human capital development programs through CDC/community partnerships. The NCDI funding reaches about 300 CDCs in 23 cities.<br><br>Core values include: 1) collaboration; 2) innovation through risk-taking, catalyze fresh thinking, and test new approaches in order to creatively disrupt the status quo and change broken systems; 3) provide leadership; and 4) make an impact through material improvements in the lives of low-income people, cities, and the systems that affect them.<br><br>Source: www. livingcities.org | The NCDI is one of the largest funder for collaboratives in the U.S. with $254 million in loans/grants between 1991 and 2001 to 23 cities. Another $110 million was committed for the second decade of work.<br><br>During the first decade, $174 million of NCDI funding was used for real estate projects; approximately 91% for high-risk, up-front, interim financing through lines of credit and other bridge loans, typically unavailable to CDCs at reasonable terms from other sources.<br><br>By 2006, the NCDI had leveraged its contributions to fund over $540 million to build or renovate more than 140,000 homes.<br><br>Over the past 18 years, Living Cities' members have collectively invested over $600 million which has, in turn, leveraged more than $16 billion in tangible community assets (http://www.livingcities.org/press).<br><br>The NCDI itself has very few staff (2–3) with the intermediaries in charge of most administration. High-level executives from the partner organizations are involved in semi-annual meetings, resulting in quick decisions. | CDCs obtained lines of credit or grants to build stores, schools, childcare options, health care, and job training centers.<br><br>More than 17,000 rental units or homes were developed or improved across the 23 sites.<br><br>In October 2010, Living Cities chose five sites for its new Integration Initiative. The sites participating in place-based community development from 2011 to 2013 are: Baltimore, MD; Cleveland, OH; Detroit, MI; Newark, NJ; and the twin cities of Minneapolis and St. Paul, MN.<br><br>In aggregate, the sites receive an investment of $85 million in grants, flexible debt, and commercial debt by Living Cities and its members. They also participate in an array of formal and informal partnership and knowledge exchange opportunities including one-on-one meetings, site visits, online collaboration tools, and cross-site convenings known as "Learning Communities." | Living Cities has a clearly articulated accountability goal: "We hold ourselves accountable for evaluating our effectiveness and are intentionally self-reflective as we strive to continuously improve, adapt, and inform future innovation" (www.livingcities. org/ about/ values).<br><br>Annual reports, analysis of projects, and program evaluations are available at www. livingcities.org/ knowledge. |

| Name and governing principles | Funding | Program dimensions and outcomes | Accountability |
|---|---|---|---|
| *Pew Charitable Trusts—Neighborhood Preservation Initiative; 1993–1997*<br><br>Foundation established in 1948.<br><br>Type: private operating foundation.<br><br>The Pew Charitable Trusts, an independent nonprofit, is the sole beneficiary of seven individual charitable funds established between 1948 and 1979 by Sun Oil Company founder Joseph N. Pew and his wife Mary Anderson Pew.<br><br>Ten groups in nine cities were chosen for funding: five were community or economic development corporations, and five were community or resident groups.<br><br>*Governing principles:*<br><br>The NPI philosophy is that the energy and commitment of community groups is more important than targeting specific activities. Regardless of what revitalization tools are used, energy and momentum from a committed community will produce the greatest "bang for your buck" (Turnham and Bonjorni, 2004, p. 34).<br><br>The NPI focused on working-class neighborhoods, as Pew argued that foundations and government agencies focus on the most distressed areas, allowing transitional neighborhoods to decay even further.<br><br>Source: www.pewtrusts.org | Pew made three-year project grants totaling $6.6 million to nine community foundations in Boston, Cleveland, Indianapolis, Greater Kansas City, Memphis, Milwaukee, Philadelphia, St. Paul, and San Francisco.<br><br>The community foundations received up to $800,000 over three years on the condition of a 50% local match.<br><br>The cities that were chosen had a community foundation with annual grant activity of $2.5 million or more.<br><br>Total investment was $85 million with combined local and national funding yielding $1 million per site (ten sites) per year for three years (Turnham and Bonjorni, 2004, p. 34). | The three-year project aimed to promote the growth and stability of diverse urban neighborhoods threatened by deterioration and decline. Four areas were identified as "critically important for neighborhood stability": crime prevention, economic opportunity, physical revitalization, and youth development.<br><br>In Kansas, the neighborhood association more than quadrupled its membership; volunteers repaired 415 homes; and numerous blighted and vacant buildings were demolished or rehabilitated. | Although specific outcome measures were not specified by the NPI, the program did require local sites to submit a strategic plan. The NPI conducted site visits and follow-ups to ensure that sites were following their strategic plan and provided assistance when needed to overcome barriers.<br><br>However, after the demonstration phase was over, the sites found it difficult to obtain additional funding without concrete outcome measures.<br><br>An evaluation was conducted by the Rockefeller Institute and David J. Wright published the findings in a book—*It takes a neighborhood: Strategies to prevent urban decline* (The Rockefeller Institute Press, 2001). |

| Name and governing principles | Funding | Program dimensions and outcomes | Accountability |
| --- | --- | --- | --- |
| *Robert Wood Johnson Foundation—Urban Health Initiative (UHI); 1995–2005* <br><br> Foundation established in 1936 as the Johnson New Brunswick Foundation. Type: originally a family foundation, it is a non-exempt charitable trust treated as a private foundation (IRS, 990PF, 2009). <br><br> The UHI is a five-city, ten-year investment to make a measurable impact on children's health and safety by using data to develop community-wide systems reform. <br><br> The UHI targeted five major urban areas (Baltimore, Detroit, Oakland, Philadelphia, and Richmond) with each community identifying or developing a "change agent" (either a lead agency or an organizational collaborative) to provide leadership and manage the initiative. <br><br> Governing principles included a strong belief in large-scale, regional strategies through which cities could enlist the involvement of suburbs and other communities. Regional focus on developing interventions at the county, state, and federal levels. | The Robert Wood Johnson Foundation (RWJF), the nation's fourth-largest foundation, awards between $400 million and $500 million a year in a $2 trillion health economy (Jellinek, 2008, p. 1). <br><br> Twenty cities were invited to apply based on staff visits, research, and analysis. Each received two years of development funding under "America's Promise" program. Eight cities were chosen for the program. The Initiative's National Program Office (NPO) was created to provide technical support. <br><br> The foundation funded the sites directly but the NPO monitored the sites' fiscal operations and negotiated all site budgets before submitting them to the RWJF. For grants under $50,000, the NPO's decisions would be honored without lengthy foundation staff review for quick turnaround. Larger grants went through a more extensive internal foundation process but the NPO's recommendations constituted a key basis for decisions. | *Detroit's Mayor's Time:* at the end of ten years, after-school strategies touched over 40,000 young people. *Philadelphia Safe and Sound:* reached over 45,000 young people with its after-school effort, and about 600 with its Youth Violence Reduction Partnership, which targeted high-risk offenders. *Baltimore Safe and Sound Campaign:* reached nearly 3,000 families with home visitation and center-based care, and its after-school strategy reached nearly 24,000 young people. In 2005, the city added more than $12 million into strategies advocated by Safe and Sound. The city also created the Baltimore City Data Collaborative to gather data for evaluation. | A national evaluation of the National Health Initiative (1998–2005) is available at http://www.icpsr.umich.edu/icpsrweb/HMCA/studies/23241. <br><br> The University of Chicago's Chapin Hall also conducted an evaluation with a focus on intermediaries. Available at www.chapinhall.org/sites/default/files/old_reports/283.pdf. |

*Continued*

| Name and governing principles | Funding | Program dimensions and outcomes | Accountability |
|---|---|---|---|
| *Robert Wood Johnson Foundation—Urban Health Initiative (UHI); 1995–2005 (continued)* Cities would decide for themselves what specific children's health issue they wanted to tackle. This contrasted with the traditional demonstration program, in which the participating sites were generally replicating a prescribed model to address a common problem.<br><br>Source: www.rwjf.org | The eight cities could then compete for much larger implementation grants two years after initial implementation. In April 1997, $24 million was awarded over two years to five cities (Baltimore, Detroit, Oakland, Philadelphia, and Richmond); four years later, another $24 million was awarded.<br><br>It is estimated that the foundation awarded approximately $60.75 million over ten years. | *Oakland Pathways to Change:* developed a case management and mental health program for at-risk, middle-school students, an after-school strategy, and an intensive case management program targeting repeat youth offenders. Violence-related school suspensions declined by 78 percent in one year among students in the program.<br><br>*Philadelphia:* $80 million a year in new and redirected funds was raised for home visits by nurses for pregnant teenage mothers, life skills training for at-risk youth, youth violence reduction, and expanded after-school programs. | The principal investigator on the evaluation concluded that the UHI has had a measurable but modest impact in its major areas of focus (Jellinek, 2008). |

| Name and governing principles | Funding | Program dimensions and outcomes | Accountability |
|---|---|---|---|
| *Obama Administration—Neighborhood Revitalization Initiative, Promise Neighborhoods; 2010–present*<br><br>Reflecting many of the principles of CCIs, the federal government launched this place–based initiative in 2010. Seeking to establish public–private partnerships, the implementation grants range from $4–$6 million over 3–5 years.<br><br>The initiative's theory of change calls for an integrated, coordinated effort to increase the quality of educational, physical, commercial, recreational, and social assets, sustained by local leadership over an extended period of time.<br><br>It seeks to address the interconnected problems in distressed neighborhoods through an interdisciplinary approach that aligns the requirements of federal programs so that local communities can more readily braid together different funding streams. It is place–based, to leverage investments by geographically targeting resources; it is data– and results–driven, to facilitate program monitoring and evaluation, to guide action to make adjustments in policy and to learn what works and develop best practices; and it is flexible, to adapt to changing conditions.<br><br>Source: www.promiseneighborhoods.org | In 2010, one–year grants ranging from $400,000–$500,000 were awarded to collaboratives and nonprofit organizations to develop a Promise Neighborhood plan in 21 communities across the country. In 2011, five new implementation grants were awarded of up to $6 million each, totaling up to $30 million across the life of the grant.<br><br>Promise Neighborhoods implementation grant applicants are required to obtain matching funds equal to at least 100% of the award (unless they applied as a rural or tribal community, in which case the matching requirement is 50%).<br><br>The federal government has pledged $60 million for this program in FY2012. The Promise Neighborhoods Initiative is now in 18 states and the District of Columbia. | Modeled after the HCZ, and funded through the U.S. Department of Education, Promise Neighborhoods seeks to encourage schools and nonprofits to work in collaboration with communities to improve the future of children. Twenty recipients of 2011 promise Neighborhood grants are implementing programs focusing on early learning, arts/humanities, affordable housing, and the integration of services to serve children and their families. | The Promise Neighborhoods Institute was established by PolicyLink to assist communities participating in the Promise Neighborhoods program including the establishment of evaluation metrics. Each site will be working with a national evaluator. |

## II. Foundations as CCI managing partners

| Name and governing principles | Funding | Program dimensions and outcomes | Accountability |
|---|---|---|---|
| *Jacobs Family Foundation—JCNI Initiative; 1988–present*<br><br>Type: private operating foundation. Targets the 60 acres in southeastern San Diego that encompass the Diamond Neighborhoods.<br><br>The Jacobs Family Foundation was founded on the belief that "people must own their own change" and fosters an approach based on resident ownership of community change. It created an operating foundation, the Jacobs Center for Neighborhood Innovation (JCNI) in 1995 that quickly became one of the largest and most comprehensive organizations in the community.<br><br>Source: www.jacobscenter.org | Jacobs has invested over $26 million, and it also leveraged funds from the Annie E. Casey Foundation, the Irvine Foundation, and the Ford Foundation. In 2006, Jacobs offered equity opportunities for community residents through an IPO for shares in Market Creek Plaza. At $10 per share, 415 local stakeholders invested $500,000 and own shares in the plaza.<br><br>The Village is located adjacent to a trolley stop that is intended to serve as the hub of transit-oriented development. JCNI plans to develop 1,000 units of affordable housing in the Village. Jacobs contributed $4.5 million toward its construction and that was leveraged into $23.5 million in investment. | Adhering to its mission of community owning the change, Jacobs has developed a rich network of more than 40 resident teams responsible for civic engagement, economic development, social capital, and physical development.<br><br>The foundation developed a master plan for the Village at Market Creek, a 60-acre site that includes Market Creek Plaza and a commercial mall that includes a major grocery store. Adjacent to Market Creek Plaza is the 78,000-square-feet Joe and Vi Jacobs Community Center, which houses JCNI's offices and offers community meeting rooms. | Jacobs is prolific in documenting and sharing its progress. Annual reports along with other documentation are available on its two websites: www.jacobsfamilyfoundation.org and www.jacobscenter.org.<br><br>JCNI's model of working teams is designed to foster collaboration between the foundation and the community and promote transparency.<br><br>Jacobs has worked closely with PolicyLink, a national research institute, to document and analyze its work to date. |

| Name and governing principles | Funding | Program dimensions and outcomes | Accountability |
|---|---|---|---|
| Enterprise Foundation—Community Building in Partnership (CBP), now Enterprise Community Partners, Inc.; 1990–present | Between 1990 and 1998, approximately $70 million was raised from more than 65 public and private funders to support the various programs in Sandtown–Winchester. | The foundation and city staff focused on four clusters: community building, physical and economic development, health and human services, and education. | Reports of outcomes include: |
| Foundation established in 1982. | In 1998, CBP's operating budget of $2,223,000 was supported in | During the planning phase, new construction of 227 homes by the | Community Building in Partnership, Inc. (2000) |
| Type: private corporate foundation. Later changed to Enterprise Community Partners, with for-profit subsidiaries. | part by CDBG ($330,000) plus in-kind contributions from the city of Baltimore, and $375,000 plus in-kind support from The Enterprise | Enterprise Construction Company began (now Enterprise Homes); the city also opened a community support center. | The Sandtown-Winchester Neighborhood Transformation Initiative: Lessons learned about community building and implementation (2001) |
| The Enterprise Foundation and Baltimore's mayor focused on Sandtown–Winchester—a 72-block | Foundation. | In 1998, the Neighborhood Transformation Center (NTC) trained | CBP, Baltimore, MD— Case study from On |
| African American neighborhood that is primarily residential, with a commercial corridor on Pennsylvania | Partners included the VHF- Community Care Network (a national demonstration program), | 11 community residents who went door-to-door to 130 of their neighbors to complete a resident survey to | the Ground with CCIs. Available at http://www. knowledgeplex.org/ |
| Avenue. Later it expanded its projects to other parts of the country, including Oregon. | The W.K. Kellogg Foundation (Community Voices: Health Care for the Underserved Initiative), the Duke Endowment, the Enterprise Foundation, | measure the quality of life in Sandtown–Winchester. | showdoc.html?id=163430. |
| Enterprise Foundation develops spin- off of nonprofits and for-profits to fit each community's revitalization needs. | Baltimore Mental Health System, and the Baltimore City Health Department. | In February 1998, the Enterprise Foundation and St. Vincent de Paul Society of Lane County, Oregon, established Environmental Enterprise Incorporated (EEI) as a nonprofit affiliate that trains resident to fix and sell appliances. | |

Continued

| Name and governing principles | Funding | Program dimensions and outcomes | Accountability |
| --- | --- | --- | --- |
| *Enterprise Foundation—Community Building in Partnership (CBP), now Enterprise Community Partners, Inc.; 1990–present (continued)* | The Urban Youth Corps, funded through a $244,000 grant by the Baltimore City Department of Public Works and the Federal Highway Administration assisted in revitalizing the neighborhood. | Sandtown Works was established in 1996 to provide employability assessment, life skills, and job readiness training and job placement services to teens and adults; Jobs Plus and Sandtown Works also provide jobs and training. | Enterprise Community Partners, Inc., is a 501(c)(3) charitable organization that provides expertise on affordable housing and sustainable communities. Financing for affordable housing is offered through its tax-exempt subsidiary, Enterprise Community Loan Fund, Inc., and its for-profit subsidiary, Enterprise Community Investment, Inc. Housing development is offered through Enterprise Community Investment's subsidiary, Enterprise Homes, Inc. |
| Its comprehensive vision is founded on finding solutions to poverty that are interrelated and respond to a comprehensive approach. It uses an all-encompassing strategy by addressing social, economic, and physical conditions at the same time; seeks to improve service delivery as well as effect system change; seeks to maintain long-standing partnership between mayor, residents, and the foundation; highlights the value of individual and community capacity and ownership, and including building local leadership. Believes in financial and political leverage, and advocates for public and private financial investment as a way of producing long-term tax savings (Clark, L. Council for Children's Rights, n.d.). | The NTC operates the Sandtown education reform initiative with an annual budget of over $500,000 from foundation sources.<br><br>The EEI was funded by the W. Alton Jones Foundation, the U.S. Department of Education, and the Enterprise Foundation, plus a working capital loan from the Abell Foundation. | Compact Schools improvements occurred in three elementary schools. Funds were provided by the Walter A. Annenberg Foundation, W.K. Kellogg Foundation, and the Enterprise Foundation.<br><br>Seeking to expand development opportunities beyond Baltimore, CBP is building 1,500 affordable homes on the site of the former Lafitte public housing site in New Orleans using Hope IV funding http://www.providencecommunityhousing.org/enterprise_providence_release.pdf. | |
| Source: enterprisecommunity.com | | | |

| Name and governing principles | Funding | Program dimensions and outcomes | Accountability |
|---|---|---|---|
| *The Carter Center—The Atlanta Project (TAP); 1991–1999* <br><br> Foundation established in 1982. <br><br> Type: private/nonprofit partnership initiated by former President Jimmy Carter and the Carter Center. TAP focused on 20 neighborhood "clusters" in Atlanta and three surrounding counties identified as containing high concentrations of poverty. <br><br> The Atlanta Project had four major goals: (1) unite Atlanta as a community; (2) foster cooperation among service providers and other groups; (3) foster empowerment; and (4) enhance the quality of life in neighborhoods. <br><br> The governance structure of TAP was envisioned as a "process," rather than a "mechanism," one that would disband as projects within and across clusters became independently sustainable. <br><br> TAP intentionally avoided a formal connection with local government, in favor of reliance on donations from the private sector and local charities, along with the extensive use of on-the-ground volunteers to support the efforts of each cluster. | $32.8 million was donated over five years including $12 million in goods and services. <br><br> Corporate partners provided funding and loaned executives to work alongside residents, providing organizational and technical skills. Private partners included IBM, Cox Enterprises, Equifax, Marriott Corporation, Arthur Anderson Consulting, and most major corporations based in Atlanta at the time, including Coca-Cola, Atlanta Gas Light, NationsBank, United Parcel Service, Delta Airlines. <br><br> TAP's Collaboration Center, with over 40 staff housed in a 30,000-square foot office, supported a basic infrastructure of 20 small community offices located in public high schools staffed by two local residents as community organizers. The center also helped to coordinate programs, seek funding, evaluate programs, provide resources, and facilitate communication among the clusters. A 36-member policy advisory board drawn from high-profile community leaders provided general guidance and links to resources. | The Children's Health Initiative engaged 7,000 volunteers going door-to-door to distribute information that led to 16,000 children receiving immunizations in a one-week period. <br><br> The Georgia Common Access Application project engaged ten state and federal agencies in consolidating forms for government assistance, saving $1.1 million for every 100,000 applicants. | The project established new relationships, particularly between poor communities and corporations, but struggled with establishing a common language, shifting players, programmatic efficacy, and coordination of a large and fluid group of 20 clusters engaging corporate partners, loaned executives, local residents, community organizers, and nonprofits (Barbash, 1994). |

*Continued*

| Name and governing principles | Funding | Program dimensions and outcomes | Accountability |
|---|---|---|---|
| *The Carter Center—The Atlanta Project (TAP); 1991–1999, continued*<br><br>Source: www.cartercenter.org/news/documents/doc184.html | | Micro-lending: six major banks and the Atlanta Chamber of Commerce launched an $11.5 million lending program, seeded with startup money from TAP, that offered business loans, mentoring, and technical support for entrepreneurs who might not otherwise qualify for credit. | Information available at: www.cpn.org/topics/community/atlanta.html.<br><br>In 1999, Georgia State University took over the project by establishing the Neighborhood Collaborative to continue the work. Evaluators estimate that overall, sustainable programs took root in eight clusters. |

| Name and governing principles | Funding | Program dimensions and outcomes | Accountability |
|---|---|---|---|
| Surdna Foundation—Comprehensive Community Revitalization Program (CCRP); 1992–1998 | The CCRP sought to establish replicable projects to develop a model scale of funding through multiple partners. | New entities were created including the Bronx Health Insurance Program and the Bronx Maintenance Company. The Bronx Employment Services placed 2,000 residents in jobs; three CDC-sponsored health care centers were also established. | No formal board of directors exists for the CCRP. A Funders Advisory Committee served as an informal, quasi board that met 3–4 times per year to review progress. Foundation staff were active in the field, providing guidance to residents and feedback to the foundation. |
| Foundation established in 1917. | Surdna made an initial grant of $3 million, followed by $9.4 million from 21 public and private funders. | | |
| Type: private foundation. | | | |
| Approximately 250,000 residents in four South Bronx neighborhoods were targeted. | Surdna, in partnership with the neighborhood CDCs, leveraged an additional $44 million in support, excluding housing (Sviridoff and Ryan, 1996). Funders included the Annie E. Casey Foundation, Chase Bank, Citigroup, Edna McConnell Clark Foundation, LISC, NY Department of Health, Open Society Institute, SEEDCO, Pew and the Rockefeller Foundations, Uris Brothers Foundation, and Wells Fargo Foundation. | Four CDCs joined forces under the CCRP, Inc. banner to win a $320,000 award from HUD's Hope II program for cooperative ownership of 401 units in city-owned buildings. | CCRP, Inc. contracted with the Organization and Management Group (OMG), to determine if supporting mature CDCs as neighborhood intermediaries is an effective approach for achieving comprehensive neighborhood change. The OMG produced three assessment reports on the CCRP. |
| The foundation relied on existing CDCs rather than creating new organizations. The CDCs were tasked with directing neighborhood community revitalization efforts. | | Three CDCs received grants totaling $600,000 from the federal Urban Resources Partnership for open space projects. | |
| The CCRP sought to implement a pragmatic approach to community initiatives, seeking "doable" projects and quick results. | | A training program in partnership with the hotel industry was also established. | |
| Source: www.surdna.org | | | Report available at http://www.knowledgeplex.org/showdoc.html?id=437741. |

| Name and governing principles | Funding | Program dimensions and outcomes | Accountability |
|---|---|---|---|
| The Los Angeles Urban Funders (LAUF); 1992–present | Described by LAUF Director Elwood Hopkins as a "bimodal funding pattern," foundations made a five-year commitment to an unrestricted communal pot used to fund interventions identified by residents of targeted neighborhoods and to respond to unconventional opportunities. | In Vermont/Manchester, residents targeted land use and its impact on the crack epidemic: liquor stores that were sites for drug sales and seedy motels were targeted; residents worked to develop abandoned lots that were sites for drug use and crime. | LAUF argue that as a collaborative, foundations hold each other accountable and seek to develop improved measures of "success." |
| Type: foundation collaborative. | | | |
| Established after the 1992 Los Angeles uprisings, this consortium of family, corporate, and community foundations began with seven foundations and ultimately totaled approximately 30 on its governing board. It targeted three underserved L.A. neighborhoods—Vermont/Manchester, Hyde Park, and Pacoima—focusing on employment and jobs. | | In Hyde Park, a group of block clubs and neighborhood safety watches already working to lower crime, beautify the area, and increase economic development were strengthened through technical and financial support. | For summary reports and analysis of LAUF efforts, please see: |
| | The funders also provided individual grants in each of the three neighborhoods to support a coordinated approach to place-based change. Each neighborhood received approximately $5 million over five years. | | Sharp, Marcia. 2002. *Foundation collaborations: Incubators for change?* Los Angeles, CA: The Center on Philanthropy and Public Policy, USC. Available at http://cppp.usc.edu/doc/RP14.pdf. |
| LAUF believe that pooling resources can have a greater effect in changing underserved neighborhoods. Funder collaboratives allow for smaller foundations to have greater impact than they could alone through greater sharing of data and nonfinancial resources such as expertise. | | In Pacoima, LAUF developed a list of obstacles facing the largely Latino population—English literacy, lack of work experience, lack of childcare—and a corresponding list of projects or programs that would provide solutions—adult-literacy classes, work-experience programs, and a childcare cooperative. In 1998, they hired an organizer to work with four "career coaches," residents who would act as advisors and bridges between social services and those who seek them. | Hershey, Christine. 2012. "Los Angeles: America, only sooner." Council on Foundations Annual Conference. Available at: www.cofinteract.org/ rephilanthropy/?p=4062. |
| Each foundation gets one vote on the board regardless of size or resources. As a group they participate in "visioning processes" that help coordinate interventions in underserved areas. | | | |

| Name and governing principles | Funding | Program dimensions and outcomes | Accountability |
|---|---|---|---|
| The *Los Angeles Urban Funders; 1992–present* (continued) <br><br> Interventions are developed in collaboration with existing neighborhood organizations that were already working for change. <br><br> Source: LAUF no longer maintains a website | The foundations engaged in LAUF included: the California Wellness Foundation, CalEndow, the Prudential Foundation, James Irvine Foundation, Freddie Mac Foundation, California Community Foundation, Liberty Hill Foundation, Durfee Foundation, Rockefeller Foundation, Wells Fargo Foundation, and the Lawrence Welk Foundation. | Local schools with thriving parents' groups where immigrant and first-generation Latinos congregated were supported by the collaborative as they developed programs to help solve immigration and job issues. <br><br> Several community gardens were built and urban grocery stores were pressured to improve the quality of their products. | Hopkins, Elwood. 2005. *Collaborative philanthropies: What groups of foundations can do that individual funders cannot.* Lanham, MD: Lexington Books. |

| Name and governing principles | Funding | Program dimensions and outcomes | Accountability |
| --- | --- | --- | --- |
| CF Foundation, Inc.—East Lake Initiative, Atlanta, Georgia; 1993–present<br><br>Type: private corporate foundation.<br><br>In 1993, Tom Cousins bought the historically significant, but decayed, golf club that was at the center of the East Lake community and donated it to his foundation with the goal of restoring the golf course and using the club as an "economic engine" to help the families of the Villages of East Lake to revitalize their community. The effort aims for cradle-to-college education, safe and affordable housing, and community wellness.<br><br>The CF Foundation supports innovative development models of social service delivery that attack the underlying causes of poverty, rather than simply treating symptoms; also supports future social entrepreneurs—what the foundation terms, the next generation of innovators who are committed to addressing social concerns. | The foundation has donated approximately $25 million since 1993 to buy and rebuild the golf facilities and improve the surrounding area.<br><br>The foundation funded the construction of a public school at East Lake without school board involvement because it wanted to move quickly. It owns the land and the 100,000-square foot building and leases it to the district for $1 a year. It also built and then found partners to operate a child development center for about 150 children (run by Sheltering Arms, one of Atlanta's premier providers of affordable day care).<br><br>New members to the golf course, largely corporate executives, donate $200,000 each to the foundation to join. | The CF Foundation established an intermediary, the East Lake Community Foundation, that worked in partnership with the Housing Authority and the residents' association to design and create a new mixed-income community. It built 541 housing units on 200 acres, Atlanta's first K–8 charter school, and a state-of-the-art, 50,000-square foot YMCA.<br><br>Among other strategies underway is a caddie program for youth, ages 14 and older, who earn money, learn golf, get help with their homework, and have the opportunity to earn college scholarships.<br><br>The foundation is also encouraging middle-class people from churches and seminaries to live in East Lake and be "strategic neighbors" to those in need. Currently, an interdenominational chaplain is provided a rent-free apartment and asked to mentor residents. | The foundation's annual reports and quarterly newsletters are available at www.eastlakefoundation. org/sites/courses/view. asp?id=346&page=8815. The CF Foundation also launched a coaching and technical assistance organization Purpose Built Communities with help from Warren Buffett to accelerate holistic revitalization of underserved communities. See http:// purposebuiltcommunities. org/index.php. |

| Name and governing principles | Funding | Program dimensions and outcomes | Accountability |
|---|---|---|---|
| *CF Foundation, Inc.—Eastlake Initiative, Atlanta, Georgia; 1993–present (continued)* | Total capital investment is estimated at $128 million, including $32 million in bonds and tax credits for multi-family housing, $5 million to bring a new grocery store to the area, and $22 million in state funds and 2007 funding from the Atlanta Housing Authority. | Since the development's completion in 2001, the crime rate has fallen 70% in the surrounding neighborhood and more than 90% within the Villages (from the highest rate of the 56 police beats in the city). | |
| CF Foundation trustees believe the principles inherent in the game of golf— discipline, honesty, hard work, and integrity—contribute to youth development. | | The first residential construction in 30 years is taking place. The charter school has a waiting list of more than 200 students. Public housing residents at East Lake are working for significantly higher median salaries than those living in other developments. | |
| Source: www.eastlakefoundation.org | | | |

| Name and governing principles | Funding | Program dimensions and outcomes | Accountability |
| --- | --- | --- | --- |
| *Rockefeller Foundation and Cleveland Foundation—Cleveland Community Building Initiative (CCBI); 1993–2004*<br><br>Type: the CCBI was chartered as a nonprofit 501(c)(3) organization in 1994.<br><br>In 1989, the Rockefeller Foundation commissioned a study of Cleveland's neighborhoods that led to the formation of the Commission on Poverty, a joint effort of the Cleveland Foundation (founded 1913) and the Rockefeller Foundation's (founded 1914) Community Planning and Action Program.<br><br>A board of trustees governed the initiative along with four village councils: Fairfax, King–Kennedy Estates, Ohio City and a portion of the Detroit Shoreway, and Mount Pleasant. Village councils, CCBI staff, members of the board, and a representative from each of the village councils jointly developed action plans. | Seven city–wide partners with expertise and resources applicable to the program areas were engaged: Neighborhood Progress, Inc.; the Council of Economic Opportunities; the Cleveland Initiative for Education; Metrohealth Medical Center; Case Western Reserve University; and others.<br><br>The Cleveland Foundation awarded a $907,603 grant to the CCBI for core support for the 2002–2003 program year. | A family education center in the Mount Pleasant Village was created to deliver integrated services to improve family economic self-sufficiency and comprehensive family supports.<br><br>In the Eastern council area, a different family resource center addressed the lack of integrated service delivery by working cooperatively with state, county, and city education, human, and social service systems.<br><br>The Children At Risk Project, a collaboration between the CCBI, the Central Village Council, the county Criminal Justice Service Agency, and the Friendly Inn Settlement House, sought to reduce poverty, violence, teen pregnancy, infant mortality, school dropout rates, and substance abuse among the neighborhood's children, while increasing opportunities for employment, affordable housing and home ownership, health and wellness, childcare, transportation, and improved academic performance. | Case Western Reserve's Center on Urban Policy and Social Change provided the primary support to the CCBI for data collection, analysis, and other evaluation tasks.<br><br>Evaluation available at www.hfrp.org/var/hfrp/storage/original/application/5d578838c1279448b0f2292d9d5aca8c.pdf.<br><br>The CCBI was one of the first CCIs to use a theory-of-change approach to evaluation (Milligan, Nario–Redmond and Coulton, 1997). The evaluators supported the four village councils with qualitative and quantitative data as well as with technical skills on assessment of neighborhood assets, agenda formation, and project development. The center's staff assisted residents in identifying short-, medium-, and long-term benchmarks to measure progress at the neighborhood level in such areas as youth and family development, access to institutions and services, indicators of safety and security, indicators of economic opportunity, and neighborhood identity. |

| Name and governing principles | Funding | Program dimensions and outcomes | Accountability |
|---|---|---|---|
| *Rockefeller Foundation and Cleveland Foundation—Cleveland Community Building Initiative (CCBI); 1993–2004, (continued)*<br><br>Five principles guided work in Cleveland: (1) the city's plan should be comprehensive and integrated; (2) strategies should be tailored to individual neighborhoods; (3) the development of strategies should begin with an inventory of a community's assets, not deficits; (4) local communities should be involved in shaping strategies and choices; and (5) the approach should be piloted and evaluated before being taken to scale.<br><br>Source: CCBI no longer maintains a website | | The West Village Housing Task Force was created as a clearinghouse for residents and developers, through which village residents can provide input on public and private community development and housing rehabilitation. | In 2003–2004, the CCBI merged with the Neighborhoods Centers Association and ceased to exist as a 501(c)(3). |

| Name and governing principles | Funding | Program dimensions and outcomes | Accountability |
|---|---|---|---|
| *NY Community Trust—Neighborhood Strategies Project (NSP); 1994–2000*<br><br>Type of organization under IRS 501(c)(3) categories: trust.<br><br>The trust established a community foundation to create economic opportunities for youth and adults in three New York City neighborhoods: Mott Haven in the South Bronx, Washington Heights in Northern Manhattan, and Williamsburg in Brooklyn.<br><br>Three core strategies that guided the programs included: increasing resident employment; stimulating local economic activity; and strengthening neighborhood institutions and affiliations.<br><br>The foundation believes that a comprehensive approach that encompasses all these elements is the most effective way to foster community revitalization. | The New York Community Trust committed $6 million in funds for six years to the NSP—one year of planning and design and five years for implementation in each of the three sites. Approximately $4 million was raised from 12 different foundations and the remainder came from the NY Trust's resources.<br><br>Planning grants of $250,000 were awarded to each neighborhood in the first year and the collaboratives received up to $350,000 per year for implementation.<br><br>In 2010, the New York Community Trust's fund balance was $1.7 billion. | *Mott Haven Programs:*<br><br>The Job Match program referred residents to educational, job training, and support services; the Entrepreneurship Training Program targeted both adults and youth. The summer open-air community market focused on neighborhood vendors. Mott Haven Matters, a bilingual community newspaper, was launched; it had a community-building and employment focus.<br><br>*Washington Heights/Inwood Programs:*<br><br>The Workforce Development Center, a job development and placement program was created. Model Blocks, a project to beautify three areas of the neighborhood, and an Institute for English for Speakers of Other Languages were opened.<br><br>Planning is underway for a retail real estate development project in which youth-oriented stores will be housed with youth services.<br><br>*Williamsburg Projects:*<br><br>An Annual Training and Job Fair began and was linked to Williamsburg Web, which provides support for individual computer centers and the development of a community network of computer resources; Catering Entrepreneurs, a culinary arts training program also started. | The NY Trust contends that the NSP is accountable to its residents through the community-based collaboratives that manage and provide oversight of the NSP. The largest collaborative is in Washington Heights. It is made up of over 200 community-based organizations, agencies and individual residents. The Mott Haven collaborative includes approximately 60 community-based organizations, religious institutions, and local service agencies. |

| Name and governing principles | Funding | Program dimensions and outcomes | Accountability |
| --- | --- | --- | --- |
| NY Community Trust—Neighborhood Strategies Project (NSP); 1994–2000 (continued)<br><br>The NSP demands that local plans and strategies integrate all three initiative components, thereby highlighting the intersections across human resource development, institutional development, and community development.<br><br>The initiative no longer maintains a website. The Chapin Hall evaluation provides the most comprehensive analysis and summary. | | Three NSP collaboratives joined together with assistance from the Non-Profit Assistance Corporation to win a $4.9 million grant from the U.S. Department of Labor for NSP Works, a welfare-to-work program that none of the neighborhood organizations could have won alone (Auspos, Brown, and Hirota, 2000). | The final report was prepared by the Chapin Hall Center for Children at the University of Chicago, and is available at: http://www.chapinhall. org/sites/default/files/ CB_25.pdf. |

| Name and governing principles | Funding | Program dimensions and outcomes | Accountability |
| --- | --- | --- | --- |
| *Price Charities—City Heights Initiative; 1994–present*<br>Foundation established in 1983.<br>Type: private family foundation.<br>The foundation implicitly seeks to have physical change drive broader community social change and believes that the free market can play a key role in revitalization. Developed by the founder of discount "big box" stores such as Costco, the initiative strives for a holistic approach that addresses the interconnected problems in distressed neighborhoods in San Diego.<br>Its values are based on a business model of community development: efficiency, quick reaction to opportunities, and spreading cost among partners.<br>The foundation believes strongly in collaboration with other entities—community nonprofits, foundations, and the city—an element that is at the core if its governing principles. | By some estimates, the foundation has invested approximately $50 million and leveraged those funds into approximately $400 million for City Heights. The foundation loaned the city's redevelopment agency $5.25 million to build the City Heights Public Library and $41.8 million for the Townhomes and Office Center Project.<br>Price Charities' comprehensive community development project is located in the heart of the City of San Diego's largest redevelopment project area at 1,984 acres. As of 2007, the city's redevelopment agency had outstanding loan debt of $15.02 million for projects in City Heights, several in partnership with Price Charities. As of June 2009, the city had accrued $13.98 million in tax increments from the City Heights project area. | The foundation developed a master plan for a nine-block area and constructed the City Heights Urban Village project, which has earned multiple awards and national attention as a model for comprehensive urban revitalization. Public and private partners have invested approximately $137 million to construct a Police Substation, a Public Library/Performing Arts Annex, a Retail Center, a recreation center with tennis courts and a swimming pool, and a new public elementary school as an anchor for the core area.<br>Price Charities donated $18 million to the SDSU to create an Education Collaborative that funds innovative practices at three schools. Each school has active parent volunteer groups, social workers, and full-time nurses. Price also funds a program whereby 3rd, 4th, and 5th graders spend 25% of their school time in San Diego's Balboa Park, home to dozens of museums that become classrooms away from school. | Price Charities does not produce or publish annual reports, and the founders shy away from publicity for their work.<br>A webpage was created by the foundation to help market 116 townhomes in the Urban Village, completed in 2003; www.pricecharities.com.<br>The foundation has contracted various entities for evaluations of its programs, including the Urban Institute, but the results are not publicly available. |

| Name and governing principles | Funding | Program dimensions and outcomes | Accountability |
|---|---|---|---|
| *Price Charities—City Heights Initiative*; 1994–present *(continued)* Source: www.pricecharities.org | | It established a 2.3-acre urban garden in partnership with a nonprofit that works with refugees. Residents farm 85 garden plots and sell produce at the City Heights Farmers market. | Selected findings and information on the Education Collaborative are available at http://thechec.org. |

| Name and governing principles | Funding | Program dimensions and outcomes | Accountability |
|---|---|---|---|
| *The Edna McConnell Clark Foundation's—Neighborhood Partners Initiative (NPI), 1996–2003* Type: private foundation. The foundation supported five community-based organizations that work with residents to produce concrete, measurable/quantifiable change in small neighborhoods in Central Harlem and the South Bronx: two CDCs, two multi-service agencies, and an organizing group (ACORN). The foundation believes that neighborhood organizations know the community best and are the primary levers for neighborhood change, and embedded foundation staff can help effect change. A block-by-block approach within a small geographic area can develop momentum for community-wide change (in densely populated NYC a block can be a significant social, economic, and political unit). An underlying NPI belief is that the lead organizations need new or strengthened organizational capacities and approaches to demonstrate that they can make things happen. | The program began in 1996 with initial grants of $200,000 to each of the five neighborhoods. The lead agencies included Abyssinian Development Corporation and HCZ in Harlem, and Bronx ACORN, Mid-Bronx Council, and Highbridge Community Life Center in the South Bronx. The organizations' budgets ranged from $400,000 to $7.4 million, with staff size ranging from 11–285. The program shifted in 1995 from targeting families that had experienced homelessness to addressing the underlying causes of homelessness. This new strategy, signaled by changing the name of the program to New York Neighborhoods, incorporated issues such as lack of affordable housing, little economic opportunity, deteriorating housing, poor neighborhood conditions, and public safety. | NPI staff were embedded in each neighborhood to help build on a range of human, political, and social assets in each site and to engage residents and other neighborhood stakeholders. These assets included individuals and organizations with an array of talents and resources, and broader forces that could be harnessed to create powerful pressures for change. The first phase focused on developing a governance framework, resident engagement, and grantee capacity. Notable successes: improvements to formerly distressed properties, the refurbishing of parks and playgrounds, public safety improvements such as the installation of speed bumps near schools, and the creation of job placement programs, computer technology centers, and youth programs. | No formal governance mechanism was prescribed by the NPI. Each site developed its own vehicles for resident engagement, leadership, and ownership of the effort. The foundation ended up "doing business differently" as a result of this experience: it decided to customize its approach upon re-funding the sites: three sites were invited to apply for two-year renewal grants, one site for an 18-month grant, and one site for a 12-month grant. Each site was given a different proposed funding range for its request. |

| Name and governing principles | Funding | Program dimensions and outcomes | Accountability |
|---|---|---|---|
| *The Edna McConnell Clark Foundation's— Neighborhood Partners Initiative (NPI); 1996–2003 (continued)* The foundation is interested in developing sustainable improvements in living conditions for the poor that are quantifiable. The foundation began in late 1997 to describe this cluster approach as "building social capital." Source: http://www.emcf.org/our-values-and-history/past-programs/new-york-neighborhoods/ | In 1999 total expenditures were approximately $4.8 million. In 2000, the foundation awarded $4.875 million to the NPI; in 2001, $3.7 million; in 2002, $4.5 million, and in 2003, it awarded $1.7 million. In total, the NPI received more than $20 million from the Edna McConnell Clark Foundation. | NPI residents strengthened block associations, advocated for better public services, started campaigns to encourage participation in the 2000 U.S. Census, and provided testimony regarding large-scale public works projects affecting their neighborhoods. | Essentially, the foundation staff saw the need to respond with flexibility to the realities of implementation, while keeping the initiative on track and its core tenets intact. A thorough evaluation of the initiative is available at: www.chapinhall.org/sites/default/files/old_reports/15.pdf. |

| Name and governing principles | Funding | Program dimensions and outcomes | Accountability |
|---|---|---|---|
| *California Endowment—Building Healthy Communities (BHC); 2010–2020*<br><br>Type: health care conversion foundation. The foundation was created in 1996 as Blue Cross of California transitioned from a nonprofit health care provider to the private WellPoint Health Networks. In 2009, the Endowment selected 14 communities for a ten-year $100 million commitment. Each community chosen was charged with identifying a "host agency" and developing a nonprofit and resident collaborative. CalEndow believes that place impacts a community's health, particularly that of children in low-income neighborhoods.<br><br>Two parallel principles guide the foundation's work: systemic change and community organizing.<br><br>CalEndow believes that community change can be modeled, replicated, and inspire policy changes.<br><br>CalEndow has its own training center—The Center for Healthy Communities—that works to build leadership and capacity within the nonprofit health sector to mobilize communities for social change.<br><br>Source: www.calendow.org | The Center for Community Engagement (CCE) at CSU Long Beach is serving as "host agency"/fiscal agent for the first two years of the grant.<br><br>Additional funding (approx. $125,000) was made available to other nonprofits/partners that can support Healthy Communities Initiatives in target neighborhoods. | *City Heights, San Diego*—over 14 months more than 3,379 residents, in a myriad of languages and various levels of engagement, contributed towards the development of the plan. Resident-driven momentum teams focus on: food justice, access to healthcare, peace promotion, built environment, and school attendance.<br><br>*Santa Ana*—the collaborative is focusing on affordable housing, voter registration/support of the DREAM Act, youth, and job creation.<br><br>*Coachella Valley*—the collaborative is focusing on community organizing and advocacy to strengthen the voice of the farm-worker community.<br><br>*South Kern*—goals for the collaborative include reduction of the use of pesticides, land use/zoning, environmental education, safe drinking water, and youth development, and increased parental involvement in education.<br><br>A team of leaders from each of the communities was developed, with a focus on communication including the management of community web pages. BHC workgroups meet weekly for cross-community collaboration and training on maximum use of technology. | CalEndow's focus changed from 1996–2009 when it made 9,200 grants to nonprofits totaling $1.7 billion. Self-reflection and stakeholder interviews led it to become more focused and targeted in its grant-making, and the foundation shifted to supporting place-based investments.<br><br>CalEndow has extensive expertise in evaluation and believes that quantitative analysis is important for organizational learning. Ongoing evaluation available at http://www.calendow.org/learning.aspx. |

# NOTES

## 2 The origins of community development philanthropy

1 In January of 2012 the most well-known settlement house, Hull House in Chicago, abruptly closed its doors leading to speculation about the causes of its demise. One observer noted its unsustainable business model that originally shunned philanthropic support and government funding, depending instead on the efforts of volunteers. In a fundamental change in approach, by the time it shut down approximately 90 percent of its budget came from state and local funding. This reliance on unreliable public sources is posited as one of the primary contributors to the failure of Hull House's viability (see: www.nonprofitquarterly.org/management/20758-death-of-the-hull-house-a-nonprofit-coroners-inquest.html).

2 Due to rounding, figures may not add up, according to the Foundation Center.

## 3 The intersection of philanthropy and community development

1 See www.brookings.edu/research/reports/2010/07/20-hcz-whitehurst.
2 For a comprehensive list of health care conversions, see Grantmakers in Health (2009).
3 See http://foundationcenter.org/getstarted/tutorials/ft_tutorial/compare.html.
4 See http://foundationcenter.org/gainknowledge/research/pdf/keyfacts_fam_2011.pdf.
5 See http://foundationcenter.org/gainknowledge/research/pdf/keyfacts_familyfdns2012.pdf.
6 For a list see http://fex.org/memberfoundations.
7 Criterion 1: Values—recommends that grant makers allocate at least 50 percent of their grants to benefit marginalized groups. Criterion 2: Effectiveness—stipulates that grant makers allocate at least 50 percent of grants dollars for operating support for nonprofits and at least 50 percent of grants should be in the form of multi-year awards. Criterion 3: Ethics—calls for foundations to assemble a diverse board of directors including representatives from the communities served by the grants. Criterion 4: Commitment—recommends that foundations expend at least 6 percent of their assets on grants on an annual basis and ensure that at least 25 percent of their assets are invested in ways that shape their mission (Jagpal, 2009).

## 4 Typology of comprehensive community initiatives

1 Defined as place-based, comprehensive, using a public/private mix of funding, actively engaging residents and community, and committed to community change.
2 *Governing principles* focuses on the mission and values expressed by the CCI or leading foundation that guides their community change agenda; *Funding* alludes to the amount of funding received by the CCI and the sources of this funding, whether foundational, public, or private. *Program dimensions and outcomes* lists the specifics of the CCI effort; and *Accountability* refers to transparency and access to data on process and outcomes.
3 Available at www.frameworksinstitute.org/blogs/alumni/2011/10/communicating-place-based-initiatives.
4 For an excellent and detailed analysis of the collaboratives and the Ford Foundation's NFI, see Chaskin, Dansokho et al. (1997).

## 5 Systems change theory: advancing complex community change

1 Letts and McCaffrey's (2003) study of LAUF was prepared for the John F. Kennedy School of Government, Harvard University, Case Program. As the most definitive and complete analysis of LAUF to date, it served as a primary source for the preparation of this case study.
2 In 2002 and 2009, the Office of Community Services (OCS) within the U.S. Department of Health and Human Services awarded 1,285 grants, and findings from an assessment of the programs funded found that many significant gains were made across all five areas of capacity—organizational development, program development, revenue development, leadership development, and community engagement—among the nonprofits served. Source: www.acf.hhs.gov/programs/opre/other_resrch/ccf/repo]rts/ccf_impact_study/ccf_impact_study_rsrch_brief.pdf.

## 6 Price Charities and the Jacobs Center for Neighborhood Innovation: an introduction to the case studies

1 The majority of data for this section was obtained from the U.S. Census Bureau including decennial reports from 1990, 2000, and the American Community Survey five-year estimates from 2006–2010. Data were obtained from the following tables. U.S. Census Bureau 1990: STF11: P11, STF3: P17A, P80A, STF3: H61A, STF3: H43A, STF3: P117, STF3: P70, STF3: P57, STF3: P28, STF3: P42, STF3: P31, STF3: H29. U.S. Census Bureau 2000: SF1: P13, SF1: PCT13, SF1: P33, SF3: P53, SF3: H85, SF3: H63, SF3: P87, SF3: P43, SF3: P37, SF3: P19, SF3: PCT 19, SF3: PCT 10, SF3: H38. U.S. Census Bureau American Community Survey 5-Year Estimates 2010: B19013, B25077, B25064, S1701, B15002, B16007, B05006, B25038. U.S. Census Bureau 2010: SF1: P13, SF1: P12, SF1: P37. Social Explorer Tables (based on U.S. Census Bureau American Community Survey 5-Year Estimates): SE T21.
2 The term "Diamond District," or "Diamond Neighborhoods," was coined by the Jacobs Family Foundation to delineate the geographic target of its community development efforts located in the larger area of southeastern San Diego. Residents of the community who tend, instead, to use the names of specific neighborhoods in southeastern San Diego, do not necessarily use this term. "Southeastern San Diego" is also a relatively new descriptor for the community. Formerly known as "southeast San Diego," in 1992 George Stevens, the city council member who represented the community at the time, held a mock funeral for "southeast San Diego" and renamed it "southeastern San Diego." Stevens sought to bury a term that was often perceived as synonymous with high crime rates and community dysfunction.
3 Due to unreliability with the American Community Survey's data on median housing values in 2010, DataQuick statistics on home sales recorded in July of

2012 were used instead (www.dqnews.com/charts/monthly-charts/sdut-charts/zipsdut.aspx). The DataQuick statistics should also be used as estimates since the values for southeastern San Diego are based on an average of several neighborhoods located within the community and not all of the census tracts are included in JCNI's boundaries for the Diamond Neighborhoods.

4  We use the terms "Diamond Neighborhoods" and "southeastern San Diego" interchangeably in discussions on the efforts of the Jacobs Family Foundation.

## 7 The Jacobs Center for Neighborhood Innovation

1  Jacobs has a unique approach to its work. The Jacobs Family Foundation is a grant-making foundation with the singular purpose of supporting the efforts of JCNI, its operating foundation. To ensure continuity, the two foundations share the same board of directors and officers.
2  In July 2008, SEDC's executive director faced allegations of misconduct and a clandestine effort to provide bonuses and extra compensation to high-ranking staff members, including herself. In May of 2011 the state of California filed criminal charges against the former executive director accusing her of embezzlement and misappropriation of public funds. In November of the same year she pleaded guilty to the charges.
3  According to U.S. Securities and Exchange Commission Filings, IRS 990 Forms for the year ending June 30, 2010, JCNI had $143,887,857 in assets and the Jacobs Family Foundation had $23,989,760.
4  See for example Mayer (1984); Pierce and Steinbach (1987); Stoutland (1999); Vidal (1992); Walker (1993).
5  See http://thevillageatmarketcreek.com/plan_history.htm.

## 8 Price Charities

1  Price Charities website: www.pricecharities.com. 1/29/02.
2  Wedemeyer, Dee, "Those Low Priced Price Clubs." *New York Times*, May 18, 1986. Section 3, page 4, Financial Desk.
3  The list of grants awarded by the Price Family Charitable Fund is available at www.pricecharities.com/News.
4  Issuance of Tax Allocation Bonds by the Redevelopment Agency of the City of San Diego for the City Heights Redevelopment Project, 2010. Available at http://munibase.elabra.com/CityHeights2010FOS/doc/fos.pdf.
5  Laura Gibney, 2004. Community Survey in City Heights. Unpublished report.

## 9 Applying systems theory to Price Charities and the Jacobs Center for Neighborhood Innovation

1  See http://prod031.sandi.net/propmm/index.htm.
2  Residential and business occupants displaced by school construction are guaranteed relocation assistance by California Government Code Section 7260 *et seq.* and Title 25 of the California Code of regulations, but there is no requirement or funding for districts to replace affordable housing.

## 10 Conclusion

1  In 2007 the LISC invested approximately $1.1 billion in support of its Building Sustainable Communities program, which is designed to facilitate comprehensive, holistic community development.

# REFERENCES

Abraham, S. (2007). New heights: The City Heights district of San Diego is on its way back, thanks to a long-term initiative led by Price Charities and the deep personal commitment of Robert Price '64. *Pomona College Magazine Online, 41*(2). Retrieved from http://pomona.edu/Magazine/PCMsp07/FScityheights.shtml.

Abu-Lughod, J. L. (1999). *New York, Chicago, Los Angeles: America's global cities.* Minneapolis, MN: University of Minnesota Press.

Ackoff, R. L. (1994). Systems thinking and thinking systems. *System Dynamics Review, 10,* 175–188.

Alpert, E. (2008). Gauging the success of three schools, 10 years and millions of dollars later. *Voice of San Diego.* Retrieved from www.voiceofsandiego.org/education/article_0a3c1fff-d52a-51a6-9de2-b33ec597a30a.html?mode=image&photo=.

Anheier, H. and Leat, D. (2006). *Creative philanthropy: Towards a new philanthropy for the twenty-first century.* London and New York, NY: Routledge.

Annie E. Casey Foundation. (1995). *The path of most resistance: Reflections on lessons learned from new futures.* Baltimore, MD: The Annie E. Casey Foundation. Retrieved from www.aecf.org/upload/publicationfiles/the%20path%20of%20most%20resistance.pdf.

Appleyard, D. and Lynch, K. (1974). *Temporary paradise? A look at the special landscape of the San Diego region: A report to the city of San Diego.* Cambridge, MA: Dept. of Urban Studies and Planning, Massachusetts Institute of Technology.

Auspos, P., Brown, P., and Hirota, J. (2000). *Neighborhood strategies project: A final assessment.* Chicago, IL: Chapin Hall Center for Children, University of Chicago.

Auspos, P., Brown, P., Kubisch, A. C., and Sutton, S. (2009). Philanthropy's civic role in community change. *The Foundation Review, 1*(1), 135–145.

Baker, C. M. (2001). Hospital conversion foundations: Issues in creation, operation, and evaluation. *Journal of Nursing Administration's Healthcare Law, Ethics, and Regulation, 3*(1), 19–29.

Barbash, S. (1994). The Atlanta project. *Boston Review.* Retrieved from http://bostonreview.net/BR19.3/barbash.html.

Bauder, D. (2012). San Diego rents third highest in nation. *San Diego Reader.* Retrieved from www.sandiegoreader.com/weblogs/news-ticker/2012/mar/13/san-diego-rents-third-highest-in-nation.

Bernard, R. M. and Rice, B. R. (1983). *Sunbelt cities: Politics and growth since World War II.* Austin, TX: University of Texas Press.

Bernholz, L., Fulton, K., and Kasper, G. (2005). *On the brink of new promise: The future of U.S. community foundations.* Blueprint Research and Design and the Monitor Group. Retrieved from http://www.monitorinstitute.com/downloads/what-we-think/new-promise/On_the_Brink_of_New_Promise.pdf.

Bernstein, I. (1996). *Guns or butter: The presidency of Lyndon Johnson.* Oxford: Oxford University Press.

Bhattacharyya, J. (1995). Solidarity and agency: Rethinking community development. *Human Organizations, 54*(1), 60–69.

Blackwood, A. and Roeger, K. (2011). *Revoked: A snapshot of organizations that lost their tax-exempt status.* Washington, DC: The Urban Institute.

Bockmeyer, J. L. (2003). Devolution and the transformation of community housing activism. *Social Science Journal, 40*(2), 175–188.

Bratt, R. G. (2009). Challenges for nonprofit housing organizations created by the private housing market. *Journal of Urban Affairs, 31*(1), 67–96.

Bratt, R., Stone, M. E., and Hartman, C. (2006). A *right to housing: Foundation for a new social agenda.* Philadelphia, PA: Temple University Press.

Bremner, R. H. (1988). *American philanthropy* (2nd edn). Chicago and London: University of Chicago Press.

Bridges, A. (1997). *Morning glories: Municipal reform in the southwest.* Princeton, NJ: Princeton University Press.

Brown, P. and Fiester, L. (2007). *Hard lessons about philanthropy and community change from the neighborhood improvement initiative.* Menlo Park, CA: William and Flora Hewlett Foundation.

Brown, P., Branch, A., and Lee, J. (1998). *The neighborhood partners initiative: A report on the start-up period.* Chicago, IL: The Chapin Hall Center for Children, University of Chicago.

Brown, P., Chaskin, R., Richman, H., and Weber, J. (2006). *Embedded funders and community change: Profiles.* Chicago, IL: The Chapin Hall Center for Children, University of Chicago.

California Department of Education. (2010). 2010–2011 accountability progress reporting. Retrieved from http://www.cde.ca.gov/ta/ac/ar.

California Endowment. (2009). *Building healthy communities: California living 2.0.* Retrieved March 5, 2010, from www.calendow.org.

California Endowment. (2010). *Building healthy communities.* Retrieved September 23, 2011, from www.calendow.org/healthycommunities.

California Tax Data. (1986). Retrieved September 3, 2012, from www.californiataxdata.com/pdf/Prop13.pdf.

Carson, M. J. (1990). *Settlement folk: Social thought and the American settlement movement, 1885–1930.* Chicago, IL: University of Chicago Press.

Chaskin, R. and Karlström, M. (2012). *Beyond the neighborhood: Policy engagement and systems change in the new communities program.* New York, NY: MDRC.

Chaskin, R., Dansokho, S. C., and Joseph, M. (1997). *The Ford Foundation's neighborhood and family initiative. The challenge of sustainability: An interim report.* Chicago, IL: The Chapin Hall Center for Children, University of Chicago.

Chaskin, R., Dansokho, S. C., Joseph, M., and Richards, C. (2001). *An evaluation of the Ford Foundation's neighborhood and family initiative.* Chicago, IL: University of Chicago, Chapin Hall.

Checkland, P. (1981). *Systems thinking, systems practice.* New York, NY: John Wiley & Sons.

Checkland, P. B., and Scholes, J. (1990). *Soft systems methodology in action.* New York, NY: John Wiley & Sons.

City of San Diego Redevelopment Agency. (2009a). *Annual report*. San Diego, CA: City of San Diego City Planning and Community Investment Department.

City of San Diego Redevelopment Agency. (2009b). *Fourth implementation plan for the City Heights redevelopment plan, for the period July 2009–June 2014*. (No. D-04405b). San Diego, CA: City of San Diego.

Clark, L. (n.d.). *Comprehensive community initiatives*. Council for Children's Rights. Retrieved from http://cfcrights.org/wp-content/uploads/2011/10/Comprehensive-Community-Initiatives-Summary-Info1.pdf.

Cohen, R. (2008). *A foundation changes course: Kellogg's complex overhaul, new focus challenges staff and raises questions for its grantees*. Retrieved, April 10, from www.Youthtoday.org/publication/article.cfm?article_id=2332.

Coleman, J. S. (1988). Social capital and the creation of human capital. *American Journal of Sociology, 94*(Special Issue), 95–120.

Council on Foundations. (2008). *Definition of "community foundation," adopted by community foundations leadership team*. Unpublished manuscript.

Council on Foundations. (2010). Retrieved from http://www.cof.org/whoweserve/terms/index.cfm.

Council on Foundations. (n.d.). Retrieved from http://www.cof.org/whoweserve/community/resources/index.cfm?navItemNumber=15626#locator.

Covington, S. (1994). *Community foundations and the disenfranchised: At the margins of change*. Unpublished paper presented at the annual meeting of ARNOVA, Berkeley, CA.

Covington, S. (2005). Moving public policy to the right: The strategic philanthropy of conservative foundations. In D. R. Faber and D. McCarthy (eds) *Foundations for social change: Critical perspectives on philanthropy and popular movements* (pp. 89–114). Lanham, MD: Rowman & Littlefield Publishers.

Cytron, N. (2010). Improving the outcomes of place-based initiatives. *Community Investments, 22*(1), 2–7.

DataQuick. (2012). *San Diego Union Tribune zip code chart for home sales recorded in July 2012*. Retrieved August 22, 2012, from www.dqnews.com/charts/monthly-charts/sdut-charts/zipsdut.aspx.

Davis, A. F. (1967). *Spearheads for reform: The social settlements and the progressive movement, 1890–1914*. New York, NY: Oxford University Press.

Davis, M., Miller, J., and Mayhew, K. (2003). *Under the perfect sun: The San Diego tourists never see*. New York, NY: New Press.

Dear, M. (ed.) (2002). *From Chicago to L.A.: Making sense of urban theory*. Thousand Oaks, CA: Sage.

Dear, M. and Dahmann, N. (2008). Urban politics and the Los Angeles school of urbanism. *Urban Affairs Review, 44*(2), 266–279.

DeFilippis, J. (2008). Paradoxes of community-building: Community control in the global economy. *International Social Science Journal, 59*(192), 223–234.

DeFilippis, J. and Saegert, S. (2008). *The community development reader*. New York, NY: Routledge.

Department of Housing and Urban Development (HUD) (1993). Section 4 Capacity Building for Community Development and Affordable Housing. Retrieved from http://www.hud.gov/offices/cpd/about/capacitybuilding.cfm.

Dillick, S. (1953). *Community organization for neighborhood development, past and present*. New York, NY: Woman's Press and W. Morrow.

Dolan, M. (2011, July 2). Revival bid pits Detroit vs. donor. *Wall St. Journal*. Retrieved from http://online.wsj.com/article/SB10001424052702304887904576397760319014524.html.

Dowie, M. (2001). *American foundations: An investigative history*. Cambridge, MA: MIT Press.

Dreier, P. (1997). Philanthropy and the housing crisis: The dilemmas of private charity and public policy. *Housing Policy Debate, 8*(1), 235–293.

Dreier, P. (2002). Social justice philanthropy: Can we get more bang for the buck? *Social Policy, 33*(1), 27–33.

Dreier, P., Mollenkopf, J. H., and Swanstrom, T. (2001). *Place matters: Metropolitics for the twenty-first century*. Lawrence, KS: University Press of Kansas.

Edwards, M. (2008). *Just another emperor? The myths and realities of philanthrocapitalism*. New York, NY: The Young Foundation.

Ehrenreich, J. (1985). *The altruistic imagination: A history of social work and social policy in the United States*. Ithaca, NY: Cornell University Press.

Ellis, R. H. (1984). The Calhoun School, Miss Charlotte Thorn's "lighthouse on the hill" in Lowndes County, Alabama. *The Alabama Review, 37*(3), 183–201.

Emshoff, J., Darnell, A. J., Darnell, D. A., Erickson, S. W., Schneider, S., and Hudgins, R. (2007). Systems change as an outcome and process in the work of community collaboratives for health. *American Journal of Community Psychology, 39*(3–4), 255–267.

Erie, S. P. (2004). *Globalizing L.A.: Trade, infrastructure, and regional development*. Stanford, CA: Stanford University Press.

Erie, S. P., Kogan, V., and MacKenzie, S. A. (2011). *Paradise plundered: Fiscal crisis and governance failures in San Diego*. Stanford, CA: Stanford University Press.

Faber, D. and McCarthy, D. (2005). *Foundations for social change: Critical perspectives on philanthropy and popular movements*. Lanham, MD: Rowman & Littlefield Publishers.

Ferguson, R. F. and Dickens, W. T. (eds) (1999). *Urban problems and community development*. Washington, DC: Brookings Institution Press.

Ferguson, R. F. and Stoutland, S. E. (1999). Reconceiving the community development field. In R. F. Ferguson, and W. T. Dickens (eds) *Urban problems and community development* (pp. 33–75). Washington, DC: Brookings Institution Press.

Ferris, J. M. and Williams, N. (2009). *Foundation strategy for social impact: A systems change perspective*. Los Angeles, CA: University of Southern California, Center on Philanthropy and Public Policy.

Flaspohler, P., Wandersman, A., Keener, D., Maxwell, K., Ace, A., Andrews, A., and Holmes, B. (2003). Promoting program success and fulfilling accountability requirements in a statewide community-based initiative. *Journal of Prevention and Intervention in the Community, 26*(2), 37–52.

Fleishman, J. (2007). *The foundation: A great American secret: How private wealth is changing the world*. New York, NY: Public Affairs.

Ford, L. (2005). *Metropolitan San Diego: How geography and lifestyle shape a new urban environment*. Philadelphia, PA: University of Pennsylvania Press.

Foster-Fishman, P. G. (2002). *How to create systems change*. Lansing, MI: Michigan Developmental Disabilities Council.

Foster-Fishman, P. G. and Behrens, T. R. (2007). Systems change reborn: Rethinking our theories, methods, and efforts in human services reform and community-based change. *American Journal of Community Psychology, 39*(3–4), 191–196.

Foster-Fishman, P. G., Nowell, B., and Yang, H. (2007). Putting the system back into systems change: A framework for understanding and changing organizational and community systems. *American Journal of Community Psychology, 39*(3–4), 197–215.

Foster-Fishman, P. G., Van Egeren, L., and Yang, H. (2005). Using a systems change approach to evaluate comprehensive community change initiatives. Presentation to the Kellogg Foundation, Toronto, Canada.

Foundation Center. (2009). *Annual report 2009*. New York, NY: The Foundation Center.

Foundation Center. (2011). *Key facts on family foundations.* New York, NY: The Foundation Center.

Foundation Center. (2012). *Key facts on family foundations.* New York, NY: The Foundation Center.

Frisch, M. and Servon, L. J. (2006). CDCs and the changing context for urban community development: A review of the field and the environment. *Journal of the Community Development Society, 37*(4), 88–108.

Garigan, M. (2004). *Health conversion foundations.* (Working Paper No. 2). The Center for Public and Nonprofit Leadership, Georgetown University Center. Retrieved from http://cpnl. georgetown.edu/doc_pool/WP02Garigan.pdf.

Gilliam, F. (2011, October 6). Communicating place-based initiatives. [Web log comment]. Retrieved from www.frameworksinstitute.org/blogs/alumni/2011/10/ communicating-place-based-initiatives.

Glickman, N. and Servon, L. J. (1998). More than bricks and sticks: Five components of community development corporation capacity. *Housing Policy Debate, 9*(3), 497–539.

Gould, S. K. (2011). *Diminishing dollars: The impact of the 2008 financial crisis on the field of social justice philanthropy.* New York, NY: The Foundation Center.

Graddy, E. A. and Morgan, D. L. (2006). Community foundations, organizational strategy, and public policy. *Nonprofit and Voluntary Sector Quarterly, 35*(4), 605–630.

Granovetter, M. S. (1973). The strength of weak ties. *American Journal of Sociology, 78*(6), 1360–1380.

Grantmakers in Health. (2009). *A profile of foundations created from health care conversions.* Washington, DC: Grantmakers in Health.

Grantmakers in Health. (2011). Encouraging multi-sectoral, place-based strategies to support children's healthy development. Meeting report. Retrieved from www.gih.org/.../GIH_ Children's_Health_Strategy_Session_Final_Paper_UPDATED_SEPT_2011.pdf.

Green, G. P. and Haines, A. (2012). *Asset building and community development.* New York, NY: Sage Publications.

Hall, P. D. (1987). A historical overview of the nonprofit sector. In W. W. Powell, and R. Steinberg (eds) *The nonprofit sector: A research handbook* (pp. 32–65). New Haven, CT: Yale University Press.

Halpern, R. (1995). *Rebuilding the inner city: A history of neighborhood initiatives to address poverty in the United States.* New York, NY: Columbia University Press.

Hamilton, R. (2002). *Moving ideas and money: Issues and opportunities in funder funding collaboration.* Chicago, IL: The Funders' Network on Smart Growth and Livable Communities; The Program on Philanthropy and Community Change of the Chapin Hall Center for Children.

Hammack, D. C. (1999). Foundations in the American polity, 1900–1950. In E. C. Lagemann (ed.) *Philanthropic foundations: New scholarship, new possibilities* (pp. 43–68). Bloomington and Indianapolis, IN: Indiana University Press.

Hancock, J. (1996). "Smokestacks and geraniums": Planning and politics in San Diego. In M. C. Sies and C. Silver (eds) *Planning the twentieth-century American city* (pp. 161–186). Baltimore, MD: The Johns Hopkins University Press.

Hapke, N. (2004). New ideas in community development. *American Thinker.* Retrieved from http://www.americanthinker.com/2004/07/new_ideas_in_community_develop.html.

Hayden, D. (1981). *The grand domestic revolution: A history of feminist designs for American homes, neighborhoods, and cities.* Cambridge, MA: MIT Press.

Hayes, C. D., Lipoff, E., and Danegger, A. (1995). *Compendium of comprehensive, community-based initiatives: A look at costs, benefits, and financing strategies.* Washington, DC: The Finance Project.

Hays, R. A. (1995). *The federal government and urban housing: Ideology and change in public policy* (2nd edn). Albany, NY: State University of New York Press.

Heskin, A. D. (1991). *The struggle for community*. Boulder, CO: Westview Press.

Hirsch, G. B., Levine, R., and Miller, R. L. (2007). Using system dynamics modeling to understand the impact of social change initiatives. *American Journal of Community Psychology, 39*(3–4), 239–253.

Hopkins, E. (2005). *Collaborative philanthropies: What groups of foundations can do that individual funders cannot*. Lanham, MD: Lexington Books.

Hopkins, E. (2010). Understanding the different types of low-income neighborhoods. *Community Investments, 22*(1), 13–18.

Hughes, A. and Hughes, T. (eds) (2000). *Systems, experts, and computers: The systems approach in management and engineering, World War II and after*. Cambridge, MA: MIT Press.

Jacobs Center for Neighborhood Innovation. (2004). *Perspective: Jacobs re-engineering: 10 reasons why comprehensive community initiatives don't work and the questions Market Creek Plaza raises in the field*. San Diego, CA: Jacobs Center for Neighborhood Innovation.

Jacobs Center for Neighborhood Innovation. (2007). *President's report*. San Diego, CA: Jacobs Center for Neighborhood Innovation.

Jacobs Center for Neighborhood Innovation. (2009). *The Village at Market Creek: Social and economic impact report calendar year 2008*. San Diego, CA: Jacobs Center for Neighborhood Innovation.

Jacobs Center for Neighborhood Innovation. (2010). *The Village at Market Creek: Breaking new ground together, social and economic impact report calendar year 2009*. San Diego, CA: Jacobs Center for Neighborhood Innovation.

Jacobs, J. (1961). *The death and life of great American cities*. New York, NY: Random House.

Jacobs, J. (1996). *The compassionate conservative: Assuming responsibility and respecting human dignity*. Richmond, CA: ICS Press.

Jacobs, M. (1999). Constructing a new political economy: Philanthropy, institution-building, and consumer capitalism in the early twentieth century. In E. C. Lagemann (ed.) *Philanthropic foundations: New scholarship, new possibilities* (pp. 101–118). Bloomington and Indianapolis, IN: Indiana University Press.

Jagpal, N. (2009). *Criteria for philanthropy at its best: Benchmarks to assess and enhance grantmaker impact*. Washington, DC: National Committee for Responsible Philanthropy.

Jargowsky, P. A. (1997). *Poverty and place: Ghettos, barrios, and the American city*. New York, NY: Russell Sage Foundation.

Jellinek, P. (2008). The urban health initiative. In S. Isaacs and D. C. Colby (eds) *To improve health and health care* (pp. 151–173). Princeton, NJ: Robert Wood Johnson Foundation.

Jenkins, J. C. (1989). Social movement philanthropy and American democracy. In R. Magat (ed.) *Philanthropic giving: Studies in varieties and goals* (pp. 292–314). New York, NY: Oxford University Press.

Jenkins, J. C. and Halcli, A. L. (1999). Grassrooting the system? The development and impact of social movement philanthropy, 1953–1990. In E. C. Lagemann (ed.) *Philanthropic foundations: New scholarship, new possibilities* (pp. 229–256). Bloomington and Indianapolis, IN: Indiana University Press.

Katz, M. B. (1986). *In the shadow of the poorhouse: A social history of welfare in America*. New York, NY: Basic Books.

Keil, R. (1998). *Los Angeles, globalization, urbanization, and social struggles*. New York, NY: John Wiley & Sons.

Kellogg Foundation. (2007). *Philanthropy in the spirit of our times: 2007 annual report*. Battle Creek, MI: W.K. Kellogg Foundation.

Kelly, J. G., Ryan, A. M., Altman, B. E., and Stelzner, S. P. (2000). Understanding and changing social systems: An ecological view. In J. Rappaport, and E. Seidman (eds) *Handbook of community psychology* (pp. 133–159). New York, NY: Kluwer Academic/Plenum.

Killory, C. (1993). Temporary suburbs: The lost opportunity of San Diego's national defense housing project. *The Journal of San Diego History, 39*(1 and 2). Retrieved from www.sandiegohistory.org/journal/93spring/suburbs.htm.

King, J. A. and Vile, J. R. (2006). *Presidents from Eisenhower through Johnson, 1953–1969: Debating the issues in pro and con primary documents.* Westport, CT: Greenwood Press.

Kretzmann, J. and McKnight, J. (1993). *Building communities from the inside out: A path toward finding and mobilizing a community's assets.* New York, NY: Acta Publications.

Kubisch, A. C., Auspos, P., Brown, P., and Dewar, T. (2010). Community change initiatives from 1990–2010: Accomplishments and implications for future work. *Community Investments, 22*(1), 8–12.

Kubisch, A., Weiss, C., Schorr, L., and Connell, J. (1995). Introduction. In J. Connell, A. Kubisch, L. Schorr, and C. Weiss (eds) *New approaches to evaluating community initiatives: Concepts, methods, and contexts* (pp. 1–21). Washington, DC: The Aspen Institute.

Lasch-Quinn, E. (1993). *Black neighbors: Race and the limits of reform in the American settlement house movement, 1890–1945.* Chapel Hill, NC: University of North Carolina Press.

Lasker, R. D., Weiss, E. S., and Miller, R. (2001). Partnership synergy: A practical framework for studying and strengthening the collaborative practice and research. *Milbank Quarterly, 79*(2), 179–205.

Laszlo, A. and Krippner, S. (1998). Systems theories: Their origins, foundations and development. In J. S. Jordan (ed.) *Systems theories and a priori aspects of perception* (pp. 47–74). Amsterdam: Elsevier Science.

Lemann, N. (1991). *The promised land: The great black migration and how it changed America.* New York, NY: Knopf.

Letts, C. and McCaffrey, A. (2003). *Los Angeles urban funders.* Cambridge, MA: Harvard University John F. Kennedy School of Government Case Studies in Public Policy and Management.

Letts, C. W., Ryan, W., and Grossman, A. (1997). Virtuous capital: What foundations can learn from venture capitalists. *Harvard Business Review, 75*(2), 36–42.

Leung, L. (2011, December 2). Demand for rentals is expected to grow. *San Diego Union Tribune.*

LISC Chicago. (2009). *LISC launches great neighborhoods program.* Retrieved from www.lisc-chicago.org/display.aspx?pointer=7370.

Lotchin, R. W. (1992). *Fortress California, 1910–1961: From warfare to welfare.* New York, NY: Oxford University Press.

Lowe, J. E. (2004). Community foundations: What do they offer community development? *Journal of Urban Affairs, 26*(2), 221–240.

Lowe, J. S. (2008). Limitations of community development partnerships: Cleveland Ohio and Neighborhood Progress Inc. *Cities, 25*(1), 37–44.

Lubove, R. (1962). *The progressives and the slums: Tenement house reform in New York City, 1890–1917.* Pittsburgh, PA: University of Pittsburgh Press.

Maani, K. E. and Cavana, M. (2000). *Systems thinking and modelling: Understanding change and complexity.* New York, NY: Prentice Hall.

MacArthur Foundation. (2007). *Community and economic development in Chicago neighborhoods.* Retrieved from www.macfound.org/press/press-releases/macarthur-invests-26-million-for-community-and-economic-development-in-16-chicago-neighborhoods.

Macy, J. (1991). *Mutual causality in Buddhism and general systems theory: The dharma of natural systems.* Albany, NY: State University of New York Press.

Magee, M. (2011, November 28). Price Charities donate $50 million to USC. *U-T San Diego.* Retrieved from http://www.utsandiego.com/news/2011/nov/28/price-charities-donate-50-million-to-usc.

Martinez-Cosio, M. (2003). Redefining civic participation: Redevelopment and democracy. (Unpublished doctoral dissertation). University of California, San Diego, La Jolla, CA.

Marwell, N. (2007). *Bargaining for Brooklyn: Community organizations in the entrepreneurial city*. Chicago, IL: University of Chicago Press.

Mayer, N. S. (1984). *Neighborhood organizations and community development: Making revitalization work*. Washington, DC: Urban Institute Press.

Medoff, P. and Sklar, H. (1994). *Streets of hope: The fall and rise of an urban neighborhood*. Boston, MA: South End Press.

Melendez, E. and Servon, L. J. (2007). Reassessing the role of housing in community-based urban development. *Housing Policy Debate, 18*(4), 751–783.

Meyer, P. (2007, March 24). West vows to fight proposed expansion of eminent domain. *The Dallas Morning News*, p. 2A.

Midgley, G. (2000). *Systemic intervention: Philosophy, methodology and practice*. New York, NY: Kluwer Academic/Plenum.

Miller, A. and Burns, T. (2006). *Going comprehensive: Anatomy of an initiative that worked—CCRP in the South Bronx*. New York, NY: Local Initiatives Support Corporation.

Milligan, S. E., Nario-Redmond, M., and Coulton, C. J. (1997). *The 1995–1996 Cleveland community-building initiative baseline progress report: Village council formation, asset appraisal, agenda formation, and action projects*. Cleveland, OH: Center on Urban Policy and Social Change, Case Western Reserve University.

Milofsky, C. (2008). Remembering Warren's interorganizational field. *Community Development Journal, 43*(1), 93–96.

Mondell, A., Mondell, C.S., and Allen, P. (Producers), Mondell, A. and Mondell, C. S. (Directors). (2007). *A fair to remember* [Motion picture]. United States: Media Projects, Inc.

Morikawa, M. and Berardino, M. (2010). *Block by block: An overview of current place-based anti-poverty initiatives in Boston*. Boston, MA: Action for Boston Community Development Inc.; The Planning Department.

Mossberger, K. (2010). *From gray areas to new communities: Lessons and issues from comprehensive U.S. neighborhood initiatives*. (GCI Working Paper-10-02). The Great Cities Institute at the University of Illinois at Chicago. Retrieved from http://www.community-wealth.org/sites/clone.community-wealth.org/files/downloads/paper-mossberger.pdf.

Nenno, M. K. (1983). The Reagan housing, CD record: A negative rating. *Journal of Housing, 40*, 135–141.

Nye, N. and Glickman, N. J. (2000). Working together: Building capacity for community development. *Housing Policy Debate, 11*(1), 163–198.

O'Connor, A. (1996). Community action, urban reform, and the fight against poverty: The Ford Foundation's gray areas program. *Journal of Urban History, 22*(5), 586–625.

O'Connor, A. (1999). The Ford Foundation and philanthropic activism in the 1960s. In E. C. Lagemann (ed.) *Philanthropic foundations: New scholarship, new possibilities* (pp. 169–194). Bloomington and Indianapolis, IN: Indiana University Press.

Orszag, P., Barnes, M., Carrion, A., and Summers, A. (2009, August 11). *Developing effective place-based policies for the FY 2011 budget*. Memorandum.

Osborne, D. and Gaebler, T. (1992). *Reinventing government: How the entrepreneurial spirit is transforming the public sector*. New York, NY: Plume.

Ostrander, S. A. (1999). When grantees become grantors: Accountability, democracy, and social movement philanthropy. In E. C. Lagemann (ed.) *Philanthropic foundations: New scholarship, new possibilities* (pp. 257–270). Bloomington and Indianapolis, IN: Indiana University Press.

Ostrander, S. A. (2005). Legacy and promise for social justice funding: Charitable foundations and progressive social movements, past and present. In D. R. Faber and D. McCarthy (eds) *Foundations for social change: Critical perspectives on philanthropy and popular movements* (pp. 33–59). Lanham, MD: Rowman and Littlefield Publishers.

Ostrower, F. (2011). *Sunsetting: A framework for foundation life as well as death.* Washington, DC: The Aspen Institute.

Otterman, S. (2010, October 12). Lauded Harlem schools have their own problems. *New York Times.* Retrieved from http://www.nytimes.com/2010/10/13/education/13harlem. html?pagewanted=all&_r=0.

Patterson, J. T. (2000). *America's struggle against poverty in the twentieth century.* Cambridge, MA: Harvard University Press.

Perry, S. (2012, May 9). Congressional hearing to examine nonprofit tax issues. *Chronicle of Philanthropy.* Retrieved from http://philanthropy.com/blogs/government-and-politics/ congressional-hearing-to-examine-nonprofit-tax-issues/30387.

Pew Charitable Trust. (2010). *Subsidy scope: Tax expenditures in the nonprofit sector.* Washington, DC: The Pew Charitable Trust.

Phillips, K. P. (1969). *The emerging Republican majority.* New Rochelle, NY: Arlington House.

Pierce, N. and Steinbach, C. (1987). *Corrective capitalism: The rise of America's community development corporations.* New York, NY: The Ford Foundation.

Pitcoff, W. (1997). Comprehensive community initiatives: Redefining community development. *ShelterForce Online.* Retrieved from www.nhi.org/online/issues/96/ccis.html.

Ports, U. (1975). Geraniums vs. smokestacks: San Diego's mayoralty campaign of 1917. *The Journal of San Diego History, 21*(3). Retrieved from http://www.sandiegohistory.org/ journal/75summer/geraniums.htm.

Putnam, R. (2000). *Bowling alone: The collapse and revival of American community.* New York, NY: Simon & Schuster.

Radford, G. (1996). *Modern housing for America: Policy struggles in the new deal era.* Chicago, IL: University of Chicago Press.

Ranghelli, L. and Craig, J. (2010). *Strengthening democracy, increasing opportunities: Impacts of advocacy, organizing, and civic engagement in Los Angeles.* Washington, DC: National Committee for Responsive Philanthropy.

Rawls, J. (1971). *A theory of justice.* Cambridge, MA: Belknap Press of Harvard University Press.

Richardson, V. G. and Reilly, J. F. (2003). *Public charity or private foundation status issues under IRC 509(a)(1)-(4), 4942(j)(3), and 507.* (No. 2003 EO CPE Text). Washington, DC: Internal Revenue Service.

Robinson, L. (2005). *Market Creek Plaza: Toward resident ownership and neighborhood change.* Oakland, CA: PolicyLink.

Roelofs, J. (2003). *Foundations and public policy: The mask of pluralism.* Albany, NY: State University of New York Press.

Rohe, W. M. and Bratt, R. G. (2003). Failures, downsizings, and mergers among community development corporations. *Housing Policy Debate, 14*(1–2), 1–46.

Russell Sage Foundation. (2007). *Celebrating 100 years of social science research.* Retrieved April 12, 2009, from http://www.russellsage.org/sites/all/files/u137/Brief-History.pdf.

Savage, S. (2004). *JFK, LBJ, and the democratic party.* Albany, NY: State University of New York Press.

Schachter, H. L. (1997). *Reinventing government or reinventing ourselves: The role of citizen owners in making a better government.* Albany, NY: State University of New York Press.

Schutze, J. (2007, April 5). Vox populi. wait a minute … there's democracy in Dallas? *The Dallas Observer.* Retrieved from http://www.dallasobserver.com/2007-04-05/news/vox-populi.

Scott, A. J. and Soja, E. W. (1996). *The city: Los Angeles and urban theory at the end of the twentieth century.* Berkeley, CA: University of California Press.

Scruggs-Leftwich, Y. (2006). *Consensus and compromise: Creating the first national urban policy under President Carter.* Lanham, MD: University Press of America.

Seidman, E. (1988). Back to the future, community psychology: Unfolding a theory of social intervention. *American Journal of Community Psychology, 16*, 3–24.

Senge, P. M. (1990). *The fifth discipline.* New York, NY: Doubleday.

Sharp, M. (2002). *Foundation collaborations: Incubators for change?* (Research Paper–14). The School of Policy, Planning, and Development, University of Southern California: The Center on Philanthropy and Public Policy. Retrieved from http://cppp.usc.edu/research/research-reports-papers.

Shiroma, S. (2001). *New health foundations: Providing new resources for philanthropy.* Washington, DC: The Foundation Center.

Shragge, A. (1994). "A new federal city": San Diego during World War II. *Pacific Historical Review, 63*(3), 333–361.

Silver, I. (2006). *Unequal partnerships: Beyond the rhetoric of philanthropic collaboration.* New York, NY: Routledge.

Smedley, B. (2008). *Place, race, and health: Promoting opportunities for good health for all children.* Washington, DC: First Focus.

Sojourner, A., Brown, P., Chaskin, R., Hamilton, R., Fiester, L., and Richman, H. (2004). *Moving forward while staying in place: Embedded funders and community change.* Chicago, IL: Chapin Center for Children, University of Chicago.

Srivastava, P. and Oh, S. (2010). Private foundations, philanthropy and partnership in education and development: Mapping the terrain. *International Journal of Educational Development, 30*, 460–471.

Stoecker, R. (1997). The CDC model of urban development: A critique and an alternative. *Journal of Urban Affairs, 19*(1), 1–22.

Stoutland, S. E. (1999). Community development corporations: Mission, strategy, and accomplishments. In R. F. Ferguson and W. T. Dickens (eds) *Urban problems and community development* (pp. 193–240). Washington, DC: Brookings Institution Press.

Strom, S. (2010, April 23). One fourth of nonprofits are to lose tax breaks. *New York Times.* Retrieved from www.nytimes.com/2010/04/23/us/23exempt.html.

Stuhldreher, A. (2007). The People's IPO: Lower-income partners of market creek plaza can now invest in shopping center. *Stanford Social Innovation Review, 5*(1), 62–63.

Suarez, D. F. (2012). Grant making as advocacy: The emergency of social justice philanthropy. *Nonprofit Management and Leadership, 22*(3), 259–280.

Sviridoff, M. and Ryan, W. (1996). *Investing in community: Lessons and implications of the comprehensive community revitalization program.* New York, NY: Comprehensive Community Revitalization Program.

Trattner, W. I. (1999). *From poor law to welfare state: A history of social welfare in America* (6th edn). New York, NY: The Free Press.

Traynor, B. (1995). Community building: Hope and caution. *ShelterForce Online.* Retrieved from www.nhi.org/online/issues/83/combuild.html.

Trolander, J. A. (1987). *Professionalism and social change: From the settlement house movement to neighborhood centers, 1886 to the present.* New York, NY: Columbia University Press.

Turnham, J. and Bonjorni, J. (2004). *Review of neighborhood revitalization initiatives.* Boston, MA: Abt Associates.

United States General Accounting Office. (2002). *Tax-exempt organizations improvements possible in public, IRS, and state oversight of charities.* (No. GAO-02-526). Washington, DC: United States General Accounting Office.

Urban Land Institute. (2007). *Awards for excellence: 2007 finalist—Market Creek Plaza San Diego, California.* Retrieved on April 24, 2013 from http://www.jacobscenter.org/news/na/uli-07.htm.

U.S. Census Bureau. (1990). *Census of population and housing.* Washington, DC: U.S. Census Bureau.

U.S. Census Bureau. (2000). *Census of population and housing.* Washington, DC: U.S. Census Bureau

U.S. Census Bureau. (2010). *American community survey.* Washington, DC: U.S. Census Bureau.

Vale, L. (2000). *From the puritans to the projects: Public housing and public neighbors.* Cambridge, MA: Harvard University Press.

Vidal, A. (1992). *Rebuilding communities: A national study of urban community development corporations.* New York, NY: New School for Social Research, Community Development Research Center.

Vidal, A. C. (1997). Can community development re-invent itself? *Journal of the American Planning Association, 63*(4), 429–438.

Viederman, S. (2005). Preface. In D. R. Faber and D. McCarthy (eds) *Foundations for social change: Critical perspectives on philanthropy and popular movements* (pp. ix–xii). Lanham, MD: Rowman and Littlefield Publishers.

von Hoffman, A. (2003). *House by house, block by block: The rebirth of America's urban neighborhoods.* New York, NY: Oxford University Press.

von Hoffman, A. (2011). *Into the wild blue yonder: The urban crisis, rocket science, and the pursuit of transformation housing policy in the great society, part two.* (Working Paper W11-3). The Joint Center for Housing Studies, Harvard University. Retrieved from http://www.jchs.harvard.edu/sites/jchs.harvard.edu/files/w11-3_von_hoffman.pdf.

Walker, C. (1993). Nonprofit housing development: Status, trends, and prospects. *Housing Policy Debate, 4*(3), 369–414.

Walsh, J. (1996). *Stories of renewal: Community building and the future of urban America.* New York, NY: Rockefeller Foundation.

Walsh, J. (1997). *The eye of the storm: Ten years on the front lines of new futures—an interview with Otis Johnson and Don Creary.* Baltimore, MD: Annie E. Casey Foundation.

Warren, R. L. (1967). The interorganizational field as a focus for investigation. *Administrative Science Quarterly, 12*(3), 369–419.

Watson, F. D. (1971). *The charity organization movement in the United States.* New York, NY: Macmillan.

Wiebe, R. H. (1967). *The search for order, 1877–1920.* New York, NY: Hill and Wang.

Williams, D. (2010). *A message from Don Williams.* Retrieved from fcedallas.org.

Williams, M. V. and Brelvi, S. S. (2000). A closer look: Profiling foundations created by health care conversions. *Health Affairs, 19*(2), 257–259.

Wilson, W. J. (1990). *The truly disadvantaged: The inner city, the underclass, and public policy.* Chicago, IL: University of Chicago Press.

Wolch, J. R. (1990). *The shadow state: Government and voluntary sector in transition.* New York, NY: The Foundation Center.

Wolch, J. R., Pastor, M., and Dreier, P. (2004). *Up against the sprawl: Public policy and the making of Southern California.* Minneapolis, MN: University of Minnesota Press.

Wooley, B. (2010, 15 May). At its peak, Ku Klux Klan gripped Dallas. *The Dallas Morning News.* Retrieved from http://www.dallasnews.com/section-archives/125th-anniversary/headlines/20100515-at-its-peak-ku-klux-klan-gripped-dallas.ece.

Wright, G. (1981). *Building the dream: A social history of housing in America.* New York, NY: Pantheon Books.

Ylvisaker, P. N. (1987). The nonprofit sector. In W. W. Powell (ed.) *Foundations and nonprofit organizations* (pp. 360–379). New Haven, CT: Yale University Press.

# INDEX